EVANGELICAL SCHOLARSHIP, RETROSPECTS *and* PROSPECTS

EVANGELICAL SCHOLARSHIP, RETROSPECTS *and* PROSPECTS

Essays in Honor of STANLEY N. GUNDRY

Dirk R. Buursma, Katya Covrett,
and Verlyn D. Verbrugge,[†] *editors*

ZONDERVAN®

ZONDERVAN

Evangelical Scholarship, Retrospects and Prospects
Copyright © 2017 by Zondervan

This title is also available as a Zondervan ebook.

Requests for information should be addressed to:
Zondervan, *3900 Sparks Dr. SE, Grand Rapids, Michigan 49546*

ISBN 978-0-310-08701-4

Cover design: Tammy Johnson
Cover photo: 123RF
Interior design: Kait Lamphere

Printed in the United States of America

17 18 19 20 21 22 23 24 25 26 27 /DHV/ 15 14 13 12 11 10 9 8 7 6 5 4 3 2 1

CONTENTS

PREFACE

Five Views on Stan Gundry:
Pastor, Scholar, Publisher, Mentor, Friend

I t was a full-blown conspiracy.

Only a handful of people were in on it—not even a dozen in the whole company: the editors who had the original idea, the CEO who approved it, the trade publisher who hid the "official record" in her list, a managing editor who made it all happen, a marketer who supported the idea, a contracts director who had to keep the documents secret, an executive assistant who supported us all. The internal paperwork was done; the contributors were on board. Now we just had to keep it a secret from Stan for a measly five years. Easy. Right? . . . It's one thing to keep a *Festschrift* secret from the outside world; it's quite another to conceal it from your own publisher. We think we did it. We won't really know until we see Stan's face at the presentation.

This is probably the most multifaceted collection of essays we have ever published. But then Stan Gundry is no one-dimensional man. He has played diverse roles and worn numerous hats in his professional life—as pastor, scholar, publisher, mentor, and trusted friend to many.

While most *Festschriften* focus on the one primary area of expertise of the honoree, from the very beginning we knew that to truly honor Stan Gundry, we had to broaden our horizons and highlight this multidimensional—*counterpoint*, if you will—aspect of Stan as a way to honor him. We invited contributors from a variety of disciplines, asking them to put a Gundry-spin on a topic of their expertise and choosing—be it an evangelical-historical look at recent developments in their discipline or a topic at the center of Stan's interests. The result is the multifaceted collection before you. What is remarkable, however, is that these essays all have threads of commonalities and connections that bind ultimately to each of Stan's diverse facets.

Pastor

Stan may have left behind formal pastoral ministry at the local church years ago, but he has remained a pastor through and through. His pastoral heart is always on display as he guides his diverse crew of publishing professionals with integrity, wisdom, and compassion. His door is (almost always) open, and those who need advice or support or just a listening ear are always welcome. Many a coworker has been talked down off the ledge and given new perspective after spending a few minutes with Stan in the serenity of his office. And these gifts aren't just reserved for the office environment; throughout the publishing industry, Stan is known as a man who stands up for what is right and who disdains the spirit of competitiveness and takes joy in pointing others to our common mission as believers in the Lord Jesus.

Scholar

While Stan's own scholarly training focused on the history of American evangelicalism and fundamentalism, his passions, interests, and expertise extend far beyond the scope of his doctoral studies in historical theology to biblical studies, the evangelical doctrine of Scripture, Bible translation, theological education, academic and reflective publishing, advocacy for women's roles in the church and marketplace, and a keen concern for the Majority World. Each of these areas of Stan's scholarly prowess are addressed in this collection.

PUBLISHER

It would not be an overstatement to say that each and every contributor to this volume first began publishing with Zondervan because of Stan. Adding up the contributors' years of publishing with Zondervan, we reach an amazing 390 years!

For those of us at Zondervan Academic, we have been blessed to have Stan as our fearless leader for four decades. Stan's extensive knowledge of the publishing industry is an abundant wellspring of wisdom, even for the industry veterans. Zondervan Academic would not be what it is today without Stan.

MENTOR

Stan's pastoral heart, scholarly prowess, and publishing wisdom have made him a perfect mentor to many of us, both publishing professionals and authors, in all things Christian-academic-thoughtful publishing. In his own unassuming and gentle way, Stan is truly a leader by example, a man whose words and deeds motivate those around him to want to "be like Stan." His open-door policy and unceasing support have provided an invaluable source of learning and growth. We are deeply indebted to Stan for the way he lives out his faith and models an attitude of adventure and exploration. When it comes to mentoring, few do it better than Stan Gundry.

FRIEND

Above all, and without exception, Stan is, has been, and always will be a friend—a friend to authors and colleagues alike, as well as to those whose lives are linked with his outside the office. Like all bosses, Stan cares deeply about how his team performs professionally—whether they meet their yearly performance goals and whether they successfully accomplish the tasks that constitute their job description. But more than that, Stan cares about every member of his team as persons who have a life outside of the office. Many of the people who have worked with Stan down through the years have testified to his kind, empathetic heart that demonstrates the agape love that Jesus mandates us to show to others.

So there you have it—five views on Stan Gundry. And we're not going to publish the counterpoints to any of these views, because, well, that just wouldn't be right. We all know Stan isn't perfect, but after all, this is a volume honoring a man who has dedicated his life to serving God—a man who has carried out this mission so well. And we are filled with deepest gratitude to God for placing Stan Gundry in this role so many years ago, and we wish for him God's richest blessings in the years ahead.

Dirk Buursma
Katya Covrett
Verlyn Verbrugge[1]

---

1. Our friend and longtime colleague Verlyn Verbrugge was one of the early adopters of the *Festschrift* idea. His creativity and knowledge of evangelical scholarship have decisively shaped this book from the beginning. Verlyn went to be with the Lord in June 2015 without seeing the eschatological realization of the book he helped inaugurate. It was only fitting, then, that we honor his contribution by including his name among the coconspirators.

Contributors

Robert H. Gundry (PhD, Manchester) is a scholar-in-residence and professor emeritus of New Testament and Greek at Westmont College in Santa Barbara, California. Among his books are *A Survey of the New Testament*, commentaries on Mark and Matthew, Sōma *in Biblical Theology*, *The Old Is Better*, and *Commentary on the New Testament*.

Robert A. Fryling, now retired, has served as publisher of InterVarsity Press and vice president of InterVarsity Christian Fellowship. He is the author of *The Leadership Ellipse: Shaping How We Lead by Who We Are*. He lives in Illinois with his wife, Alice, an author and spiritual director. Together they have coauthored three books.

Millard J. Erickson (PhD, Northwestern University) has served as a pastor and seminary dean and has taught at several schools, including Southwestern Baptist Theological Seminary, Western Seminary, and Baylor University. He is the author of many books, including *Christian Theology* and *Introducing Christian Doctrine*.

John D. Woodbridge (PhD, University of Toulouse, France) is research professor of church history and history of Christian thought at Trinity Evangelical Divinity School in Deerfield, Illinois. He is the author of several books, including *Biblical Authority*, and coauthor with Frank James III of *Church History, Volume Two: From Pre-Reformation to the Present Day*.

John H. Walton (PhD, Hebrew Union College) is professor of Old Testament at Wheaton College and Graduate School. Among his many books are *The Lost World of Adam and Eve*, *The Lost World of Scripture*, *The Lost World of Genesis One*, *Ancient Near Eastern Thought and the Old Testament*, and commentaries on Genesis and Job in the NIV Application Commentary series.

Tremper Longman III (PhD, Yale University) is distinguished scholar of biblical studies at Westmont College in Santa Barbara, California. He is the author of numerous books, including *An Introduction to the Old Testament*, *How to Read Proverbs*, and commentaries on Genesis, Job, Proverbs, Ecclesiastes, Song of Songs, Jeremiah and Lamentations, and Daniel.

Karen H. Jobes (PhD, Westminster Theological Seminary) is the Gerald F. Hawthorne Professor Emerita of New Testament Greek and Exegesis at Wheaton College in Wheaton, Illinois. She is the author of *Letters to the Church* and commentaries on Esther, 1 Peter, and the Johannine Epistles. After many years on the New International Version's Committee on Bible Translation, she continues as an honorary member.

Craig L. Blomberg (PhD, Aberdeen) is distinguished professor of New Testament at Denver Seminary. His numerous books include *Interpreting the Parables*, *Neither Poverty nor Riches*, *Christians in an Age of Wealth*, *Jesus and the Gospels*, *The Historical Reliability of the Gospels*, and commentaries on Matthew and 1 Corinthians. He currently serves as a member of the New International Version's Committee on Bible Translation.

Gordon D. Fee (PhD, University of Southern California) is professor emeritus of New Testament at Regent College. His published works include *How to Read the Bible for All Its Worth* (with Douglas Stuart), *God's Empowering Presence, Pauline Christology*, and commentaries on 1–2 Timothy and Titus, Galatians, 1 Corinthians, and Philippians. He is an honorary member of the New International Version's Committee on Bible Translation.

Ruth A. Tucker (PhD, Northern Illinois University) has taught mission studies and church history at Trinity Evangelical Divinity School and Calvin Theological Seminary. She is the author of many books, including *Katie Luther, First Lady of the Reformation* and the award-winning *From Jerusalem to Irian Jaya*.

Richard J. Mouw (PhD, University of Chicago) is professor of faith and public life at Fuller Theological Seminary in Pasadena, California, where he served as president for twenty years. He is the author of numerous books, including *Uncommon Decency, Calvinism in the Las Vegas Airport, The Smell of Sawdust,* and *Adventures in Evangelical Civility*.

Christopher J. H. Wright (PhD, Cambridge) is international ministries director of the Langham Partnership. He has written many books, including commentaries on Deuteronomy, Jeremiah, Lamentations, and Ezekiel; *Old Testament Ethics for the People of God; The God I Don't Understand; The Mission of God's People; Cultivating the Fruit of the Spirit; The Mission of God;* and *Knowing Jesus through the Old Testament*.

Carolyn Custis James (BA in sociology, MA in biblical studies) is an author and speaker whose ministry is dedicated to addressing the deeper needs that confront both women and men as they endeavor to extend God's kingdom together in a messy and complicated world. She is the author of several books, including *When Life and Beliefs Collide, Lost Women of the Bible, The Gospel of Ruth, Half the Church,* and *Malestrom*.

Frank A. James III (DPhil, Oxford; PhD, Westminster Theological Seminary) is the president and professor of historical theology at Biblical Theological Seminary in Hatfield, Pennsylvania. He is the author of *Peter Martyr Vermigli and Predestination*, the coauthor with John D. Woodbridge of *Church History, Volume Two: From Pre-Reformation to the Present*, and one of the founding members of the Reformation Commentary on Scripture series.

Chapter 1

A Brotherly Tribute

ROBERT H. GUNDRY

Writing a tribute to Stan Gundry puts me in mind of biblical comparisons between older brothers and their younger brothers: Cain and Abel, Esau and Jacob, What's-His-Name and the Prodigal Son. Not a happy comparison for me as Stan's older brother, though Jacob and the Prodigal Son (scoundrels both) give me a half-measure of comfort. I'll start my tribute with an envy-tinged identification of Stan's personality traits—three of them in particular—as perceived by one who grew up in the same home with him and who in adulthood viewed him usually from a lamentable distance. Following the identification of personality traits will come an analysis of influences on him from his background, especially of influences early on (since I am most familiar with them), and—in keeping with the Christian identity of the Zondervan Corporation—a very partial inventory of Stan's theological persuasions and attitudes. Then I'll take up the effect of all the foregoing on what he has contributed to the ministry of Zondervan, and I'll append some personal words addressed directly to him.

Personality Traits

High sociability marks the Stan Gundry whom I know and whom I suspect a good many others know. What an unusually wide circle of acquaintances and friends he can call his own! In small parties, he has dined a couple of times with Rupert Murdoch. In his own Avanti, which he himself beautifully restored, he once transported the automobile magnate John DeLorean.[1] In a crowd, Ollie North has hailed him down with "Hi, Stan!" Dr. Ben Carson owes a good deal of his fame to Stan's seeking him out for the publication of his life story. Chuck Colson counted Stan a friend. And these are not to mention the names of other luminaries, as well as many lesser lights, especially throughout the wide spectrum of evangelical Christianity. So outgoing is Stan, furthermore, that he has gone to high school reunions despite living far away and has pursued his family history not only in genealogical and historical records but also in face-to-face visits with distant relatives both in the United States and in Cornwall, England.

It is hard to know whether Stan's sociability is the cause or the effect of his generosity of spirit. In either case, and to take but one example, this generosity showed itself in his 1978 presidential address to the Evangelical Theological Society, where on the thorny issue of biblical inerrancy he spoke of "assuming the integrity and intellectual honesty of those with whom we [inerrantists] disagree." Naturally, such an assumption led him to hope for dialogue ("engaging the opposing view in open discussion") and to posit for the sake of genuine dialogue the need for both self-criticism and sympathy with other points of view. Stan's own defense of inerrancy on the threefold basis of Scripture's view of itself, the historic view of the church, and consistent logic looks like the three-legged stool of Episcopalism—Scripture, Tradition, and Reason—though he treads cautiously on "the turn of some well-known evangelical personalities to the Episcopal Church and the issuance of the Chicago Call" and its "crypto-episcopalism."[2]

---

1. See Stan's book, *What the Shop Manual Won't Tell You: Tips for Studebaker Avanti Restoration and Maintenance* (Grand Rapids: AvantiPublishing.com, 1999). As a youth, Stan worked in an auto parts shop and traces his interest in the restoration of old automobiles to that job. Besides, our first family automobile was a 1930s Studebaker.

2. For full discussion, see Stanley N. Gundry, "Evangelical Theology: Where *Should* We Be

Though it has not choked off Stan's core convictions, openness to dialogue has also enabled him to be forward-looking, as in the subtitle of the aforementioned presidential address: "Where *Should* We Be Going" (emphasis original or, as I would shift it to make the present point, "Where Should We Be *Going*"). Given Stan's sociability, generosity of spirit, and openness to dialogue, it is no wonder that he has the previously mentioned broad-based personal associations not only in this country but also in other parts of the world.

Background Influences

The preceding identification of Stan's personality traits suffers from brevity, but I go on to ask, What influences enhanced those traits, so far as it is humanly possible to determine such influences? Since Stan got his middle name, "Norman," from our father, it is Norman Gundry (usually "Dad" from now on) who deserves first mention. Converted as a young man, Dad matriculated at the Bible Institute of Los Angeles (or "BI" as he called it; now Biola University), where he met and then married Lolita Hinshaw, an alumna of Pacific University (now George Fox University). Later, our parents took us occasionally to Torrey Memorial Bible Conferences at Biola. It's understandable, then, that upon graduation from college Stan attended Talbot Theological Seminary, a division of Biola, where he got a good dose of dispensational evangelical theology (in addition to the same that he had gotten at home) and where as a teaching fellow he gave instruction in Hebrew under the wing of Charles Feinberg, a Jewish Christian Old Testament scholar. It's also understandable that Stan later joined the faculty of Moody Bible Institute, a school after which Biola had been modeled.

Norman and Lolita Gundry went as missionaries to Nigeria, West

---

Going?" *JETS* 22.1 (1979): 3–8. This address appears also in Quo Vadis, *Evangelicalism: Perspectives on the Past, Direction for the Future*, ed. Andreas J. Köstenberger (Wheaton, IL: Crossway, 2017), 75–90.

Africa, under the Sudan Interior Mission (SIM) and with me in tow. But after several years there, for a medical reason we had to return and stay in the US. Nevertheless, missionaries from various countries subsequently paraded through our home quite often; and I can't help but think that this missionary influence contributed to Stan's interest in and concern for worldwide Christianity.

Now both Biola and SIM were, and are, interdenominational (or nondenominational, according to currently preferred terminology). But Dad was converted in a Baptist church and eventually gravitated to the Baptist communion, in particular to the General Association of Regular Baptist Churches when he learned of its existence and opposition to what was then called "modernism" in theology, and of the ecclesiastical separatism advocated by that association. He became a GARBC pastor, in fact. So Stan spent a good deal of his later boyhood growing up in a GARBC church and home. Not surprisingly, then, prior to his time at Talbot Theological Seminary, for a year he attended the Baptist Bible Seminary in Johnson City, New York, and completed his bachelor of arts degree at the Los Angeles Baptist College, these two undergraduate institutions approved as they were by the GARBC. Nor is it surprising that following his years in college and seminary, Stan pastored a GARBC church in Everson, Washington.

Stan also diverged from our father, however. You could even call the divergence something of a rebellion. Dad believed strongly not only in ecclesiastical separation—so strongly, in fact, that you should separate not only from modernists but also from fellow evangelicals who haven't separated from modernists—but also in separation from worldliness, which for him included the use of tobacco and alcohol, dancing and gambling, watching movies and television, and women wearing lipstick, short hair, and pants. Along with strong evangelistic and Bible-teaching emphases, Dad felt it his pastoral duty to preach regularly and explicitly against those vices. As Stan himself has pointed out in print, multiple copies of John R. Rice's book *Bobbed Hair, Bossy Wives and Women*

Preachers occupied a prominent place on Dad's bookshelf; and he gave copies "to those he thought needed instruction," including Stan upon his leaving home for college (even a GARBC-approved college being dangerous as compared with a Bible school).[3]

Stan would have none of such heavy-handed fundamentalism with respect to worldliness, so that as a pastor himself he preached biblical principles of godly living but left it to his congregants to apply those principles to their own conduct as the Holy Spirit led them. Catching wind of such homiletic lassitude, as he thought it to be, Dad was not pleased. But here we have further evidence of Stan's openness and generosity of spirit.

In addition to Torrey Memorial Bible Conferences and matriculation at Talbot Theological Seminary, earlier influences probably broadened Stan's outlook—or at least prepared him for the broadened outlook that now characterizes him. Our mother grew up an evangelical Quaker and attended the Greenleaf Quaker Academy in Idaho prior to her time at college. It was only natural, then, that after her and Dad's return from Nigeria (again with me in tow), they settled temporarily on her father's farm near Greenleaf, during which period she gave birth to Stan. We all attended the Friends (i.e., Quaker) church in Greenleaf, but soon moved thirty-five miles away to Boise, where to his everlasting, baptistically theological regret ("the worst thing I ever did"), Dad founded the Whitney Friends Church of Boise.[4] Back on the farm several years later, Stan started going to an elementary school that, though public, was dominated by Quakers.

The nearby town of Nampa, Idaho, was dominated by Nazarenes,

---

3. Stan Gundry, "From *Bobbed Hair, Bossy Wives, and Women Preachers* to *Woman Be Free*: My Story," *Priscilla Papers* 19.2 (2005): 19. This article reappeared in the collection of essays by various authors, *How I Changed My Mind about Women in Leadership: Compelling Stories from Prominent Evangelicals*, ed. Alan F. Johnson (Grand Rapids: Zondervan, 2010). I have to wonder whether in titling his book *Bourgeois Babes, Bossy Wives, and Bobby Haircuts: A Case for Gender Equality in Ministry*, published by Zondervan in 2012, Michael F. Bird drew on Stan's recollections of Rice's book, published by Sword of the Lord Publications in 1941.

4. Quakers do not practice baptism or celebrate the Lord's Supper.

kissing cousins of evangelical Quakers. Stan had been born there in a Nazarene hospital, and our family occasionally attended Nazarene camp meetings on the grounds of Nampa Nazarene College (now University) during the summertime. In his boyhood, then, Stan was exposed to a fair amount of Holiness and Arminian influence; and to this day he expresses admiration for the deep piety of his friends and acquaintances in that sector of evangelicalism.

Since our father vehemently disagreed with Calvinism because in his view its doctrine of election crushes evangelistic effort and missionary zeal, collusion (if that's the right word) with Arminians made a certain amount of sense to him and surely made at least a subtle impression on Stan's theological and ecclesiastical outlook. Strangely, for Dad was a cessationist when it comes to miraculous gifts of the Holy Spirit, he would take us even to a Pentecostal revival meeting of the wildfire sort. Whether this particular exposure affected Stan at all, I can't tell. But of some Southern Baptist influence I'm fairly sure, because Dad brought a Southern Baptist evangelist more than once to hold revival meetings at his GARBC church in Brawley, California, where Stan spent the major part of his elementary and high school years. Many of the church members, moreover, had Southern Baptist backgrounds.

Add to these exposures the strains of radio broadcasts such as "The Old Fashioned Revival Hour" (with Charles E. Fuller), "The Radio Bible Class" (with Dr. M. R. DeHaan), and "The Young People's Church of the Air" (with Percy Crawford) that regularly coursed through our home—also subscriptions to *Moody Monthly* and *The Sunday School Times*, as well as the GARBC's *Baptist Bulletin*, Rice's *Sword of the Lord*, Carl McIntire's *Christian Beacon*—and you can appreciate the wide and varied background of which Stan is a product and to which as a big-tent evangelical he has now contributed for a number of decades. I shouldn't forget our frequent attendance at massive Youth for Christ rallies in downtown Los Angeles (Bob Pierce, later the founder of World Vision, in charge and Rudy Atwood at the piano) during the winter of 1944–1945. The earning of a master of sacred theology degree at Union College of British Columbia and of a doctor of sacred theology degree at the Lutheran School of Theology at Chicago broadened Stan's outlook even beyond evangelicalism.

Theological Persuasions and Attitudes

How has Stan reacted to the just-delineated family, church, parachurch, and educational influences that impinged on him? (There are doubtless others, but I have to concentrate on those most familiar to me.) Specifically, what theological persuasions and attitudes represent Stan's reactions? Broadly speaking, he has reacted by developing a keen sense of both strengths and weaknesses evident in the various sectors of evangelical Christianity, especially in the United States. This sense has translated into a fine-tuned appreciation of theological proportion and balance and thus enabled Stan to vary his expressions in accordance with circumstances, just as the telescoping slide mechanism on his trombone enables him to vary the musical pitch of its sound. Though a staunch inerrantist himself, for example, he declared that "discussion of inerrancy should not be allowed to become the preoccupation of evangelical theology. Theology is more than prolegomena."[5] And he reminded his fellow inerrantists that "even James Orr, who did not subscribe to inerrancy, was a contributor to *The Fundamentals* and a valiant defender of orthodoxy," and that "even [J. Gresham] Machen . . . admitted, 'There are many who believe the Bible is right at the central point, and yet believe that it contains many errors. Such men are not really liberals, but Christians.'"[6]

Stan also opined, "Perhaps [Harold] Lindsell's historical and theological argument [for biblical inerrancy] can be faulted in certain minor

---

5. Gundry, "Evangelical Theology," 7.
6. Ibid., 4.

details."[7] Those who, unlike Stan, qualify inerrancy might reapply his descriptor "minor" and object that it is the supposedly minor details in *biblical* texts, not Lindsell's text, that demand a qualification of the doctrine if evangelicals are to avoid a slippery slide into obscurantism—a slide as dangerous as the one ending in a denial of scriptural inspiration. To a limited degree, however, Stan seems to recognize as much when admitting that "a solution [to a textual problem] which theoretically or technically is possible" may produce "something less than a natural or obvious meaning" and therefore a (presumably errant) denial of "the clarity of Scripture."[8]

Despite this recognition, Stan resists what he considers the "magnification of minor points" in scriptural texts, particularly with regard to redaction criticism; and over against those points he stresses "logical consistency and epistemology, Scripture's view of itself, Christ's view of and use of Scripture, and the historic view of the church."[9] But unlike many, Stan is broad-minded enough to recognize the textual problems and call for discussion. In this respect, he takes after the subject of his published doctoral dissertation, *Love Them In: The Proclamation Theology of D. L. Moody*. Fitting Stan to a T, in fact, is his description of Moody as "bringing various theological traditions together in cooperative effort. His was an ecumenism of spirit and practice based on a shared evangelical understanding of the Gospel."[10]

Not so broad-minded or easygoing, perhaps, is Stan on the issue of feminism or, as he calls it, egalitarianism versus hierarchicalism. For he

---

7. Ibid., 3. See Harold Lindsell, *The Battle for the Bible* (Grand Rapids: Zondervan, 1976).

8. Gundry, "Evangelical Theology," 5–6.

9. Robert L. Thomas and Stanley N. Gundry, *The NIV Harmony of the Gospels* (San Francisco: HarperSanFrancisco, 1988), 283; Gundry, "Evangelical Theology," 4. Though Thomas may be mainly responsible for the quotation from his and Stan's NIV harmony, Stan has expressed the same opinion in conversation with me.

10. Stanley N. Gundry, *Love Them In: The Proclamation Theology of D. L. Moody* (Chicago: Moody, 1976), 220. Moody Press republished this book in 1999 with a new preface and a slightly revised title, *Love Them In: The Life and Theology of D. L. Moody*. Here is the place to mention Stan's discovery, in MBI's archives, of the only known recording of Moody, reading Matthew's version of Jesus' beatitudes, as it turned out.

goes so far as to suggest, though not quite to affirm, that "the traditional subjection of women to male leadership" has "perpetuated *sinful* male dominance."[11] But what are we to expect? Stan lost his job at MBI over the women's issue! His wife, Patricia Gundry, gets full credit from him for his conversion to egalitarianism; and he is well-known to have played a leading role in the evangelical feminist movement, especially in connection with Christians for Biblical Equality.

Stan subtitled his manifesto on egalitarianism "My Story." With one exception, the manifesto avoids what he calls "theological and exegetical arguments" and thus suits nicely his resistance to a supposed magnification of minor scriptural points in the practice of redaction criticism. It would be nice to know how Stan harmonizes his appeal to the church's historic view on the question of scriptural inerrancy, on the one hand, and the church's historic view on the question of women's roles, on the other hand. I'll have to ask him someday, though I have a hunch how he'll answer.

Exceptionally, Stan's manifesto does advance a theological argument for egalitarianism, namely, "the grand sweep of biblical or redemptive history" in "the restoration of broken human relationships in general and male/female and husband/wife relationships in particular."[12] Left open for discussion is how this line of argument might link up with the same line in regard to currently lively questions of homosexual intercourse and same-sex marriage; divorce and remarriage; economic injustice and ecological responsibility; and soteriological exclusivism, inclusivism, and universalism.

The women's issue raises the larger issue of hermeneutics. To what extent, if at all, are biblical teachings culturally conditioned? To what extent are our perceptions of them culturally conditioned? As in the definition of worldliness according to Stan, are we dependent on the

---

11. Gundry, "Evangelical Theology," 9 (emphasis added).

12. Gundry, "From *Bobbed Hair*," 19, 21–23. With his attention to the grand sweep of biblical or redemptive history, compare his article "Typology as a Means of Interpretation: Past and Present," *JETS* 12.4 (1969): 233–40.

Holy Spirit's leading to answer these questions? In any case, Stan advises that we become "aware of our own culturally conditioned rationalizations" while at the same time "submitting them to the full authority of what Scripture teaches as the ideal that transcends culture."[13] Then, though he remains a pretribulationist and thus a dispensationalist, there comes a hint that such submission may be drawing covenant theologians and dispensationalists closer together than they used to be.[14] But Stan has broader concerns having to do with missiology and the contextualization of theology for churches throughout the world. And his work at Zondervan has displayed these concerns.

Stan's Contributions to the Ministry of Zondervan

An insider at Zondervan should be writing this section, but I'll do my best as an observer from outside. The close of the preceding section featured Stan's concerns with missiology and the worldwide church. I can't help but imagine that they originated from his having been conceived in Nigeria (as he likes to make known) though born in the United States. How else do you explain his conceiving the *Africa Bible Commentary*, written by Africans for Africans and published by Zondervan?[15] Though not his original idea, Zondervan's *NIV Application Bible Commentary* suits perfectly the emphasis on practicality that he inherited from our father (who was a pragmatist without ever having heard of William James). Also suiting this emphasis is a bevy of books: Gordon D. Fee and Douglas K. Stuart's *How to Read the Bible for All Its Worth*; the

---

13. Gundry, "Evangelical Theology," 9. See also his article, "Hermeneutics or *Zeitgeist* as the Determining Factor in the History of Eschatologies?" *JETS* 20.1 (1977): 45–55, where Stan displays his knowledge of historical theology.

14. Gundry, "Evangelical Theology," 9–10. His pretribulationism came up not so long ago in a conversation between Stan, Craig Keener, and me.

15. See too Samuel Waje Kunhihop's *Africa Christian Theology* and *Africa Christian Ethics*, both published by Zondervan.

NIV Study Bible and the *NIV Zondervan Study Bible* (together replacing the Scofield Reference Bible, on which Stan and I were raised); *The Expositor's Bible Commentary*; Rick Warren's *Purpose Driven* books; and many others.

Under Stan's leadership, the scholarly breadth and depth of Zondervan's academic books have increased dramatically. A sampling of those books includes various Hebrew, Greek, and exegetical helps; the *Zondervan Exegetical Commentary on the New Testament*; the Counterpoints Series of books in which authors of opposing views (on the question of a historical Adam, for instance) debate each other; and more than one volume on Wesleyanism (reflecting Stan's embracing of Wesleyans as an important segment of American evangelicalism). Not to be omitted are Stan's working with the Committee on Bible Translation for the wildly popular New International Version of the Bible, helping forge Zondervan's way into digital publishing, and the creation of tools for online learning. In numerous ways, then, God has used Stan to further the gospel and build up the church through the ministry of Zondervan.

Personal Words Directed to Stan

Stan, I've tried to avoid making my tribute to you overly hagiographic. But your accomplishments joined my justifiable pride in you and brotherly love for you to make the effort difficult. So let me unofficially add another summa cum laude to those you earned longer ago than either of us cares to remember. Because *tempus fugit*, I'm sure to have suffered lapses of memory, lapses leading to mistakes and omissions that shouldn't have been made. Please draw on your generosity of spirit to forgive them as unintentional. More importantly, please forgive the merciless teasing to which our cousin Milas and I subjected you in your early boyhood. In partial atonement thereof I'll buy you another cold cream soda next time you and I are together in Coaldale, Nevada, though making the purchase may prove difficult now that Coaldale has been torched and abandoned.

God bless you, and congratulations on your eight decades of a rich and useful life—with more to come!

Chapter 2

A KEY TO A PUBLISHING FRIENDSHIP

ROBERT A. FRYLING

I probably first met Stan for an introductory handshake at a publishing conference about twenty years ago. It may have been at the ETS (Evangelical Theological Society) conference in Santa Clara or the SBL (Society of Biblical Literature) conference in San Francisco, or perhaps it was the ECPA (Evangelical Christian Publishers Association) leadership summit in Santa Fe.

I have been at so many of these conferences over the years that the hotels, restaurants, and conference venues all meld together into an extended experience of walking, standing, talking, and strategically planning one's meal appointments! Exhibiting as a publisher at these events is a physically demanding time not for the weak of leg or for one needing to diet.

In the midst of exhibiting and selling books, these conferences are relationally rich times when authors and publishers get to exchange book ideas and pursue the common desire to successfully publish new ideas, research, and insights. But they are also times for publishers to get to know each other both personally and professionally. We see each other's booths and often publish the works of some of the same authors. We follow the same schedules and continually bump into each other in hotels and restaurants. We are necessarily all on our guard so as not to engage in collusion or give/take unfair advantage of one another. Yet there is frequently a genuine sense of common mission that transcends the reality of marketplace competition. We are all in the same business, and the bonds of mutual respect and friendship grow over time.

Such has been the case with Stan Gundry and me. Whenever our first handshake was, I vividly remember the first dinner we had together. It was at a traditional Southern restaurant in Atlanta called Pittypat's Porch, which I discovered was a favorite of Stan's—and especially their peach cobbler with homemade ice cream for dessert. But far more important than the delightful calorific intake was the time of exchanging stories with each other.

Although we grew up on opposite coasts and have no known family connections or less than six degrees of separation, we immediately connected at a personal and spiritual level. Some of this was due to similar conservative influences in our lives. Stan was from a GARB (General Association of Regular Baptists) church, while I was raised in a Plymouth Brethren home and local assembly. I'm not sure these groups ever talked with each other or even knew of each other, but they both had a strong commitment to the Bible and to their particular interpretation of it.

Stan's context was probably a bit more legalistic than mine, but we both struggled with how to grow in our understanding of the Scriptures while still being appreciative of the strong biblical roots that shaped our youth. Neither one of us are rebels by nature, but neither were we content to allow certain interpretations of Scripture to be seen as inerrant and ironically trump the essential authority of the Scriptures themselves. So we shared many stories of our spiritual journeys that were taking us beyond the limits of our backgrounds, but in strikingly similar ways.

One profound way was in our shared understanding of God's calling of women in ministry. My background strongly taught that women could not teach in the public worship of the church and that women also needed to wear head coverings. I was perplexed by what seemed to be a lack of a unified witness and clarity in the Bible on this topic, but had concluded that the weight of biblical evidence led to an egalitarian position.

In that first dinner conversation, I discovered that Stan had not only come to a similar conclusion, but he had done so with a far deeper exegetical rigor and a public stance that provided important scholarly support for the egalitarian movement of the CBE (Christians for Biblical Equality). Since InterVarsity Press (IVP) published many books along these lines, we found ourselves talking about these matters in both personal and theological ways.

These shared convictions led Stan to ask my wife, Alice, and me to write a chapter for the Zondervan book *How I Changed My Mind about Women in Leadership*. We were honored to do so, as it is unusual for a publisher to ask another publisher to write for them—but such has been the unusual nature of our relationship.

After that first dinner conversation, we decided to try to have a meal whenever we were at a conference together, and in the spirit of friendship, we would take turns picking up the tab. But we often couldn't remember whose turn it was—until one year at a National Pastors Convention in San Diego, Stan suggested we use a hotel key card as a reminder. So for many years, we would pass that same hotel key card back and forth after our meal as a reminder of whose turn it was to buy the next time!

I'm not sure how many meals we've had together, but they have always been times of relaxed friendship and rich discussions about theological issues and trends. One such topic of conversation has been our mutual respect and appreciation for Tom Oden, who has published books with both Zondervan and InterVarsity Press.

In the course of our conversations, I discovered it was Stan who urged Tom to become a member of ETS to help bridge a chasm between conservative evangelicals and mainline evangelicals and moderates. Stan also invited Tom to be on the Zondervan editorial board for their

Methodist imprint initiative called Francis Asbury Press. Although the imprint did not last, the friendship between Tom and Stan endured. In fact, in Tom Oden's theological memoir, *A Change of Heart*, which InterVarsity Press published, Tom writes with deep appreciation for Stan's encouragement and support for Tom's remarkable spiritual journey.

Interestingly, though, when Tom presented his vision for a multi-volume Bible commentary based on the writings of the church fathers, it was IVP and not Zondervan that accepted this publishing challenge, which became the tremendously successful twenty-nine-volume *Ancient Christian Commentary on Scripture*. Stan and I laugh at how it worked out, but I have never felt any sense of Stan not being able to rejoice with those who rejoice. He has been truly glad that this huge project worked out so well for both Tom and IVP. The mutual affection and respect of Stan and me with Tom Oden are wonderful expressions of Stan's gracious spirit.

Another issue that took more than a few salads and main courses has been our ruminations on the future of evangelicalism. We have lamented the shrinking theological middle between the pulls of a rigid fundamentalism on one side and an uncentered progressivism on the other. In response, we see our publishing houses as meaningful vehicles for providing space and opportunity for genuine scholarly debate and disagreement. We both believe in iron sharpening iron, and our conversations have reflected that dynamic in tone and in substance.

I must eagerly acknowledge, though, that I have been the greater beneficiary in these discussions. Rarely has there been a topic that Stan has not read more widely on or thought more deeply about than I have. His scholarly mind and prodigious work habits have equipped him to engage in almost any theological issue with clear understanding, insights, and opinions. I am glad that Stan knows his own mind and is able to express his convictions with civility and true humility. After some meals, I felt like I owed him tuition!

As I mentioned previously, we needed to be careful to not engage in any conversations as competitors that would be inappropriate or even illegal. We also both had an obligation to protect and promote the interests of our two companies. Keeping these boundaries is especially easy with Stan, as his standards of integrity and scrupulous honesty are of the highest order.

In addition to Stan's external adherence to the letter of the law, he also has demonstrated his Christian character by not descending into matters of gossip or attacks on others. Stan has made some difficult decisions in letting go of successful authors who changed their theological positions beyond what Stan thought was compatible with Zondervan's theological spectrum. Yet he did so without demeaning or denouncing them. He just disagreed with them. Stan never compromised on issues of truth, but he also did not compromise on matters of grace.

One of the most difficult and delicate areas of publishing has to do with publishers getting caught up in disagreements or conflicts with authors that affect both publishing houses. One such instance happened with an author who had published one book with IVP and had signed a contract to write another IVP book.

Unfortunately, the author got caught up in other opportunities and wasn't able to write the new book, despite some contract extensions. But when a Zondervan acquisitions editor innocently approached this author about writing a book for Zondervan, she naively signed a contract with Zondervan without telling Zondervan of her prior obligation to IVP. Consequently, we had the dilemma of an author with two contracts for essentially the same book.

When I realized this awkward situation, I called Stan and explained the situation without knowing how he would respond. To his great credit, he immediately responded that he would be willing to cancel the Zondervan contract. We were able to work out what had become a stressful relationship with the author and released her to publish with Zondervan. But it was Stan's attitude of doing what was right that enabled us to forge a resolution.

Then within several months, we had an opposite situation develop where an author signed a contract and wrote a book with IVP without realizing that he had an exclusive relationship through his agent with Zondervan for a similar book. Again I talked with Stan, and we were able to work out a solution that enabled IVP to publish the book in a way that honored all parties involved. Not all publishing conflicts get resolved so cleanly without resorting to legal wrangling and costs. But I am thankful for Stan and his integrity in enabling us to work out these problems.

The last time I was with Stan at a SBL conference was once again in Atlanta, and again we had a Southern fried chicken meal and pie à la mode. It was a different restaurant, but our time was filled with the same careful and delightful style of conversation. But it was a sad time for us, as I had just announced my retirement, and we realized we probably would not have another publishing conference meal opportunity again. The key card was put away, but the trusting relationship continues.

Thank you, Stan, for being such a disciplined scholar, worthy publishing competitor, and godly man of integrity and convictions. I am deeply grateful for your example and for our two decades of delightful friendship in the arena of Christian publishing. May you continue to think and write and shape Christian publishing for the sake of God's kingdom—and by the way, the next pie à la mode is on me!

Chapter 3

EIGHTY YEARS OF AMERICAN EVANGELICAL THEOLOGY

MILLARD J. ERICKSON

I t is not often that an author receives advice on a Festschrift essay from the person being honored. This chapter, in a somewhat different form, was presented to the Midwest Region of the Evangelical Theological Society in Grand Rapids on March 11, 2016. Stan was present at that session and agreed to read my paper and offer suggestions. His comments were of great help, though, of course, all shortcomings of this chapter are my responsibility. Thanks, Stan!

Any attempt to define evangelicalism is becoming increasingly difficult as the terminology becomes more elastic. The adjective *evangelical* has even been applied to atheism![1] For purposes of this paper, we will use an oversimplified definition: evangelicals are those Christians who hold to the historic doctrines of orthodoxy, who regard a personal acceptance of Jesus Christ as Savior as indispensable to a positive relationship with the triune God, and who seek to encourage others to enter such a relationship.

The past eighty years have been interesting ones for evangelicalism and specifically for evangelical theology. This paper will first sketch

---

1. Martin Miller, "Evangelical Atheists Need to Learn Civility," *Star Tribune Newspaper of the Twin Cities*, July 24, 2002, A21.

the situation in 1937, then trace the developments since that time, draw some lessons from that history, describe the present scene, and offer some suggestions as to how to proceed.

The Situation Eighty Years Ago

By 1937, the fundamentalist-modernist controversy was largely over. The liberal element had prevailed in those denominations where the battle had been engaged. In each case, the conservative group had either remained as a minority voice or had withdrawn. The denominational theological seminaries were under the control of liberals. Conservatives who remained within their larger denominations founded seminaries as alternatives to the more liberal schools. The fundamentalists who withdrew turned to Bible institutes for their leadership, or started their own institutions, such as Dallas and Westminster Seminaries. Conservative Christians were depicted by the press as ignorant and negative persons. Further, rather than presenting a united front against liberalism, evangelicalism had begun to divide further. In some cases, these divisions took place over secondary and even tertiary issues.[2]

Developments during the Past Eight Decades

Any attempt to divide a section of history into subdivisions inevitably involves some arbitrariness and overlap.[3] Nonetheless, some broad delineations may be helpful.

---

2. See Joel Carpenter, *Revive Us Again: The Reawakening of American Fundamentalism* (Oxford: Oxford University Press, 1997), 13–20.

3. The dates here are somewhat fluid and designate the primary character of the periods rather than sharp and discrete separation.

THE PERIOD OF CONSOLIDATION, 1937–1947

Even in the midst of this marginalization of evangelicalism, there were signs of vitality. The conservative churches were growing numerically more rapidly than their more liberal counterparts and were outstripping them in financial giving, missionary activity, and candidates for the ministry.[4]

Among some more educated evangelical leaders, there was a sense of discontent with fundamentalism. Two of them were Harold John Ockenga, pastor of Park Street Church in Boston, and Carl F. H. Henry, a professor at Northern Baptist Seminary in Chicago. Ockenga expressed his concern in an article titled "Can Fundamentalism Win America?" to which his answer was basically, "Not as presently constituted."[5] Henry was even more declarative in his book *The Uneasy Conscience of Modern Fundamentalism*.[6]

Those who were unhappy with fundamentalism gradually came to accept the designation "new evangelicalism."[7] In a sense, they represented a return to the fundamentalism of the very first years of the twentieth century rather than that movement's later development. The specifics of their concern with fundamentalism also constituted the basis for the future direction. They involved several:

---

4. See William Hordern, *New Directions in Theology Today: Volume I: Introduction* (Philadelphia: Westminster, 1966), 75–76. Herman C. Weber, ed., *Yearbook of American Churches* (New York: Round Table, 1933), 300–305; see also 1939 ed., 6–17; 1941 ed., 129–38.

5. Harold John Ockenga, "Can Fundamentalism Win America?" *Christian Life and Times* 2 (June 1947): 13–15.

6. Carl F. H. Henry, *The Uneasy Conscience of Modern Fundamentalism* (Grand Rapids: Eerdmans, 1947).

7. Although Ockenga is usually credited with coining the name in a convocation address in the fall of 1948, Carl Henry had used the term in articles published earlier that year ("The Vigor of the New Evangelicalism," *Christian Life and Times* 3 [January 1948]: 30–32; see also *Christian Life and Times* 3 [March 1948]: 35–38; *Christian Life and Times* 3 [April 1948]: 32–35, 65–69) and affirmed to me in a personal conversation that this was the first public use of the term. I see a development from new evangelicalism—more a mood than a school—to New Evangelicalism a more clearly identified movement, to Neo-Evangelicalism, which redefined some tenets of the earlier evangelicalism. Since about 2000, a group of "postconservative evangelicals" has become increasingly vocal.

1. **A concern for academic scholarship.** This expressed itself most notably in the founding of Fuller Seminary in 1947 as an alternative to liberal mainline schools and a sort of West coast version of what Princeton Seminary had been in the nineteenth century.[8] In 1949, a small group of conservative scholars formed the Evangelical Theological Society for the exchange of scholarly research, and it has since grown to several thousand members. In 1956, *Christianity Today* was launched as an evangelical theological organ rivaling *The Christian Century*.

2. **An emphasis on unity rather than separatism.** Essentials of Christian faith were to be distinguished from secondary and tertiary matters. This led to the formation of the National Association of Evangelicals in 1942, a group positioned between the more liberal Federal (later National) Council of Churches and Carl McIntyre's separatist American Council of Churches. It also showed itself in the inclusion of less than conservative churches and denominations in the evangelistic crusades led by Billy Graham, who came to real prominence in 1949 in connection with his Los Angeles crusade.

3. **An apologetic for the Christian faith in the face of secular opposition.** Early markers of this development were Carl Henry's *Remaking the Modern Mind*, Edward Carnell's *Introduction to Christian Apologetics*, and Bernard Ramm's *The Christian View of Science and Scripture*.[9]

4. **Insistence on social concern, without a diminution of emphasis on evangelism.** Both Ockenga and Henry stressed this in the writings mentioned earlier.

---

8. See George Marsden, *Reforming Fundamentalism: Fuller Seminary and the New Evangelicalism* (Grand Rapids: Eerdmans, 1987), 115.

9. Carl F. H. Henry, *Remaking the Modern Mind* (Grand Rapids: Eerdmans, 1946); Edward John Carnell, *An Introduction to Christian Apologetics* (Grand Rapids: Eerdmans, 1948); Bernard Ramm, *The Christian View of Science and Scripture* (Grand Rapids: Eerdmans, 1954).

THE PERIOD OF CONSTRUCTION, 1947–1977

A number of doctrines received thorough definition at this time. Several dealt with the span of Christian doctrines, often multiauthored, although there was no single exhaustive survey of systematics.[10]

1. Much of the discussion related to the doctrine of Scripture, since this was foundational to the rest of evangelical belief and practice. In fact, biblical inerrancy was the sole article in the Evangelical Theological Society's doctrinal basis.

2. Other works concentrated on the interpretation and authority of the Bible.[11] Initially, these sought to elaborate a methodology for determining the intent of the author and then expanded to grappling with the larger hermeneutical issues of semantics and broader cultural origin.[12]

3. Carl Henry began a multivolume treatment of God, as well as of revelation. In this, he interacted not only with a wide range of biblical and theological scholarship, but also with the philosophical issues of epistemology.

4. Some explorations of Christology began to explore the wider dimensions of the person and work of Christ.[13] Because liberalism had challenged the deity of Christ and especially his virgin birth, some statements of the fundamentals had been silent on his humanity, since this was not at issue.

---

10. Merrill C. Tenney, ed., *The Word for This Century* (New York: Oxford University Press, 1960); Carl F. H. Henry, ed., *Basic Christian Doctrines* (New York: Holt, Rinehart and Winston, 1962); Carl F. H. Henry, ed., *Revelation and the Bible: Contemporary Evangelical Thought* (Grand Rapids: Baker, 1958). Edward John Carnell, *The Case for Orthodox Theology* (Philadelphia: Westminster, 1959).

11. Bernard Ramm, *Protestant Biblical Interpretation: A Textbook of Hermeneutics for Conservative Christians* (Boston: Wilde, 1956); A. Berkeley Mickelsen, *Interpreting the Bible* (Grand Rapids: Eerdmans, 1963); Bernard Ramm, *The Pattern of Authority* (Grand Rapids: Eerdmans, 1957).

12. Anthony Thiselton, *The Two Horizons: New Testament Hermeneutics and Philosophical Description with Special Reference to Heidegger, Bultmann, Gadamer, and Wittgenstein* (Grand Rapids: Eerdmans, 1980); Grant R. Osborne, *The Hermeneutical Spiral: A Comprehensive Introduction to Biblical Interpretation* (Downers Grove, IL: InterVarsity, 1991).

13. See Bernard L. Ramm, *An Evangelical Christology: Ecumenic and Historic* (Nashville: Nelson, 1985).

5. In eschatology, George Eldon Ladd elaborated a nondispen-
sational view of premillennialism.[14] His understanding of the
kingdom included some aspects of the presence of the kingdom
that fundamentalists had neglected because of liberals' emphasis
on God's present earthly reign.

Two general observations about this period are in order. There was
no currently informed evangelical introductory systematic theology
textbook. Professors had to adapt older or less conservative works. As
this period extended, numerous evangelical surveys began to pour from
the pens of scholars representing a variety of evangelical viewpoints.[15]

Secondly, much of this discussion took place within a relatively
homogeneous context. Consequently, much of the scholarship elaborated
the positions of the older theology such as that of nineteenth-century
Princeton theology, although not without new and creative contributions. As noted, some of the work was designed to deal with aspects of
doctrine that had been neglected during the fundamentalist-modernist
controversy. It was when major challenges to these positions arose that
evangelical theologians were forced to define more fully what these
doctrines really meant.

The Period of Controversy, 1977–

The conflicts within evangelicalism during the constructive period
were often between older-line fundamentalists and those who identified themselves as "new evangelicals."[16] Within the latter group,

---

14. George Eldon Ladd, *Crucial Questions About the Kingdom of God* (Grand Rapids: Eerdmans,
1952); *The Blessed Hope: A Biblical Study of the Second Advent and the Rapture* (Grand Rapids:
Eerdmans, 1956).

15. Among the many, some of the first were Millard J. Erickson, *Christian Theology* (Grand
Rapids: Baker, 1986); Wayne Grudem, *Systematic Theology: An Introduction to Biblical Doctrine* (Grand
Rapids: Zondervan, 1994); Alistair McGrath, *Christian Theology: An Introduction* (Cambridge,
MA: Blackwell, 1994); Stanley J. Grenz, *Theology for the Community of God* (Nashville: Broadman
& Holman, 1994). Many more have followed.

16. Edward Carnell's *Case for Orthodox Theology*, for example, had been critical of fundamentalism, and in return received similarly sharp criticism from fundamentalists.

however, some theologians began to express somewhat broader views, resulting in conflict both with fundamentalists and the conservative new evangelicals.

Specific Doctrinal Loci

Biblical inerrancy. The first of these cracks to appear was over inerrancy. An early sign was the faculty retreat at Fuller Seminary in 1962 on "Black Saturday," which revealed significant differences among faculty members. This tended to be a divergence between those who held that the Bible was inerrant in all its assertions, including those on matters of history and science, and those who held that inerrancy applied only to the theological matters, those things related to "making us wise unto salvation."[17] By the 1970s, the issue was becoming more sharply etched. Harold Lindsell held that inspiration involved a very specific interpretation of Scripture, so that the relationship of the circumference to the diameter of the furnishing described in 2 Chronicles 4:1–2 must be exactly equal to pi.[18] The International Council on Biblical Inerrancy was formed and held its first summit in Chicago in October 1978. It drew up the Chicago Statement on Biblical Inerrancy, signed by more than three hundred attendees. This highly nuanced statement defined inerrancy between the views of Lindsell and those who regarded the Bible's inerrancy as applying only to revelational matters.[19] For several years, the issue has arisen as an implication of other doctrines. It has gained prominence more recently in connection with the writings of persons such as Peter Enns.[20]

Gifts of the Holy Spirit. Within evangelicalism there has been a division between cessationists, who believe that the supernatural gifts

---

17. See Marsden, *Reforming Fundamentalism*, 208–15.
18. Harold Lindsell, *The Battle for the Bible* (Grand Rapids: Zondervan, 1976), 165–66.
19. See Daniel P. Fuller, "Benjamin B. Warfield's View of Faith and History," *Bulletin of the Evangelical Theological Society* 11.2 (Spring 1968): 75–83.
20. Peter Enns, *Inspiration and Incarnation: Evangelicals and the Problem of the Old Testament* (Grand Rapids: Baker, 2005).

such as tongues speaking and healing ceased with the close of the apostolic age, and those who believe that God is bestowing these in the present time and believers should seek to receive them. There had been a sort of agreement to disagree. In the 1980s, however, under such nomenclature as the third wave of the Holy Spirit, signs and wonders, and power evangelism, there was a renewed emphasis on the powerful working of the Holy Spirit. John Wimber, Charles Kraft, and Peter Wagner were among the strongest proponents of this emphasis, although even Calvinist theologian Wayne Grudem became part of the movement.[21]

Gender roles. Although there is no established position within evangelicalism on the relationship of men and women, historically a majority have held to the traditional position that in a marriage, the husband and father is to exercise loving leadership, and the wife and children are to submit to this leadership. With respect to the officers of the church, this position also held that ministry, particularly that of administration and preaching and teaching of the Word, was reserved to men.

Some evangelicals became advocates for marital equality of authority and for full access to offices of teaching and leadership for women. Others, however, emphatically rejected this view, believing that the Bible taught the traditional view, especially in passages such as 1 Corinthians 11:3; 14:33–36; Ephesians 5:22–24; 1 Timothy 2:11–15; 3:2, 12; Titus 1:6.[22] The former group regard these as culturally conditioned, like the references to slavery and female attire, which sometimes occur in juxtaposition to the instructions about male leadership.[23]

---

21. John Wimber and Kevin Springer, *Power Evangelism* (New York: Harper & Row, 1986); Charles H. Kraft, *Christianity with Power: Your Worldview and Your Experience of the Supernatural* (Ann Arbor, MI: Vine, 1989); C. Peter Wagner, *How to Have a Healing Ministry Without Making Your Church Sick* (Ventura, CA: Regal, 1988); Wayne A. Grudem, *The Gift of Prophecy in the New Testament and Today* (Westchester, IL: Crossway, 1988).

22. John Piper and Wayne A. Grudem, eds., *Recovering Biblical Manhood and Womanhood: A Response to Evangelical Feminism* (Wheaton, IL: Crossway, 1991); Wayne Grudem, *Evangelical Feminism and Biblical Truth: An Analysis of More Than One Hundred Disputed Questions* (Sisters, OR: Multnomah, 2004).

23. See Craig S. Keener, *Paul, Women & Wives: Marriage and Women's Ministry in the Letters of Paul* (Peabody, MA: Hendrickson, 2004); Philip Barton Payne, *Man and Woman: One in Christ: An Exegetical and Theological Study of Paul's Letters* (Grand Rapids: Zondervan, 2009).

The nature of doctrine. Stanley Grenz challenged the traditional view of doctrine as the systematic compilations of the doctrinal teachings of Scripture.[24] In its place, he defined doctrine as the Christian community's reflection on its beliefs.[25] Grenz acknowledged the similarity of his view of doctrine to that of the postliberal scholar George Lindbeck.[26]

Salvation of the unevangelized. In the 1990s, Clark Pinnock and John Sanders argued that large numbers of those who do not hear of Jesus during their earthly lives nonetheless will be saved. The principal argument was that they will come to saving faith through the general revelation.[27] This concept of implicit faith was supplemented with the idea of "eschatological evangelism": that those who do not hear the gospel within their earthly life will have an opportunity to hear and choose after death.[28] Finally, these men also held to annihilationism—the doctrine that the finally impenitent will not live on in endless agonizing separation from God, but will rather simply cease to exist.[29]

These views were vigorously opposed by more conservative evangelicals, many of whom held that not only would those who had not heard not be saved, but they could not possibly be saved without the benefit of the special revelation.[30] Most of their critics also rejected any form of annihilationism and in some cases held a literal view of hell, involving physical suffering from literal flames. The Consultation on Evangelical Affirmations did not include a statement on annihilation in its articles of belief.[31]

---

24. Stanley J. Grenz, *Revisioning Evangelical Theology: A Fresh Agenda for the 21st Century* (Downers Grove, IL: InterVarsity, 1993), 65–72.

25. Ibid., 75–76, 87.

26. Ibid., 77–78.

27. See Clark H. Pinnock, *A Wideness in God's Mercy: The Finality of Jesus Christ in a World of Religions* (Grand Rapids: Zondervan, 1992), 157–63; John Sanders, *No Other Name: An Investigation into the Destiny of the Unevangelized* (Grand Rapids: Eerdmans, 1992), 233–36.

28. Pinnock, *Wideness in God's Mercy*, 168–72.

29. See Clark H. Pinnock, "The Destruction of the Finally Impenitent," *Criswell Theological Review* 4.2 (Spring 1990): 43–59.

30. See John Piper, *Let the Nations Be Glad: The Supremacy of God in Missions*, 2nd ed. (Grand Rapids: Baker, 2003), 113–34.

31. Carl F. H. Henry and Kenneth Kantzer, eds., *Evangelical Affirmations* (Grand Rapids:

Divine foreknowledge. A dispute over the nature of God, and particularly his knowledge of the future, came to the fore in the 1990s. The traditional view was that God knows all events that will ever occur, and some also held that he knows all the possible events that could occur. Over against this view were the "open theists." One aspect of their theology was that God knows all of the future with the exception of future actions of free moral agents. These theologians based their view on biblical passages in which God seemed to profess ignorance of the future, repented of his intentions, and changed his mind when certain events occurred or in response to human petitions.[32]

Those who opposed this open view did so on the basis of two types of biblical considerations: texts that declared that God knew even human actions in advance, and instances of such knowledge, particularly in connection with prophecy.[33] To them, the open theist view was inconsistent with the doctrine of biblical inerrancy. A thorough examination of the views of Clark Pinnock and John Sanders led to the acquittal of both.[34] There has been no further major open discussion of the issue within the Evangelical Theological Society.

The Trinity. More recently, discussion has arisen over the relationships of authority among the members of the Trinity. One group insists that the Father is eternally supreme in authority and that the Son and the Spirit are, always have been, and always will be subordinate to him.[35] They base this on Jesus' statements while on earth that he came to do the Father's will, his sitting now at the Father's right hand, and

Zondervan, 1990), 36–37.

32. Clark Pinnock, Richard Rice, John Sanders, William Hasker, and David Basinger, *The Openness of God: A Biblical Challenge to the Traditional Understanding of God* (Downers Grove, IL: InterVarsity, 1994).

33. John Piper, Justin Taylor, and Paul Kjoss Helseth, eds., *Beyond the Bounds: Open Theism and the Undermining of Biblical Christianity* (Wheaton, IL: Crossway, 2003).

34. "Reports Relating to the Fifty-Fifth Annual Meeting of the Society," *Journal of the Evangelical Theological Society* 47.1 (March 2004): 171.

35. Bruce Ware, *Father, Son, and Holy Spirit: Relationships, Roles, and Relevance* (Wheaton: Crossway, 2005); Wayne Grudem, *Systematic Theology: An Introduction to Biblical Doctrine* (Grand Rapids: Zondervan, 1994), 248–52; *Evangelical Feminism and Biblical Truth*, 433.

his model prayer in which he told his followers to pray to the Father. Another group of evangelicals contends that the Son's submission to the Father was part of his ministry on earth, but that he (and the Spirit) are co-equal with the Father in authority. They note biblical statements that Jesus became obedient (Philippians 2:8) and that he learned obedience (Hebrews 5:8).[36] Some philosophers of religion contend that if the superordination/subordination is eternal and inherent in the Trinity, then these are essential attributes; thus the essence of the Father and the Son are different, so their opponents' views are implicitly Arian.[37]

Conversion. The traditional understanding of conversion was that it included both repentance and faith. Some theologians, such as Zane Hodges, distinguished between these two. While faith is necessary for conversion, repentance is not a condition for eternal salvation.[38] While accepting Jesus as Savior is essential to salvation, accepting his lordship is not, although it is necessary for discipleship.[39]

Atonement. For the most part, twentieth-century evangelicals held to the substitutionary-penal interpretation of the atonement. Some evangelicals have recently begun to contend that such a view arose out of a societal structure of feudal lord and serf, so that this view is historically conditioned rather than biblically based.[40] Some have even questioned whether the picture of a Father who puts his Son to death is faithful to the biblical witness regarding the nature of God.[41] On the other hand, more traditional evangelicals contend that the biblical evidence supports the substitutionary-penal view.[42]

---

36. Kevin Giles, *Jesus and the Father: Modern Evangelicals Reinvent the Doctrine of the Trinity* (Grand Rapids: Zondervan, 2006), 117.

37. Thomas McCall, *Which Trinity? Whose Monotheism? Philosophical and Systematic Theologians on the Metaphysics of Trinitarian Theology* (Grand Rapids: Eerdmans, 2010), 175–88.

38. Zane C. Hodges, *Absolutely Free: A Biblical Reply to Lordship Salvation*, 2nd ed. (Denton, TX: Grace Evangelical Society, 2014), 128.

39. Ibid., 18–20.

40. Joel B. Green and Mark D. Baker, *Recovering the Scandal of the Cross: Atonement in New Testament and Contemporary Contexts* (Downers Grove, IL: InterVarsity, 2000), 126–36.

41. Steve Chalke and Alan Mann, *The Lost Message of Jesus* (Grand Rapids: Zondervan, 2003), 182.

42. I. Howard Marshall, *Aspects of the Atonement: Cross and Resurrection in the Reconciling of*

Justification. A number of objections have traditionally been raised to the idea of forensic justification. In the last decade or two, N. T. Wright has especially challenged the forensic view with his idea of a second justification. Whereas the initial justification is based solely on faith, the final justification will take into account faithful works done in obedience to God's commands as depicted in Matthew 25:31–46.[43] Several evangelical theologians and New Testament scholars have disagreed vigorously.[44]

Epistemology. Traditional evangelical theology had held that through God's special revelation believers have a true, objective knowledge of God. While not exhaustive, this is genuine. The biblical revelation was thought not simply to present God in an encounter with humans, but also to convey true information about him. Although this has often been labeled propositional revelation, its adherents maintain that is a somewhat inaccurate term.

Postmodernism has challenged this idea of human knowledge, which it contends is always conditioned historically, culturally, or linguistically. Postmodern or postconservative evangelicals have also maintained that the traditional view is an instance of a now discredited foundationalism, in which all knowledge is justified by being based on an absolutely certain starting point, in this case, an inerrant Scripture.[45] Rather than conceiving of the Bible as a collection of inerrant propositions, it should be understood as a grand narrative, a story. The essence of evangelicalism should not be thought of as a set of doctrines, but as a living experience with God.

God and Humanity (Colorado Springs: Paternoster, 2007).

43. N. T. Wright, *Justification: God's Plan and Paul's Vision*, 2nd ed. (Downers Grove, IL: InterVarsity, 2009), 160–62.

44. For example, Thomas R. Schreiner, *Faith Alone—The Doctrine of Justification: What the Reformers Taught . . . and Why It Still Matters* (Grand Rapids: Zondervan, 2015).

45. See Stanley J. Grenz and John R. Franke, *Beyond Foundationalism: Shaping Theology in a Postmodern Context* (Louisville: Westminster John Knox, 2001); Elizabeth Blackwell, "The Data Renaissance," *Weinberg Magazine* (Fall/Winter 2016), 20–25, www.weinberg.northwestern.edu/after-graduation/weinberg-magazine/fall-winter-2016/the-data-renaissance.html (accessed May 15, 2017).

Lessons to Be Drawn from the Periods of Construction and Controversy

1. Scripture is evangelicals' supreme authority; its modifications affect the construction of other doctrines.

2. There is a pendular tendency in theology. Thus, there is a reaction to any movement that deviates from the mean. That reaction, however, does not usually stop at the point from which departure took place, but tends to overreact and become an error in the opposite direction.

3. Theology is organic. Where a given doctrinal development stems from a particular principle, that principle will tend to produce congruent developments in other doctrines as well. So, for example, Clark Pinnock's and John Sanders's views of salvation of the unevangelized were followed by their views of divine foreknowledge.

4. Developments in the broader culture affect doctrinal developments. An example can be seen in the gender debates, where clashes of cultural positions also appear within theological circles.

5. A number of doctrines are still in need of further treatment. Some of them underlie the discussions that are taking place and in some cases are interrelated. Among these are general revelation, the salvation of those who die in infancy, Christ's ascension, the nature of the resurrection body, and the intermediate state.

6. Ignoring history can lead to a procedure similar to reinventing the wheel. In some cases, issues reappear in forms where help could be derived from an examination of earlier treatment of similar issues. Compare, for instance, the tendency toward generic church names with an article discussing a similar phenomenon more than ninety years ago![46]

---

46. John R. Scotford, "Church Names as a Liability," *Christian Century* XXXX.25 (June 28, 1923): 817.

The Present-Day Situation

SPECIFIC DEVELOPMENTS

As we look at the scene of evangelical theology today, a number of characteristics stand out:

1. **The passing from the active scene of many evangelical theologians.** In the case of the evangelical left, this has been especially notable. Stanley Grenz, Robert Webber, Clark Pinnock, John Sanders, and Gregory Boyd have either died or left full-time teaching at evangelical schools in the past ten years. Among conservative evangelicals, such theological stalwarts as Carl Henry, Roger Nicole, Donald Bloesch, and Thomas Oden are no longer with us, and others, like J. I. Packer, have reached the age where their scholarly output has reduced. A number of younger scholars have made promising contributions to the field, but at this point, no future leader on either side of evangelicalism is identifiable.

2. **Dissection of the discipline.** In the past, theology has been largely done by persons whose training was in the field of systematic theology or dogmatics. More recently, many working in the field come rather from a concentration in biblical studies,[47] history,[48] or philosophy.[49] The result tends to be theology somewhat lacking in one or more of the major elements of the discipline. Gordon Lewis and Bruce Demarest commendably attempted a more methodologically comprehensive survey.[50]

---

47. Grudem, *Systematic Theology.*

48. James Leo Garrett Jr., *Systematic Theology: Biblical, Historical, and Evangelical,* 2 vols. (Grand Rapids: Eerdmans, 1990, 1995).

49. Norman L. Geisler, *Systematic Theology* (Minneapolis: Bethany, 2011).

50. Gordon R. Lewis and Bruce A. Demarest, *Integrative Theology: Historical, Biblical, Systematic, Apologetic, Practical* (Grand Rapids: Zondervan, 1996).

3. **Popularization of discussion.** With the spread of social media, persons with only basic theological training have blogs and Twitter accounts on which they expound theology with considerable certainty but, in some cases, limited quality. This is in part a product of the popular version of postmodernism according to which anyone's opinion is of equal value to anyone else's, and to suggest otherwise is an instance of oppression. Paradoxically, there is also a tendency to follow somewhat uncritically the teachings of a few gurus. Often these are not theological professors, but pastors or other more popular figures. With the decline of theological seminaries, the traditional major locus of theological scholarship, this trend will probably continue.[51]

4. **Polarization.** The current political polarization has been well documented.[52] It is paralleled by theological and ecclesiastical polarization. Part of this is what I call "purism," in which the purity of the view is so important that one must adhere to it in its entirety. While this has usually been more characteristic of the evangelical right, it also recently has come to be true of the left, who often seem more inclined to engage in dialogue with nonevangelicals than with conservative evangelicals.

5. **Absolutism.** There is currently a tendency to maintain that one's position is absolutely certain. This frequently involves an insistence that every biblical text supports their view, even if this requires somewhat strained and dubious interpretations of some of those texts. The corollary is that finding a single problem with the opposing view is believed to invalidate it.

---

51. See G. Jeffrey Macdonald, "Oldest U.S. Graduate Seminary to Close Campus," *Washington Post*, November 13, 2015, www.washingtonpost.com/national/religion/oldest-us-graduate-seminary -to-close-campus/2015/11/13/b2dd8876-8a54-11e5-bd91-d385b244482f_story.html (accessed May 15, 2017).

52. "Partisan Polarization Surges in Bush, Obama Years: Trends in American Values: 1987– 2012," *Pew Research Center*, June 4, 2012, www.people-press.org/2012/06/04/partisan-polarization -surges-in-bush-obama-years (accessed May 15, 2017).

6. **Rhetoric.** The discussion has at times been conducted with language that has not contributed to calm and objective discussion. This has been true from both extremes. Likening one's opponents to "evangelical Taliban" is not likely to advance the discussion.[53]

GENERAL CHARACTERISTIC:
THE SHIFT OF IDEOLOGICAL ENVIRONMENT

At the beginning of the period, the struggle was with modernism. This held that there was objective truth, but that orthodox Christianity did not possess it. Today the challenge is coming from postmodernism. Although postmodernists insist that all views are conditioned and therefore relativized, they generally do not apply this to their own view. The philosopher Michel Foucault's concept of fictive history means that facts are created to substantiate a view.[54] The literary critic Stanley Fish basically recommends winning arguments by stipulative definition.[55] With the spread of postmodernism into evangelicalism, some of its approaches to truth have also begun to appear there. While it may be tempting to try to win theological arguments or ecclesiastical struggles by embellishing the truth, it is a contradiction of Paul's statement in 2 Corinthians 4:2: "Rather, we have renounced secret and shameful ways; we do not use deception, nor do we distort the word of God. On the contrary, by settling forth the truth plainly we commend ourselves to everyone's conscience in the sight of God." When views are supported not by rational argument but by coercion, an absolutism or authoritarianism generally underlies it.

---

53. Bruce A. Ware, "Rejoinder to Replies by Clark H. Pinnock, John Sanders, and Gregory A. Boyd," *Journal of the Evangelical Theological Society* 45.2 (June 2002): 251. Ware's reference to "evangelical Taliban" is to a statement by Sanders in his plenary address at the 53rd Annual Meeting of the Evangelical Theological Society in Colorado Springs on November 15, 2001.

54. Michel Foucault, "Questions of Method," in *After Philosophy: End or Transformation*, ed. Kenneth Baynes, James Bohman, and Thomas McCarthy (Cambridge: MIT Press, 1987), 111–12.

55. Stanley Fish, *There's No Such Thing as Free Speech . . . and It's a Good Thing Too* (New York: Oxford University Press, 1994), 6–7.

Going Forward

The issues I have mentioned to this point were debated within a framework of what I would call "pre-postmodernism." I use that awkward term in part to emphasize the commonality between the premodern and modern periods regarding the nature of truth and the means of getting to truth. Conversely, I use it to dispute the contention that the objective conception of truth arose as a product of the Enlightenment. The current and near future discussions will have to take place within a different environment.

POLITICAL CORRECTNESS AND OTHER RESTRICTIONS OF EXPRESSION

In other places, most notably *Truth or Consequences*,[56] I have discussed postmodernism and have challenged the epistemological issues involved therein. I would insist that given the opportunity to advance their arguments, pre-postmodernists can make a persuasive case. I also note that in a number of disciplines, a move back toward more objective positions is taking place.[57] What I am suggesting here, however, is that the real struggle will be not so much epistemological but communicational, or even political. To put it more bluntly, we will need to contend to be able even to express and argue for our views, and for them to be heard.

We are all familiar with the phenomenon known as political correctness. That is a situation in which certain views, generally of a liberal nature, are the only ones considered legitimate for consideration or even expression.[58] In political correctness, instead of argument against the

---

56. Millard J. Erickson, *Truth or Consequences: The Promise and Perils of Postmodernism* (Downers Grove, IL: InterVarsity Press, 2001).

57. Patricia Cohen, "Digital Keys for Unlocking the Humanities' Riches," *New York Times*, November 16, 2010, www.nytimes.com/2010/11/17/arts/17digital.html?ref=topics; "Analyzing Literature by Words and Numbers," *New York Times*, December 3, 2010, www.nytimes.com/2010/12/04/books/04victorian.html?ref=topics; "In 500 Billion Words, New Window on Culture," *New York Times*, December 16, 2010, www.nytimes.com/2010/12/17/books/17words.html?ref=topics (all articles accessed May 15, 2017).

58. Ben Shapiro, *Bullies: How the Left's Culture of Fear and Intimidation Silences Americans* (New York: Threshold, 2013).

truth of a view, the right of a given view to be expressed and argued for is questioned. The attempt to suppress free thought, discussion, and debate is currently taking several forms in our society and with respect to evangelical beliefs. It can even be found expressed by some evangelicals.

- **Declaring that certain references should not be used because they might offend someone.** In a session of a regional Evangelical Theological Society meeting, one member vigorously condemned a speaker's use of a particular historical figure's name in a humorous illustration, even though that person has a federal holiday named for him and the member conceded that no persons from that ethnic group were present.
- **Branding positions.** The usurping of the term *complementarian* rather than distinguishing hierarchical- and egalitarian-complementarians is an example.
- **Ruling out certain viewpoints as incredible, indefensible, or unsophisticated.** Consequently, such a view need not even be considered. A creationist view of origins is an example.
- **Simply avoiding the presentation of certain facts.** In one case, a Christian periodical stated that a certain theologian was "another who withheld his signature" from a declaration, even though the scholar involved informed the reporter *three times* that he had not even been asked to endorse it.[59]

STRATEGY FOR THE COMING DECADE

In light of these developments, I suggest that we shift our focus from *what we debate* and the position we take, to the *right to debate* and to hold conclusions. This strategy would involve certain tactics:

---

59. Millard J. Erickson, "Evangelical Theological Scholarship in the Twenty-First Century," in Quo Vadis, *Evangelicalism?* ed. Andreas J. Köstenberger (Wheaton, IL: Crossway, 2007), 192–93; see Timothy C. Morgan, "Theologians Decry 'Narrow' Boundaries," *Christianity Today* 45.7 (June 10, 2002): 18.

- We need to suspend some of our internal debates and join with other evangelicals who have the same concern for objective truth. This is not to say that these issues are not important, but that unless we are willing to become culturally marginalized, we must concentrate on establishing the very right to express and argue theology.

- We also need to recruit some neglected evangelicals to the task. There are capable women who do not enter the discipline because they perceive that they will not receive the sort of hearing that male theologians do. Minorities and Majority World theologians will have more influence as the evangelical church gains strength in different circles than we have usually attended to. White, male, middle-class Americans will need to reconsider their somewhat imperialistic attitude toward theology.

- This, in turn, will mean that theologians will need to have competence in all subdisciplines of systematic theology. Competence in biblical, historical, or philosophical studies, as well as in the social sciences, will be needed to establish the right to do evangelical theology.

- We will need to make common cause with nonevangelicals who also believe in objective truth and in free expression. To some "purists," this will seem like compromise. I would suggest that the analogy is to the way evangelicals have teamed with Roman Catholics on right-to-life issues. This will also mean we participate in professional societies where we have an opportunity to interact with them.

- Theology must be tested in the realm of practice. Theology has often been enclosed in an ivory tower. While the workability of a given theology does not establish that it is true, the lack of workability is evidence of its falsity, while allowing for debate over the measure of practicality. Theology need not be written on a lay level, but it should be translatable to those not trained theologically. Antecedent and ongoing experience in ministry should be requirements for those who teach and write theology.

• With the decline of the influence of print media and broadcast and channel television, especially among millennials, other opportunities for expression and influence are growing. I have in mind the social media. The problem, of course, is that because anyone can express himself or herself in these media, there is a lot of nonsense, and the sheer quantity of information detracts from notice of our expressions. In the big picture, however, I am hopeful that the persons we want to influence will be able to discern and take seriously the message we are attempting to communicate.

• We will need to find creative ways to express the message if we expect to be heard. This includes finding ways to sneak up on people with the truth. The primary biblical instance of this is Nathan's approach to David in 2 Samuel 12:1–14, where he posed the situation in a parable, so that David unknowingly pronounced judgment on himself: "The man should die!" (verse 5). That type of creativity, in which we are able to get past the defenses of others, is what will be needed.

• Rather than simply attempting to relate to the present situation, we need to be preparing for the next era. I expect, on the basis of some preliminary indications, that at some point our culture will enter a new period of objectivism, but one that will be different from the previous ones.[60] We need to be developing a neo-objectivism that will be successful in reaching those in that age. Generals sometimes are guilty of preparing to fight the last war, but the next war will probably not be military warfare but rather economic, energy, currency, or cyberwarfare. We need similarly to be prepared to deal with the next cultural setting, not the last one or even the present one. One of the ways we can anticipate the future for theology is

---

60. In addition to the *New York Times* articles cited earlier, see my *Truth or Consequences*, 319–28.

to observe developments in other areas of culture, since religion is often the last to respond to such changes. Another is to observe where the momentum in the world community is. For example, not only politically and economically but in Christianity, the influence has for some time been moving both east and south. We can expect those societies to have a greater impact on developments in the days ahead.

I do not expect to be part of that future, but I am both pessimistic and optimistic about it. Short term, evangelicalism may well have some difficult times theologically. Longer term, however, God has raised up over the centuries persons from sometimes surprising places to perpetuate his church and his mission. The younger men and women of evangelicalism have a great opportunity. May God use those who serve in the decades to come.

Chapter 4

THE FUNDAMENTALIST-
MODERNIST CONTROVERSY

JOHN D. WOODBRIDGE[1]

The story of the fundamentalist-modernist controversy constitutes a signally important chapter of American religious history. The present modest study constitutes a reception history of Charles Woodbridge's personal glimpses and perceptions of Professor J. Gresham Machen and Professor Adolph von Harnack. It provides additional historical background with which to understand the careers of these two iconic figures in the fundamentalist-modernist controversy. The study also sheds further light on the long reach of this controversy's influence into the foreign mission fields of the day.

Introducing the Controversy

During 1924–1927—the period when Charles J. Woodbridge attended Princeton Theological Seminary—the fundamentalist-modernist

---

1. The author is the son of Charles J. Woodbridge. This filial relationship should be factored into any assessment of the objectivity of this essay. The author expresses his sincere thanks to Karla Fackler Grafton, Archives and Rare Books Librarian at Westminster Theological Seminary, for her generous help in providing access to the Machen/Woodbridge correspondence in the archives of the Montgomery Library at Westminster Theological Seminary in Philadelphia. The author also expresses

controversy was raging in the United States. On May 21, 1922, Harry Emerson Fosdick (1878–1969), an ordained Baptist supply pastor of the First Presbyterian Church of New York City, had fired up the smoldering controversy when he preached a provocative sermon titled "Shall the Fundamentalists Win?" To his own rhetorical question, Fosdick trumpeted a famous, clarion, and prophetic response: "No."[2]

Fosdick indicated divisive fundamentalists could not "drive out from the Christian churches all the consecrated souls who do not agree with their theory of inspiration." He alleged that the fundamentalist view of biblical inspiration encompassed a literalistic hermeneutic, a mechanical dictation theory of inspiration, and a useless belief in the inerrancy of the "original documents of the Scripture."[3] He also succinctly explained the agenda of liberalism or modernism: "It is primarily an adaptation, an adjustment, an accommodation of the Christian faith to contemporary scientific thinking. It started by taking the intellectual culture of a particular period as its criterion and then adjusting Christian teaching to that standard." Fosdick's sermon was printed under a revised title, "The New Knowledge and the Christian Faith," and distributed to

---

thanks to Stan Gundry for his warm friendship and generosity in sharing a profound knowledge of the history of evangelicalism and fundamentalism. Stan Gundry knew Charles Woodbridge.

2. Harry Emerson Fosdick, "Shall the Fundamentalists Win?" *Christian Work* 102 (June 22, 1922): 716–22. Concerning Fosdick's sermon, see Robert Miller, *Harry Emerson Fosdick, Preacher, Pastor, Prophet* (New York: Oxford University Press, 1985), 116–17, 130, 158.

3. Princeton theologians like B. B. Warfield, often portrayed as the originators of a "fundamentalist" view of biblical inerrancy in the original autographs, did not in fact uphold a mechanical dictation theory of biblical inspiration. See Bradley N. Seeman, "The 'Old Princetonians' on Biblical Authority," in *The Enduring Authority of the Christian Scriptures*, ed. D. A. Carson (Grand Rapids: Eerdmans, 2016), 195–227; Fred G. Zaspel, *The Theology of B. B. Warfield: A Systematic Summary* (Wheaton, IL: Crossway, 2010), 111–75; Paul Helseth, *Right Reason and the Princeton Mind: An Unorthodox Proposal* (Phillipsburg, NJ: P&R, 2010). The premise of lost "original documents of Scripture" did not constitute a useless belief. It recognized that the infallible "autographs" of Scripture no longer exist but could be very closely reconstituted through lower textual criticism—a practice extending back to the Patristic Period (see Augustine's letter to Faustus the Manichean, *Letters of St. Augustine*, 82:3: "I confess to your Charity that I have learned to yield this respect and honor only to the canonical books of Scripture: of these alone do I most firmly believe that the authors were completely free from error. And if in these writings I am perplexed by anything which appears to me opposed to truth, I do not hesitate to suppose that either the manuscript is faulty, or the translator has not caught the meaning of what was said, or I myself have failed to understand.").

130,000 ordained pastors throughout the nation. John D. Rockefeller Jr. funded this publishing initiative.

Fosdick advocated "liberal progressive Christianity." He argued that in an age enthralled by the accomplishments of "science," Christians needed to accommodate their faith to the "great mass of new knowledge," including Darwinian evolution and biblical higher criticism. If such accommodations were not forthcoming, Fosdick reasoned that people might conclude Christianity was not intellectually viable or defensible because it wasn't sufficiently compatible with the "new knowledge."

In 1925, the Scopes Trial made front-page headlines in the nation's newspapers. Many modernists believed lawyer Clarence Darrow ostensibly bested in argument William Jennings Bryan, a famous critic of evolution and a recognized fundamentalist spokesperson. For them, the Scopes Trial provided further evidence of the supposed anti-intellectualism and backward cultural attitude of fundamentalism.[4]

By contrast, fundamentalists worried that Christianity's influence in American culture was rapidly ebbing, and modernists were abetting this loss. They complained that modernists, often criticized as partisans of a form of naturalism, were commandeering Christian denominations.[5] Modernists were gaining strategic leadership positions

---

4. For a persuasive revisionary assessment of the career of William Jennings Bryan and the Scopes Trial, see Edward Larsen, *Summer of the Gods: The Scopes Trial and America's Continuing Debate over Science and Religion* (New York: Basic, 2006). Larsen traces the history of perceptions of the Scopes Trial in the twentieth century and beyond. The William Jennings Bryan described in his account does not match the laughingstock caricatures of Bryan displayed in a film like *Inherit the Wind* and in some secondary literature. Standard works on the history of fundamentalism include insider perspectives of David Beale (*In Pursuit of Purity: American Fundamentalism Since 1850* [Greenville, SC: Bob Jones University Press, 1986]) and George Dollar (*A History of Fundamentalism in America* [Greenville, SC: Bob Jones University Press, 1973]), as well as outsider perspectives of George Marsden (*Fundamentalism and American Culture* [New York: Oxford University Press, 2006] and Joel Carpenter (*The Reawakening of American Fundamentalism* [New York: Oxford University Press, 1991]).

5. In *What Is Christianity?* Professor Adolph von Harnack had advocated a form of naturalism: "We are firmly convinced that what happens in space and time is subject to the general laws of motion, and that in this sense, as an interruption of the order of Nature, there can be no such things as 'miracles'" (*What Is Christianity?* 2nd ed. [1901, repr., New York: G. P. Putnam's Sons, 1908], 28–29).

in church hierarchies, boards, schools, and mission agencies. For their part, fundamentalists believed they urgently needed to halt the advance of modernists. They might be able to do this if they united together and forthrightly defended the "fundamental" doctrines of the faith (the number of which varied among fundamentalists). Some fundamentalists sought to drive modernists from denominations—especially northern Baptist and Presbyterian churches.[6]

Fundamentalists generally rejected the modernists' agenda of making intellectual accommodations to the scientific findings of the day, especially those thought to contradict biblical teaching. Some fundamentalists attempted to expunge the teaching of evolution from the nation's schools.[7] Fundamentalists perceived themselves as faithful defenders of the historic, biblical doctrines of the Christian church. Some were determined to spread "the Old Gospel" or "the Old Time Religion."

The "Fundamentals" of the Faith

In 1907, Lyman Stewart, a wealthy businessman and a founder of Bible Institute of Los Angeles (no Biola University), reflected about a concern he said "had been on our hearts for some time, that of sending some kind of warning and testimony to the English-speaking ministers, theological teachers and students, and English-speaking missionaries of the world . . . which would put them on their guard and bring them

---

6. The controversy did reach into other Christian groups such as the Southern Baptist Convention and Methodist churches.

7. See "Theologians Rap Fight on Missing Link," *Oakland Tribune* (California), February 15, 1922: "Will instruction in the Darwinian theory of evolution lower the morals of the schools and bring out the beast in their nature? Dr. John Roach Straton, leader of the fundamentalist movement in the Baptist Church, believes it will and has made a public pronouncement to this effect. Dr. Straton has announced that the fundamentalists are preparing to start a campaign to have textbooks dealing with the theory excluded from the New York City public schools."

into right lines again."[8] His driving motivation: stem the advance of liberalism. Between 1910–1915, a group of English, Canadian, and American theological conservatives published *The Fundamentals: A Testimony to the Truth*—a series of twelve booklets designed to uphold the truthfulness of the Christian faith by answering "the various forms of error so prevalent at the present day." A. C. Dixon, Louis Meyer, and R. A. Torrey gave editorial leadership to the project. The last booklet, devoted to evangelism, emphasized another key purpose of the pamphlets: to encourage "Christians everywhere to more active effort and more earnest prayer for the conversion of a great number of the unsaved." In a publishing blitz, more than three million pamphlets, "compliments of two Christian laymen" (brothers Milton and Lyman Stewart of the Union Old Company), were distributed free of charge to English-speaking Christian pastors, evangelists, missionaries, theological professors, YMCA and YWCA secretaries, Sunday school superintendents, and others in the United States, in the United Kingdom and "throughout the earth." The rhetorical tone of the booklets was moderate and not especially militant.

In the General Assemblies of 1910, 1916, and 1923, the Presbyterian Church in the United States of America, Professor Machen's own denomination, proposed five fundamental doctrines as "essential and necessary" to historic Presbyterian Christianity: (1) the inerrancy of Scripture in the original documents; (2) Christ's virgin birth; (3) Christ's vicarious atonement; (4) Christ's bodily resurrection; and (5) the reality of biblical miracles.

After World War I (1914–1918), the conflict between fundamentalists and modernists heated up dramatically. In 1919, the World's Christian Fundamentals Association identified not five but nineteen doctrines as "fundamental." The list included as an indispensable,

---

8. Cited in Paul W. Rood II, "The Untold Story of the Fundamentals," *Biola Magazine* (Summer 2014), http://magazine.biola.edu/article/14-summer/the-untold-story-of-the-fundamentals (accessed May 15, 2017).

nonnegotiable fundamental "the personal, premillennial, and imminent return of our Lord and Savior Jesus Christ" (Article 7).[9]

In 1920, Curtis Lee Laws, a Baptist editor of the *Watchman-Examiner*, defined fundamentalists in bellicose terms:

> We here and now move that a new word be adopted to describe the men among us who insist that the landmarks should not be removed. "Conservatives" is too closely allied with reactionary forces in all walks of life. "Premillennialists" is too closely allied with a single doctrine and not sufficiently inclusive. "Landmarkers" has a historical disadvantage and connotes a particular group of radical conservatives. We suggest that those who still cling to the great fundamentals of the faith and who mean to do battle royal for the fundamentals should be called "Fundamentalists."[10]

Interestingly enough, Laws did not include premillennialism as an essential "fundamental."

Many of the nation's newspapers, including the religious press, helped stoke the fires of the fundamentalist-modernist controversy.[11] The *Lebanon Daily News* (Pennsylvania) on December 16, 1922, published an advertisement for a sermon titled "Fundamentalism versus Funnymonkeyism." It supposedly summarized the respective views of the opposing parties:

> The world seems set upon substituting Evolution for Creation, Principle animating cosmos for the Living God, Consciousness of the individual for the Authority of the Bible, Reason for

---

9. Historian George Dollar proposed that the only authentic fundamentalist was a dispensationalist premillennialist. He viewed a Presbyterian such as Professor J. Gresham Machen as an "orthodox ally." For Dollar's comparison of "fundamentalists" and "orthodox allies," see his *A History of American Fundamentalism* (Greenville, SC: Bob Jones University Press, 1973), 181–83.

10. Curtis Lee Laws, "Convention Sidelights," *Watchman-Examiner* 8 (July 1, 1920): 834.

11. References to the controversy filled columns of the nation's newspapers from Berkeley, California, to Boston, Massachusetts.

Revelation, Sight for Faith, Social Service for Salvation, Reform for Regeneration, the Priest for the Prophet, Ecclesiasticism for Evangelism, the Human Jesus for the Divine Christ, and Ideal man-made society for the Kingdom of God, and Humanitarian efforts for the Eternity of Joy in God's bright heaven. THEY ARE MONKEYING WITH THE BASIC FORMULAE OF THE TRUTH WHICH SHALL MAKE YOU FREE.[12]

The *Joplin Globe* (Missouri) for May 16, 1924, printed a front-page article titled "South Baptists Flay Modernism: Fundamentalism Is Stoutly Reaffirmed in Resolution Introduced." The article reported that at a Southern Baptist convention, a delegate had proposed a resolution calling for the convention to "at this critical time go on record before the world as affirming full and steadfast beliefs in the full inspiration, inerrancy and paramount and permanent authority of both the Old and the New Testament scriptures."[13]

Although a number of articles attacked modernism or recommended the opposing parties should compromise, other articles harshly criticized fundamentalism.[14] The *Lowell Sun* (Massachusetts) for June 7, 1923, contained a piece targeting the alleged anti-intellectualism of Fundamentalism: "An Assault upon Learning Fundamentalist Movement Attacked by Dr. Albert C. Dieffenbach of Boston." The article quoted Dr. Dieffenbach, an influential Unitarian: "Here in the United States at present we are witnessing the rise of a pernicious church movement known as fundamentalism with its characteristic doctrine of the second coming of Christ."[15] The June 18, 1923 edition of the *San Antonio Express* (Texas) published an article titled "Fundamentalism—

---

12. From an advertisement in the *Lebanon Daily News*, December 16, 1922, 1.

13. "South Baptists Flay Modernism: Fundamentalism Is Stoutly Reaffirmed in Resolution Introduced," *Joplin Globe*, May 16, 1924, 1.

14. See "Religious Rivals Warned to Find Common Ground," *Waterloo Evening Courier*, March 24, 1923.

15. "An Assault upon Learning Fundamentalist Movement Attacked by Dr. Albert C. Dieffenbach of Boston," *Lowell Sun*, June 7, 1923.

Menace to Protestantism's Teaching Says Rev. S. Arthur Huston." In the article, Huston excoriated fundamentalism not only as "crude" but "perniciously political as well as religious in its aim."[16]

Charles Woodbridge's Personal Glimpses of Professors Machen and von Harnack

In this contentious, heated religious environment, Charles Woodbridge arrived at the doorstep of Princeton Theological Seminary in the fall of 1924. At Princeton, he met Professor J. Gresham Machen (1881–1937). Professor B. B. Warfield, one of Machen's mentors, had died in 1921. At the time, Machen commented, "Dr. Warfield's funeral took place yesterday afternoon at the First Church of Princeton . . . It seemed to me that the Old Princeton—a great institution it was—died when Dr. Warfield was carried out."[17] However, in the eyes of many, Machen had assumed Warfield's mantle as the principal defender of old-school Presbyterian theology. In 1921, Machen published *The Origin of Paul's Religion*. He argued that the religion of Paul found its origins in the teachings of Jesus. Many modernists had denied this. Machen's scholarship was impressive and compelling. His volume was reviewed in both the United States and Europe.

In 1923, Machen had also published *Christianity and Liberalism*.[18] This book became a lightning-rod piece in the fundamentalist-modernist controversy. In a blurb for the book, Machen clearly explained his purpose in writing: "What is the difference between modern 'liberal' religion and historic Christianity? An answer to this question is attempted in the present book. The author is convinced that liberalism on the one

---

16. "Fundamentalism—Menace to Protestantism's Teaching Says Rev. S. Arthur Huston," *San Antonio Express*, June 18, 1923.
17. Quoted in Ned B. Stonehouse, *J. Gresham Machen: A Biographical Memoir* (Grand Rapids: Eerdmans, 1954), 310.
18. J. Gresham Machen, *Christianity and Liberalism* (1923; repr., Grand Rapids: Eerdmans, 2009).

hand and the religion of the historic church on the other are not two varieties of the same religion, but two distinct religions proceeding from altogether separate roots."[19] In the volume itself, Machen wrote:

> In the sphere of religion, in particular, the present time is a time of conflict; the great redemptive religion which has always been known as Christianity is battling against a totally diverse type of religious belief, which is only the more destructive of the Christian faith because it makes use of traditional Christian terminology . . . But manifold as are the forms in which the movement appears, the root of the movement is one; the many varieties of modern liberal religion are rooted in naturalism—that is, in the denial of any entrance of the creative power of God (as distinguished from the ordinary course of nature) in connection with the origin of Christianity.[20]

Machen's contention that liberalism found its roots in naturalism, not in historic Christianity, constituted a singularly devastating charge against modernism. The volume burnished Machen's reputation as one of the nation's premier apologists for orthodox Protestantism. In *A Preface to Morals*, Walter Lippmann, a well-respected commentator, praised the high quality of Machen's *Christianity and Liberalism*: "It is an admirable book. For its acumen, for its saliency, and for its wit this cool and stringent defense of orthodox Protestantism, is, I think, the best popular argument produced by either side in the current controversy."[21]

On May 5, 1924, a number of Presbyterians belonging to Machen's denomination, the Presbyterian Church in the United States, published the Auburn Affirmation: An Affirmation designed to safeguard the unity and liberty of the Presbyterian Church in the United States of America. The Affirmation was eventually signed by 1,293 Presbyterian

---

19. Quoted in Stonehouse, *J. Gresham Machen*, 342.
20. Machen, *Christianity and Liberalism*, 2.
21. Walter Lippmann, *A Preface to Morals* (New York: Macmillan, 1929), 32.

pastors (with another twenty signatures as an addendum and one original signee who later asked that his name be removed).[22] The authors of the document professed their full acceptance of the Westminster Confession, evangelical Christianity, and a belief in liberty of conscience. They specifically challenged the constitutional right of the General Assembly of 1923 to indicate that five fundamentals of the Presbyterian Church were binding church doctrine—for "these are not the only theories allowed by the Scriptures and our standards." For example, regarding the doctrine of biblical inerrancy, they affirmed, "The doctrine of inerrancy, intended to enhance the authority of the Scriptures, in fact impairs their supreme authority for faith and life, and weakens the testimony of the church to the power of God unto salvation through Jesus."[23] Seriously perturbed by the Auburn Affirmation, Machen wrote a letter to the *New York Times* in which he severely criticized it. He considered that any Presbyterian pastor who signed it had violated his ordination vow.[24]

Likewise, in 1924, Harry Emerson Fosdick published *The Modern Use of the Bible*. In his review of the book, Machen sharply criticized the quality of Fosdick's scholarship. Machen wrote, "We have not yet commented on the most astonishing thing about Dr. Fosdick's presentation of the modern use of the Bible. The most astonishing thing is that in exalting the historical method of approach, our author displays so little acquaintance with that to which he himself appeals. It would be difficult to discover a book which exhibits less understanding than this book does for the historical point of view."[25]

In time, Charles Woodbridge esteemed Dr. Machen not only as a great defender of the Christian faith but also as a theological mentor and a personal friend. They grew to know each other very well.

---

22. "Historic Documents in America Presbyterianism: The Auburn Affirmation," www.pca history.org/documents/auburntext.html (accessed May 15, 2017).

23. Ibid.

24. See Edwin H. Rian, *The Presbyterian Conflict* (Grand Rapids: Eerdmans, 1940), 17–51; Stonehouse, *J. Gresham Machen*, 365.

25. J. Gresham Machen, *What Is Christianity? A Selection of Notable Addresses by a Noble Defender of the Faith*, ed. Ned B. Stonehouse (1951; repr., Birmingham, AL: Solid Ground, 2013), 185–200.

Professor Machen often addressed Charles Woodbridge as "Charlie." Like other Princeton students, Woodbridge sometimes affectionately addressed Professor Machen as "Das," more frequently as Dr. Machen.[26] Dr. Machen preached at both Woodbridge's ordination to the Presbyterian ministry in the First Presbyterian Church of Princeton, New Jersey, and his installation as pastor of the First Presbyterian Church of Flushing, Long Island. And in his will, J. Gresham Machen left $2,000 to Charles Woodbridge.

Not only was Woodbridge a student of Machen at Princeton Seminary, but Machen asked him to serve as the first general secretary of the Independent Board of Presbyterian Foreign Missions founded in June 1933. For more than three years, Woodbridge worked directly under Dr. Machen's supervision as general secretary of the mission. Professor Machen was the president of the mission board.

The two men exchanged tens of letters and met regularly. Woodbridge also acted as one of Machen's three defense lawyers when the professor was put on ecclesiastical trial by the New Brunswick presbytery. The Presbyterian Church in the United States of America had ordered Machen to disband the mission, but he refused to do so.

From the privileged vantage point of a trusted protégé, Woodbridge observed up close Dr. Machen's efforts to preserve what he thought constituted the doctrinal integrity of Princeton Theological Seminary and the Presbyterian Church in the United States of America.

Charles Woodbridge also enjoyed personal contacts with Professor Adolph von Harnack (1851–1930), the world-renowned liberal church historian and theologian at the University of Berlin. In 1900, Professor von Harnack published a landmark popular apologetic for Protestant liberalism titled *What Is Christianity?*[27] The book was based on his winter term lectures, 1899–1900, given at the University of Berlin, and

---

26. See Paul Woolley, *The Significance of J. Gresham Machen Today* (Nutley, NJ: Presbyterian and Reformed, 1977), 5.

27. Von Harnack, *What Is Christianity?*; see Martin Rumscheidt, ed., *Adolf von Harnack: Liberal Theology at its Height* (London: Collins, 1989), 126–226.

in it, von Harnack emphasized three teachings that for him expressed the essence of the gospel: "Firstly, the kingdom of God and its coming. Secondly, God the Father and the infinite value of the human soul. Thirdly, the higher righteousness and the commandment of love."[28]

During the fall semester of 1927, Woodbridge, along with nine German students, gathered at Professor von Harnack's home each Tuesday night to exegete Scripture and to talk theology and church history. Professor von Harnack called this group his "Church History Society." The same fall, Woodbridge also attended a course of Professor von Harnack titled "The Origin of the New Testament."

Professor von Harnack's liberal theological influence was mediated to the United States in part through one of Harry Emerson Fosdick's principal professors at Union Theological Seminary, the Protestant church historian A. C. McGiffert.[29] McGiffert had studied under Professor von Harnack in Germany. Like his famous mentor Professor von Harnack, McGiffert emphasized a key theme of Protestant liberalism—the immanence of God. And like Professor von Harnack, Fosdick wrote a book titled *What Is Christianity?* In it, he also underscored the immanence of God, a theme highlighted by his professor, A. C. McGiffert.

Thus, Charles Woodbridge interacted personally with two of the iconic figures engaged directly or indirectly in the fundamentalist-modernist controversy of the 1920s and 1930s. He wrote in his memoirs, "Without a question the two most learned men I have ever met were Dr. Machen

---

28. Von Harnack, *What Is Christianity?* 55.

29. In his 1924 critical review of McGiffert's *The God of the Early Christians*, J. Gresham Machen wrote, "The truth is that the antitheistic religion of the present day—popularized by preachers like Dr. Fosdick and undergirded by scholars such as the author of the brilliant book [McGiffert] which we have just attempted to review—the truth is that this antitheistic Modernism, which at least in one of its characteristic forms, takes the man Jesus of naturalistic reconstruction as its only God, will have to stand at last upon its own feet. With the historic Christian church, at any rate, it plainly has little to do" (cited in D. G. Hart, ed., *J. Gresham Machen: Selected Shorter Writings* [Phillipsburg, NJ: P&R, 2004], 505–6).

of Princeton Seminary and von Harnack of the Friedrich-Wilhelm University of Berlin. Both were intellectual giants, poles apart in their theological convictions."

More Details of the Life and Times of Charles J. Woodbridge (1902–1995)

The unpublished memoirs of Charles J. Woodbridge contain a mine of colorful details about his early days in China as a missionary child; his Southern Presbyterian missionary father Samuel's close relationship with Dr. Andrew Sydenstricker, Pearl Buck's father in China; his father's last-minute deliverance by a British gun ship from near certain death at the hands of rebels of the Boxer Rebellion; his student frolics at Dwight L. Moody's Mount Herman school for boys; the introduction his mother, Jeannie Wilson Woodrow, made of her best friend, Ellen Axson, to Woodrow Wilson, her first cousin and future president of the United States [Ellen Axson became Wilson's first wife]; his career at Princeton University as a Phi Beta Kappa scholar and three-year All-American in soccer; his studies and intriguing conversations with Princeton Theological Seminary professor J. Gresham Machen; and his studies and conversations with the renowned German liberal theologian Adolph von Harnack at the University of Berlin.

Sometimes in a markedly partisan fashion, Woodbridge projects in his memoirs a sprawling panoramic and contemporary view of Presbyterian, evangelical, and fundamentalist history. A host of notable personages such as Clarence Darrow, Pearl Buck, Dr. Samuel Zwemer, Dr. Henry Sloane Coffin, Dr. John R. Mott, Dr. J. Gresham Machen, Dr. Harry Ironside, Dr. William R. Newell, Dr. Robert E. Speer, Professor Adolph von Harnack, Professor Rudolf Bultmann, and Professor Ned Stonehouse all parade across the memoirs' pages.

Charles Woodbridge's papers afford us glimpses of Professor Machen and Professor von Harnack we may have never seen before. In a number of the standard biographies of J. Gresham Machen, Charles J. Woodbridge is absent or briefly mentioned. Professor D. G. Hart's *Defending the Faith: J. Gresham Machen and the Crisis of Conservative Protestantism in Modern America* (1994) and Paul Wooley's *The Significance of J. Gresham Machen Today* (1977) constitute well-crafted studies devoted to the life of J. Gresham Machen.[30] They include no allusions to Charles J. Woodbridge. Nor does he appear in Bradley J. Longfield's *The Presbyterian Controversy: Fundamentalists, Modernists, and Moderates* (1991).[31] He is noted in the sturdy Machen biographies by Ned Stonehouse (1954) and Stephen J. Nichols (2004) and in Ed Rian's richly documented *The Presbyterian Conflict* (1940).[32]

Gaining a Passion for the Gospel of Jesus Christ

We continue our story in the fall of 1928. Charles Woodbridge had just spent a year as an exchange student in Germany. He had taken classes from Professor Adolph von Harnack at the University of Berlin and from Professor Rudolph Bultmann at Marburg, among other German theological luminaries.[33] As a recently minted graduate of Princeton Theological Seminary and Princeton University [an MA in history], he assumed the pastorate of the First Presbyterian Church in Flushing, Long Island (1928–1932). He felt deeply honored that Professor Machen graciously preached his installation sermon at the church.[34]

---

30. D. C. Hart, *Defending the Faith: J. Gresham Machen and the Crisis of Conservative Protestantism in Modern America* (Phillipsburg, NJ: P&R, 2003); Woolley, *Significance of J. Gresham Machen Today.*

31. Bradley J. Longfield, *The Presbyterian Controversy: Fundamentalists, Modernists, and Moderates* (New York: Oxford University Press, 1991).

32. Stonehouse, *J. Gresham Machen: A Biographical Memoir;* Stephen J. Nichols, *J. Gresham Machen: A Guided Tour of his Life and Thought* (Phillipsburg, NJ: P &R, 2004); Rian, *Presbyterian Conflict.*

33. In his personal memoirs, Woodbridge wrote, "I am particularly glad I could listen at length to Dr. Bultmann." He took copious notes of Bultmann's lectures.

34. On March 12, 1931, Machen playfully wrote Charles Woodbridge, thanking him for an overly generous honorarium for speaking at his church: "If I had not had the conversation on the Long Island platform last Sunday night, I should certainly have returned your generous check, which you enclose with your letter of March 10th. But you tell me that the check came from the church and not from you. If it came from the church, I don't see why the church treasurer didn't

Charles Woodbridge's sermons preached at the Flushing church reveal that, like J. Gresham Machen, he viewed the inerrancy of Scripture as a "fundamental" doctrine of the Christian faith.[35] The sermons also make clear that the central thrust of his ministry was preaching the gospel of Jesus Christ. In a sermon titled "Enduring Peace" (November 11, 1928), he noted, "The fact remains that today the world is seething. Unrest can be felt on every hand." He cited, as one illustration among many of this seething, "the old hatred between France and Germany still persists." In these circumstances, how might his parishioners find enduring peace? They needed to be "justified by faith alone." Then they would experience peace with God—a peace not available in a seething world: "It is Christ who is our enduring peace," Woodbridge declared. "If you haven't accepted Christ as your Savior from sin, you're at enmity with God" and thus do not enjoy genuine peace. In another sermon titled "Fear," preached on February 22, 1931 (the Depression was in full swing), he observed, "I love to study people's faces. It is a rare thing in New York City to find a face which is carefree and joyous. Life presses in on most of us. Many of us are just one step ahead of the sheriff, as one of our men put it . . . But perfect love casteth out fear." He continued: "A perfect love for the risen Christ means a

---

sign it, but at the same time I don't like to charge you with prevarication! I should hate to have you think that you couldn't call me in to preach for you whenever you think the congregation can stand it, without providing an honorarium. The upshot of the matter is that I am turning the check over to Westminster Seminary as a little contribution. It ought to be a contribution from you instead of from me, but we'll not start a theological controversy on that point. It was the greatest possible privilege for me to preach for you last Sunday" (archives of the Montgomery Library at Westminster Theological Seminary, Philadelphia PA [Machen/Woodbridge correspondence, Box 30–31]).

35. Charles Woodbridge's sermons are located in the personal archives of the author. In *Christianity and Liberalism* (1923), Machen had written (p. 62), "Before the full authority of the Bible can be established, therefore, it is necessary to add to the Christian doctrine of revelation the Christian doctrine of inspiration. The latter doctrine means that the Bible not only is an account of important things, but that the account itself is true, the writers having been so preserved from error, despite a full maintenance of their habits of thought and expression, that the resulting Book is the 'infallible rule of faith and practice.'" Machen also contested Fosdick's charge that those who believed in biblical inerrancy upheld a "mechanical dictation theory of inspiration"; see also J. Gresham Machen, *The Christian Faith in the Modern World* (Grand Rapids: Eerdmans, 1936), 23–86.

perfect trust in his redeeming work, and thus the assurance that nothing can separate us from the love of God, neither life, nor death . . ." In one sermon, he indicated that if a person is not witnessing for Christ, he or she will not grow in the Christian life.

In Flushing, Long Island, Charles Woodbridge practiced what he preached about witnessing. In his memoirs, he wrote, "A large part of my ministry was house-to-house visitation. My goal: one thousand visits per year. I was systematic. I kept records. I prayed, read the Bible, and witnessed for Christ in every household which would permit it. I offered to help those in trouble. New visitors began to attend our services every Sunday. The Lord honored the proclamation of his Word. Souls were being saved. It soon became apparent that we would need a larger sanctuary." He also engaged in street preaching in New York City.

In his memoirs, Charles Woodbridge rhetorically asked the question why he had been willing to give up a prominent pulpit in Flushing and go to Africa with his wife and young daughter as a missionary. After all, he indicated that an astounding seven hundred candidates wanted to replace him in the Flushing pulpit. Answer: he felt compelled by his conviction that Africans in the French Cameroon were "in desperate need of a Savior and that Christ Jesus enjoined his disciples to go into all the world with the glorious proclamation of salvation to every creature."

What was the provenance of Woodbridge's passion for gospel preaching and evangelism? As an undergrad at Princeton University, he lacked this passion; nor did he apparently evince this passion during a year spent teaching at a middle school in China before his matriculation at Princeton Theological Seminary in the fall of 1924. But during the years 1924 to 1927, the teaching and pastoral counsel of Professor Machen ignited in him a burning desire to serve the Lord in gospel ministry. Preaching on weekends and during every summer in small churches gave him an opportunity to put into practice what he was learning in the classroom.

Interacting with Professor J. Gresham Machen at Princeton Theological Seminary (1924–1927)

In his memoirs, Charles Woodbridge wrote, "Upon arriving at the seminary in 1924, I was duly matriculated by Rev. Paul Martin, affable and somewhat portly registrar of the school. Safely ensconced in Alexander Hall, I was expected to worship daily in Miller Chapel. Thus was the revered past made to live in the present." After listing the rooms and a number of dorm mates on the fourth floor in Alexander Hall, he observed, "Then the little suite of a bachelor professor who, more than any man was to influence my thinking about the Christian gospel. He was Dr. J. Gresham Machen." Machen played chess and checkers with the fellows in the hall. "Das" provided refreshments like cookies, nuts, and soft drinks to students who participated in his Checkers Club, which met in the "parlor" on Saturday nights. He won their admiration not only in the classroom but also through personal contacts in their living quarters. He loved clever humor and "stunts" (telling colorful and witty stories). He also offered free tickets as inducements to students to go with him to Princeton football games.[36]

Woodbridge afforded other details of student life at the seminary: "The students ate at eating clubs. Mine was the Bentham Club [Machen had earlier belonged to the Bentham Club as a student] founded by a Mrs. Bentham many years before my arrival on the scene. This club boasted as its emblem of culinary delight a chicken wishbone, which satisfied customers wore on the lapels of their jackets." He told of the seminary choir and its director, a nervous assistant professor of theology who "complained periodically when we were rehearsing for concerts that our numbers were decimated by our insouciance." Woodbridge also referred to "the weekend preaching assignments, when we students scattered here and there subjected docile congregations to our feeble efforts to expound the Scriptures."

---

36. On Professor Machen's personal relationships with Princeton Theological Seminary students, see Woolley, *Significance of J. Gresham Machen Today*, 2–5.

During his three years at Princeton Theological Seminary, Woodbridge did not fully sense the titanic struggle taking place between theological conservatives and moderates for the control of the school. He wrote, "In retrospect, I find it strange that during my three years at the seminary I had little more than suspicions that all was not well in Presbyterian Zion." Apparently, the professors and administration did not import their differing views about the future direction of their seminary into the classroom. Professor Machen, who was often at the center of the struggle for the control of the seminary, apparently said little about it to students.[37]

Charles Woodbridge continued: "In 1924, the seminary was fundamentally sound. The faculty, speaking generally, wanted no traffic with heresy. The Board of Directors on the whole shared the faculty's convictions . . . But the seminary Board of Trustees, to which were entrusted the temporal concerns of the institution, seemed to have on its membership men whose views were not as robust as those of their counterparts on the Board of Directors."

Woodbridge's first hint of theological struggles lingering around the seminary appeared in an anecdote involving Professor Machen and the founding of the League of Evangelical Students:

> On October 21, 1924, a month after my arrival at the seminary, a student meeting was held in Miller Chapel. The inter-seminary movement in which Princeton was interested was sharply divided on doctrinal grounds. The question arose as to whether the Princeton men should quit the larger group and form their own organization, which would be true to the faith of their fathers. The building was packed. Arguments pro and con were presented. Professor Machen was present. I sat on a back pew, vaguely interested, studying my Hebrew assignment for the following day.

---

37. See Rian, *Presbyterian Conflict*, 37–56; Stonehouse, *J. Gresham Machen*, 382–429.

A brief pause in the debate. "Where ignorance is bliss" I arose and made a brief speech, the gist of which was the whole subject under discussion was a matter of personality clashes rather than of doctrinal principles. I sat down and continued studying Hebrew. The students voted to withdraw from the inter-seminary movement. They subsequently formed their own League of Evangelical Students. On the way out of Miller Chapel, Dr. Machen said to me, and I shall never forget his subdued words: "In your speech tonight you were exactly 100 percent wrong!" I was furious. In genuinely neophytic fashion, I replied, "Dr. Machen, I did not have to come to this seminary at all. I could have gone elsewhere." He mildly went his way. I quickly went to Ed Rian's dormitory room in Brown Hall. Ned Stonehouse was there. I burst out, "Think of it, men. Dr. Machen had the audacity to tell me that I was completely wrong in what I said tonight!" My friends, more mature than I in these matters, quickly explained that Dr. Machen was right and I was wrong! For about an hour they told me exactly why I was wrong . . . Gradually over the three-year seminary period the seriousness of the doctrinal debate at the institution dawned on me.[38]

During the first two years at Princeton Theological Seminary, Dr. J. Ross Stevenson, the president of the school, and Dr. Charles R. Erdman befriended Charles, called him by his first name, and entertained him in their homes. Woodbridge wrote in his memoirs, "I thought them broad-minded and courteous. But I quickly discovered that the position they held in the great Princeton debate was wrong, and that Dr. Machen and his faithful colleagues were right." Nonetheless, he asked both Professor Machen and Professor Erdman to preach at his ordination service that also included two other students:

---

38. Personal memoirs of Charles Woodbridge.

On April 13, 1927, I was ordained to the gospel ministry . . .
My ordination took place in the First Presbyterian Church of
Princeton, New Jersey . . . Six people participated in the ordina-
tion ritual. On the platform, presiding over the proceedings, was
Dr. Sylvester Woodbridge Beach, pastor of the church and my
father's cousin. The two speakers, both professors at Princeton
Seminary, were Dr. J. Gresham Machen, professor of Greek,
who, more than any other scholar, helped to shape the theological convictions which I have held throughout my ministry, and
Dr. Charles R. Erdman, professor of English Bible, who once
presented me with a complete set of the Ante-Nicene Fathers.
When the subsequent doctrinal debate at Princeton Seminary
came to a dismal climax in 1929 . . . Dr. Machen and Dr. Erdman
took diametrically opposing theological positions.[39]

Interacting with Professor Adolph von Harnack at the University of Berlin

The other person besides Dr. Machen who influenced Charles
Woodbridge most tellingly regarding his evangelical beliefs—in this
instance, in what he thought his beliefs should not be—was the great
church historian and biblical scholar, Professor Adolph von Harnack.
Professor von Harnack provided him with a firsthand, direct knowledge
of Protestant liberalism, what Woodbridge came to think was a seriously
flawed, naturalistic set of beliefs.

Why would a young Princeton Theological Seminary graduate head
off to the University of Berlin in the fall of 1927 to study with Professor
von Harnack and others?[40] First, Charles Woodbridge wanted to take

---

39. Dr. J. Ross Stevenson became president of Princeton Theological Seminary in 1914 (see
Woolley, *Significance of J. Gresham Machen Today*, 11–12). Sylvester Woodbridge Beach (1852–1940),
pastor of the First Presbyterian Church in Princeton, presided over the funeral of President Woodrow
Wilson, former president of Princeton University and the first cousin of Charles Woodbridge's
father. Charles R. Erdman (1886–1960) was moderator of the Presbyterian Church in America
(see Longfield, *Presbyterian Controversy*, 6–7, 227–28).

40. From the early nineteenth century until Charles Woodbridge's own day (1920s), more

advantage of six hundred dollars he had won in an essay contest. He had also been awarded an American German Exchange Fellowship to study in Germany. Second, Professor Machen recommended that Princeton students be exposed to the best arguments non-Christians had to offer against the faith. Dr. Machen wrote:

> But after they [Princeton students] have studied at Princeton, indeed even while they are studying here, the more they acquaint themselves with what opposing teachers say, the better it seems to us to be. We encourage our graduates, if they can, to listen to the great foreign masters of naturalistic criticism; we desire them to hear all that can be said against the gospel that we believe.
>
> No doubt such a program is full of perils. Might it not be safer for our future ministers to close their ears to all modern voices and remain in ignorance of the objections that the gospel faces in the modern world? We reply that of course it might be *safer*. It is safer to be a good soldier in comfortable barracks than it is on the field of battle. But the great battles are not won in that way.
>
> Thus, we encourage our students to be fearless in their examination of the basis of the faith.[41]

Third, Machen, like many other young American theologians and Bible students, had himself studied in Germany, where he had wrestled with his doubts about Christian faith. He wrote, "Some of us have been through such struggles ourselves; some of us have known the blankness of doubt, the deadly discouragement, the perplexity of indecision."[42]

In his memoirs, Charles Woodbridge echoed Machen's conviction concerning the value of studying with the keenest proponents of unbelief: "Constant exposure to brilliantly defended heresy may make him

than nine thousand Americans had traveled to Germany to pursue theological studies.
41. Quoted in Hart, *J. Gresham Machen*, 316–17.
42. Quoted in Nichols, *J. Gresham Machen*, 32–34.

[the Christian student] re-examine the foundations of his own convictions . . . The buffeting which that truth appeared to me to receive at the hands of German scholarship fortified me in my desire to have a reason for the faith which was within me."

Dr. Machen particularly admired the superb quality of Professor von Harnack's scholarship. Moreover, he appreciated von Harnack's intellectual integrity demonstrated by a willingness to change his views if new persuasive evidence emerged. Addressing the Bible League of Great Britain (June 10, 1927), Machen declared (just before Charles Woodbridge departed for Germany): "You have the extraordinary phenomenon that scholars like Professor von Harnack, of Berlin, whose view as to the origin of Christianity is of a thoroughly naturalistic kind, as far removed as possible from that which is present in the Lucan writings, have been so much impressed by the argument from literary criticism that they have actually come to the traditional view that the gospel according to Luke was written by Luke the physician and companion of Paul."[43] Dr. Machen's appreciation of von Harnack may have been enhanced by another fact: Professor von Harnack had favorably reviewed a number of Machen's writings. While dismissing certain of Machen's conclusions, von Harnack did appreciate Machen's objectivity. Machen bound a collection of von Harnack's reviews of his work in a packet and sent them to the German scholar. Dr. Machen may have been the person who suggested to Charles Woodbridge to study with Professor von Harnack in Berlin.

SETTING OFF TO GERMANY

On September 1, 1927, Charles Woodbridge sailed for Hamburg, Germany, on the SS *Deutschland*. During the summer of 1927, he had given himself a crash course in German grammar. Aboard ship, he enlisted "unsuspecting German passengers and beguiled them into teaching me conversational German in exchange for a smattering of

---

43. Cited in Hart, *J. Gresham Machen*, 46.

English." Then he studied German for six weeks at a language institute in Berlin and somehow passed a German proficiency exam that permitted him to take courses at the University of Berlin. He described the garret in Berlin where he lodged as "a miserable sort of hostelry where exchange students were supposed to eke out their dreary but frugal existence." He continued: "The little gas kitchen stove in the apartment was temperamental. The bedroom was dark. The entire setup was unprepossessing." Ed Rian, another Princeton graduate, a protégé of Machen, and a close personal friend, was also studying in Berlin.[44]

German students invited Charles Woodbridge to frequent their "corps" or fraternal organization and to attend their duels. Woodbridge was shocked by what he saw: "The first duel I observed, held in an upstairs club house in a room strewn with sawdust, made me physically ill. I leaned against a piano. I watched blood streaming down the face of a young blond student whose self-protection was obviously inadequate, only to watch a blasé student observer yawn and to hear him condescendingly proclaim, 'We Germans think that your American boxing is very cruel and inhuman!'"

On October 28, 1927, Charles Woodbridge wrote to "Das" from Berlin: "Almost seven weeks over here in Germany studying German morning, noon, and night! Next week the lectures start; and today I am to be examined to see whether I know enough German to understand die Herren Professoren!" He indicated to Professor Machen that he had "a new, and developing courage [about the faith]." He added, "I thank you, largely, for that." He related that he was going to concentrate his studies on the New Testament, that Professor von Harnack was lecturing every Saturday on the New Testament, and that he had finished reading von Harnack's *Die Entstehung des Neuen Testaments*. He signed off his letter with a dose of embarrassing praise probably difficult for

---

44. Rian and Woodbridge attended parties together in Berlin. They traveled together through Europe. The Woodbridge archives contain numerous photos of the two men together. Rian later wrote *The Presbyterian Conflict* (1940).

Professor Machen to assimilate: "Every day, on my way to school, I pass a statue of Martin Luther, with open Bible in his hand. I regard you, Sir, in somewhat the same sort of light as I do him. May the courage of conviction that was his, be mine when I return to the U.S. Most sincerely, your friend, Charles Woodbridge."[45]

Interacting with Adolph von Harnack in Berlin

How did it happen that, from among the hundreds of students who attended Professor von Harnack's popular classes, Charles Woodbridge garnered direct personal access to the world-renowned scholar? Possibly Dr. Machen had sent von Harnack a letter of introduction for Charles. In any case, not only did Woodbridge know Professor von Harnack in person, but the great man graciously invited Woodbridge to his home. Woodbridge wrote in his memoirs:

> Every Tuesday night during my sojourn in Berlin, I went to Professor von Harnack's home as a member of his little Church History Society. About ten of us students (nine Germans and one American) gathered around the large dining room table. Each of us had his Greek New Testament. Von Harnack took his seat at the head of the table. He had no book with him at all. We were studying the Pastoral Epistles of Paul. It soon became evident that the professor needed no book; he knew the epistles in Greek as well as in German. To me this was an ordeal. But the system had an inbuilt escape mechanism! When my turn came to read, if I did not understand a Greek word in the verse before me, I could at the last resort gently inquire, "Let me see, what is the German word for this?" Seven students at least would come to my aid—I was the only American present, and I would quickly be in business again! One Tuesday night, Professor von Harnack asked me, "Wann sind

---

45. Archives of the Montgomery Library at Westminster Theological Seminary, Philadelphia, PA (Machen/Woodbridge correspondence, Box 27–28).

Sie geboren?" ("When were you born?") I informed him. "Ach!" he replied. "I was studying theology thirty years before you were born."

On December 20, 1927, he presented me with his year-old booklet "The Assembling of Paul's Letters." On page 11, the author writes, "When I began the study of theology 37 years ago, no more than four Pauline epistles were regarded as genuine. Since then it has become otherwise." He then lists additional letters which are almost universally recognized: 1 Thessalonians, Colossians, Philippians, and Philemon. And around his dining room table he told us, "If I had another lifetime, I should like to devote it to a study of the Pastoral Epistles" (1 and 2 Timothy and Titus).

Woodbridge was impressed that Professor von Harnack, a man of apparent scholarly integrity, could revise his thinking when faced with compelling new evidence.

The great German professor, however, had little patience with orthodox Christology. Charles Woodbridge on one occasion asked von Harnack, "Who was Jesus Christ?" Von Harnack brusquely replied, "The greatest man who ever lived." Undaunted, Woodbridge posed a follow-up question: "Was Christ more than that?" Von Harnack repeated that Jesus was the greatest man who ever lived. He would not say that Jesus was God incarnate.

On March 5, 1928, Woodbridge wrote to "Das," referencing the fact that Dr. Machen had experienced setbacks in the General Assembly of the Presbyterian Church in the United States: "The whole situation is stirring me very deeply. My coming to Germany has taught me many things. I pray to God that He may let me live to take my place in the ranks of those who are upholding the standards of the cross against this subtle but devilish attack of the forces of sin."

Woodbridge indicated he was depending on the writings of Machen and others to help him address the intellectual problems encountered daily stemming from Professor von Harnack's teaching: "Thank you for that book 'The Origin [of Paul's Religion].' One of my feet is planted on that. Another foot is planted on [Geerhardus] Vos's 'Self-Disclosure [of Jesus].'"[46]

Later, Woodbridge indicated that given the instruction he had received from Professor von Harnack, he was convinced that the critical issue residing at the very heart of the fundamentalist-modernist controversy was nothing less than the deity of Christ. He knew this, based on instruction from and direct conversations with the great German professor.

In a 1930 review of Robert E. Speer's book *Some Living Issues*, Professor Machen made the same point: "One thing at least is plain— there can be no real compromise between the naturalism of Harnack and the super-naturalism of the Bible and of the Christian faith. Was the real Jesus the Jesus reconstructed by Harnack, or was he the stupendous Redeemer whom the Bible presents? That question ought never to be trifled with, but must be resolutely and clearly faced."[47]

Engaging in Missionary Service in Africa and the Long Reach of the Fundamentalist-Modernist Controversy

By 1929, moderates had clearly triumphed at Princeton Theological Seminary, and they reorganized the school. Believing that "Old

---

46. Ibid., letter from Charles Woodbridge to Dr. Machen dated March 28, 1928. Woodbridge added, "Stevenson, who himself studied under von Harnack, said you were 'temperamentally unfit' to fill that apologetics chair. That statement ... proves one of two things. 1. Either he has never read your 'Origins' or 2. He is very, very ignorant." In June 1928, Professor Machen wrote back to Woodbridge, "Your letter, which I have read and re-read, has been an immense encouragement to me. In these days when one meets with such a blank lack of comprehension for the things which seem to us important, it is indeed refreshing to find men like you who think our labors at Princeton have not been altogether in vain. I do feel highly honored by the way in which you speak of me, and I am profoundly grateful to you for the warmth and generosity with which you give expression to your feeling not only about me but about our beloved Princeton." Machen explained in the letter what was taking place in the struggle for control of the seminary (archives of the Montgomery Library at Westminster Theological Seminary, Philadelphia, PA [Machen/Woodbridge correspondence, Box 27–28]). In his *The Origin of Paul's Religion* (6–7, 26, 33–36, 98, 119, 263, 273), Machen specifically interacted with von Harnack's writings. In 1926, Geerhardus Vos had published *The Self-Disclosure of Jesus: The Modern Debate about the Messianic Consciousness* (1926, repr. Phillipsburg, NJ: P&R, 2002).

47. Quoted in Hart, *J. Gresham Machen*, 446.

Princeton" had died, Machen, along with a number of other professors and students, left Princeton Theological Seminary. Machen founded Westminster Theological Seminary in Philadelphia.[48]

On March 4, 1930, Charles Woodbridge married Ruth Dunning, a daughter of a Presbyterian minister from Pennsylvania. Ruth had already served a term as a Presbyterian missionary in the French Cameroon, Africa. Charles and Ruth met on a blind date in New York City.

In 1932, Charles and Ruth Woodbridge, along with their young daughter, Norma, headed for the French Cameroon. *Time* magazine carried an article on their departure accompanied by a photo of the three. In page after page of his memoirs, Woodbridge described in vivid detail the joys and perils of being a missionary in West Africa in the early 1930s.

When Charles and Ruth arrived at their post, their little daughter came down with malaria. Moreover, they sadly learned that the missionary whom Charles had come to replace had just died—stung by a poisonous insect. On occasion, the Woodbridge family's living quarters were invaded by armies of driver ants. Woodbridge was also struck down by malaria. Quinine tablets apparently helped restore his health. In addition, his little daughter recovered from her own bout of malaria.

Woodbridge's mission station shepherded 103 outposts. He rode a motorcycle deep into the jungle for weeks at a time, visiting many of these outposts scattered through the countryside. He learned to preach in Bulu, an African language. Ruth, having earlier served as a missionary in the French Cameroon, already knew some Bulu. As

---

48. On the founding of Westminster Theological Seminary, see Rian, *Presbyterian Conflict*, 37–71; J. Gresham Machen, "Westminster Theological Seminary: Its Purpose and Plan," in *J. Gresham Machen*, ed. Hart, 187–94. On July, 24, 1929, Woodbridge wrote to Dr. Machen, "Have just been reading in the *NY Times* headlines regarding the new seminary. Delighted to hear about your meeting in Philadelphia. The publicity it is getting will be of incalculable value in the acquiring of funds for the seminary. I am confident that many of the students will join with you in the new venture. Thank God for men of conviction who are willing to act on their convictions . . . May God bless you in these strenuous days. With real affection—Ever sincerely, your friend Charlie" (archives of the Montgomery Library at Westminster Theological Seminary, Philadelphia, PA [Machen/Woodbridge correspondence, Box 28–29]).

a single woman, she had taken care of missionary children and drove her own motorcycle deep into the jungles to minister at a leper colony. Many Africans came to saving faith in Christ due to the ministry of this couple. Charles and Ruth Woodbridge loved the Africans and were deeply committed to evangelistic outreach.

At a gathering of Presbyterian missionaries from West Africa in Elat, however, Charles Woodbridge experienced a shock that led him to question if he could remain a missionary in the French Cameroon. The Foreign Missions Board of the Presbyterian Church in New York appeared to be yielding to the sway of modernism, and the secretary of the board, Dr. Robert Speer, was supposedly allowing this to happen. In 1932, Speer published *The Finality of Jesus Christ*. In the mid-May 1933 edition of *Christianity Today*, Dr. Machen reviewed the book and sharply criticized Dr. Speer:

> Dr. Speer possesses a truly amazing power over the hearts and minds of men. There are many evangelical Christians, moreover, who think that the vast influence is truly to the advancement of belief in the Bible and of the clear propagation of the Christian Faith. With persons who think [like this] I disagree . . .
>
> The plain fact is that in the great issue of the day between Modernism and Christianity in the Presbyterian Church Dr. Speer is standing for a palliative middle-of-the road, evasive policy, which is in some ways a greater menace to the souls of men than any clear-cut Modernism could be.[49]

Dr. Speer was a highly respected, brilliant, and warmhearted Christian man who personally believed in the deity of Christ and the

---

49. Robert E. Speer, *The Finality of Christ* (New York: Revell, 1932); see J. Gresham Machen, "Dr. Robert E. Speer and His Latest Book," *Christianity Today* 4.1 (May 1933): 15–16, 22–26. Machen and Speer had recently debated each other (see "Machen-Speer Debate—Historic Event in Presbyterian Church," *Christianity Today* 3.12 [April 1933]: 19–23). On Robert E. Speer, see John F. Piper, *Robert E. Speer* (Louisville: Westminster John Knox, 2014).

resurrection. He had contributed an article on evangelism and missions in *The Fundamentals*. However, his board had only "with regret" accepted the resignation of Mrs. Pearl S. Buck on May 1, 1933, as a Presbyterian missionary. This stance constituted a prime piece of evidence for Dr. Machen that demonstrated Dr. Speer's allegedly evasive, indifferent attitude toward modernism. In his book review, Dr. Machen pointed out that Mrs. Buck "is the author of an article in *Harper's Magazine* for January, 1933, which attacks the Christian faith at its very roots. In a subsequent article, in the May number of *The Cosmopolitan*, she says plainly, what she implies in that previous article, that to her it is a matter of small importance whether 'Christ' ever lived as in a 'body of flesh and bone' upon this earth."[50]

On June 14, 1933, Professor Machen sent to Charles Woodbridge a copy of his *Modernism and the Board of Foreign Missions of the Presbyterian Church in the U.S.A.*[51] From this work and Machen's correspondence, Woodbridge followed closely the intensifying dispute between Machen and Speer regarding the future direction and theological orientation of the Board of Foreign Missions back in the United States.

At the gathering of missionaries in Elat previously noted, a gentleman arose and proposed that the Presbyterian missionaries of West Africa should go on record as enthusiastically supporting Dr. Speer against those who were unduly attacking him in the United States (with Professor Machen apparently in mind). As a new missionary,

---

50. Machen, "Dr. Robert E. Speer and His Latest Book"; see Pearl S. Buck, "Is There a Case for Foreign Missions?" *Harper's Magazine* 166 (January 1933): 143–55.

51. Archives of the Montgomery Library of Westminster Theological Seminary, Philadelphia, PA (Machen/Woodbridge correspondence, Box 1932–33). Machen drew up this work in part as a response to the Board of Foreign Missions for its support and endorsement of the publication of William Ernest Hocking's *Re-Thinking Missions: A Laymen's Inquiry after One Hundred Years* (New York: Harper, 1932). This latter volume denied that Jesus is the only way, the truth, and the life: "Whatever its [Christianity's] present conception of the future life, there is little disposition to believe that sincere and aspiring seekers after God in other religions are to be damned: it has become less concerned in any land to save men from eternal punishment than from the danger of losing the supreme good" (p. 19). Christianity should be less concerned with other religions like Islam, Hinduism, or Buddhism than with the menace of materialism, secularism, and naturalism (p. 29); see Rian, *Presbyterian Conflict*, 87–102.

Charles Woodbridge was not entitled to cast a vote on the motion. But another missionary urged that an exception be made so that new missionaries could vote. When a voice vote was in fact taken, a wave of ayes swept across the assembly. Then the perfunctory parliamentary question "Opposed?" was asked. Woodbridge's memoirs indicate what happened next: "Quietly, but firmly, as a minority of one, I replied 'No.' A wave of incredulous consternation swept the place. Who was I, a missionary neophyte, to defy the expressed will of the Mission? I arose to my defense. Daggers of disapproval met me as I explained briefly that, in the light of the cumulating evidence, I could not in good conscience give a blanket endorsement to the Mission Board in New York. I was a leper, an outcast."

Genuinely perplexed by this development, on July 13, 1933, Woodbridge wrote to Dr. Machen seeking counsel regarding what to do. In his letter, Woodbridge expressed "righteous indignation" concerning the way Machen and others had been treated at a recent meeting in Columbus, Ohio.[52] Unbeknown to Woodbridge, Dr. Machen was at the very same time in the process of creating the Independent Board for Presbyterian Foreign Missions.

On August 23, 1933, Rev. Roy T. Brumbaugh, a pastor of the First Presbyterian Church of Tacoma, Washington, wrote to Dr. Machen and suggested the name of Charles Woodbridge, among others, as a possible candidate for the position of general secretary of the Independent Board for Presbyterian Foreign Missions.[53]

On September 1, 1933, Dr. Machen responded to Rev. Brumbaugh and provided a laudatory assessment of Woodbridge:

You mention Charles J. Woodbridge as a possibility. Well, after receiving your letter I have received a letter from him which convinces

---

52. Archives of the Montgomery Library at Westminster Theological Seminary, Philadelphia, PA (Machen/Woodbridge correspondence, Box 1933–34).

53. Copy of the letter found in the author's personal archives.

me, when taken in connection with what I previously knew about him, that he would be a splendid General Secretary for the Board. His letter was entirely unsolicited. I had not written to him about the Board at all, but he had simply read the account of what happened at Columbus and was filled with a righteous indignation. He expressed himself as doubtful whether a man of his views can well serve longer under the present Board . . . I have known Woodbridge for years. He is the son of a very distinguished missionary family. When he first began his studies at Princeton Seminary, he stood rather against the League of Evangelical Students and was therefore somewhat inclined to side with the administration. But then he very frankly acknowledged his error, and his speech in defense of the League telling his reasons for his change of attitude was one of the most eloquent student speeches that I think I ever heard. During his year of study abroad, his evangelical conviction was even strengthened beyond what it had been before, by his contact with unbelief in the raw. At Flushing, Long Island, he made a wonderful success as a pastor. There was a tremendous evangelical fervor about his preaching which was mightily used for the saving of souls. He is quite unswerving in his devotion to the evangelical cause in the church . . . He is just exactly the type of man which will appeal to evangelistic pastors in the membership of the Board. Of one thing I am sure—if he should promote the work of the Board, there will be no question about its wide popular appeal among Bible-believing Christians in the church. Woodbridge is just one of those men upon whom God has laid His hand—a man of real power such as one seldom sees in these times.[54]

Dr. Machen then wrote a letter dated September 18, 1933, to Charles Woodbridge.[55] Quite discouraged, Woodbridge described the letter as

---

54. Archives of the Montgomery Library at Westminster Theological Seminary, Philadelphia, PA (Machen/Woodbridge correspondence, Box 1933–34).

55. Ibid. (original of letter from Machen to Woodbridge in the personal archives of the author).

one of cheer and encouragement. After all, the letter came from a person whom Woodbridge profoundly admired—J. Gresham Machen.

In his memoirs, Woodbridge wrote, "The clarity of this great scholar's teaching in the good old days at Princeton Seminary, his rugged, masterly defense of the Word of God, his class exposition of the *Epistle to the Galatians*, the hours of fellowship with him some of us students enjoyed on the fourth floor of the seminary's Alexander Hall—all these items had contributed to fortifying my faith and persuading me never to yield to the blandishments of compromise."

In his letter, Dr. Machen asked Woodbridge to consider becoming the general secretary of the Independent Board for Presbyterian Foreign Missions. For the rest of his days, Woodbridge treasured Machen's carefully worded and evangelically suffused invitation as one of his prized possessions. The letter provides us with another privileged glimpse into Machen's life and thought. We turn to a brief review of its more salient points.

First, Dr. Machen explained the reasons he and his colleagues had decided to form the new board:

> At Columbus last May, it seemed perfectly clear to [H. McAllister] Griffiths and to me, as well as to others who were there, that if we really love the Bible and the gospel of our Lord Jesus Christ, the time for mere words was past and the time for really self-sacrificing action had come. We can criticize the [New York] Board all we please; we can point out its obvious unfaithfulness; we can express our longing for a really Christian and really Presbyterian missionary activity: but all this has no more effect than the wind blowing unless we prove our faith by our works and really proceed to show the Bible-believing people in our church how they can carry the gospel to the ends of the earth in a way which is obviously impossible under the official Mission Board.

Machen argued that "the latent missionary zeal of the Bible-believing part of the church, now checked and discouraged at every point by this wretched business of asking Bible-believing Christians to give through a Board that is predominantly unfaithful to the Bible, should at length be released."

Second, Dr. Machen proposed the reasons he thought Charles Woodbridge would be a good candidate to serve as general secretary for the Board: "It seems to me that the man to be the instrument in releasing that latent enthusiasm and showing a channel for that consecrated service will be a young man in the fullness of his strength who will stand forth as the representative of this great cause. You have plainly shown by the blessing of God upon your words that you have the faculty of arousing people's enthusiasm, of winning them not only to indignation against evil but also to zeal and joy in the propagation of the truth."

Third, Dr. Machen spelled out the risks Woodbridge ran if he accepted the invitation to become the general secretary. These risks included a meager salary. Dr. Machen wrote:

I understand perfectly well that from a worldly point of view that would seem to be to ask a man to take a terrible risk. But neither you nor I nor any of the rest of us is looking at this thing from the worldly point of view. Westminster Seminary frequently does not have the money to pay our salaries until almost the very day when the salaries become due. Yet it is an established institution, and we have found that God has provided for us more surely than provision made through endowment or the like. I need not point also to the example of the China Inland Mission, and other faith missions, since you know more about them than I do, and since you know that God in their case has graciously supplied the needs of His own work.

Dr. Machen closed his letter with these words: "May God guide you and bless you in all things! I am thankful to Him for His blessing so wonderfully shown in your life."

Dr. Machen followed up this letter by sending a cable dated September 18, 1933:

> EXECUTIVE COMMITTEE OF INDEPENDENT BOARD FOR PRESBYTERIAN FOREIGN MISSIONS HAS DECIDED TO NOMINATE YOU FOR GENERAL SECRETARY OF BOARD AT BOARD MEETING ON OCTOBER SEVENTEENTH (STOP) I AM TAKING THE LIBERTY OF INFORMING YOU OF THIS AND OF ASKING YOU WHETHER YOU WOULD CONSIDER THE INVITATION OF THE BOARD FAVORABLY (STOP) A WONDERFUL OPPORTUNITY IS OFFERED TO STIR THE LATENT FIRES OF MISSIONARY AND EVANGELISTIC ZEAL, AND YOU ARE THE ONLY MAN WHO CAN BE THE INSTRUMENT IN DOING THIS GREAT WORK (STOP) DOCTOR BUCHANAN IS QUITE AGREED WITH INVITATION (STOP) ED RIAN ESPECIALLY DESIRES TO JOIN IN URGING YOU (STOP) J GRESHAM MACHEN.[56]

Charles Woodbridge was thrilled by Dr. Machen's letter. But he did not immediately cable a response. His memoirs read, "I had scheduled a week's trek in the jungle in the service of the Lord. I had hours of solitude on this journey. There was time for prayer, meditation, analysis, sifting of possibilities, self-examination. I emerged from the forest convinced I should accept Dr. Machen's invitation, face squarely any missionary misunderstanding, and embark for the U.S.A."

On October 2, 1933, Dr. Machen, perhaps wondering about the delay in hearing from Woodbridge, sent another cable to him:

> I AM EAGERLY WAITING YOUR REPLY TO LETTER SENT SEPTEMBER EIGHTEENTH (STOP) DECISION TO ACCEPT INVITATION OF COURSE NOT NECESSARY NOW BUT EARNESTLY HOPE THAT YOU WILL SAY THAT YOU WOULD CONSIDER SUCH

---

56. Ibid.

INVITATION FAVORABLY (STOP) DOCTOR BUCHANAN AND I HAVE WRITTEN AT LENGTH BUT LETTERS WILL ARRIVE AFTER BOARD MEETING (STOP) YOU ARE CHIEF HOPE OF THIS GREAT CAUSE (STOP) J GRESHAM MACHEN.[57]

The very same day, October 2, 1933, Charles Woodbridge sent a return cable with his positive response:

ACCEPT INVITATION PLEASE CABLE DECISION WOODBRIDGE.[58]

On that same day, Professor Machen replied in a cable:

YOUR TELEGRAM RECEIVED REJOICE GREATLY WILL CABLE ACTION OF BOARD.[59]

The Board did in fact approve Charles Woodbridge as its general secretary of the new mission. Dr. Machen once again cabled Woodbridge:

I DESIRE TO ASSURE YOU THAT YOUR COMING IS AWAITED WITH GREAT ENTHUSIASM AND THAT WE BELIEVE WONDERFUL THINGS TO BE IN STORE.[60]

Understandably, the appointment of Charles Woodbridge as the general secretary of the Independent Board for Presbyterian Foreign Missions elicited a negative response from the national office of the Presbyterian Church in the U.S.A. After all, the new board appeared to directly challenge the constitutional authority of the established Board of Foreign Missions of the Presbyterian Church in the United States. In a letter dated October 31, 1933, Woodbridge explained to Dr. Machen the reasons his departure from Africa would need to be delayed for two months: "The bomb has exploded! It may have occasioned some surprise

---

57. Ibid.
58. Ibid.
59. Ibid.
60. Ibid.

among those connected with the new board when my cable reached [Paul] Woolley, to the effect that 'obligations detain me two months. I wish first to explain this delay' . . . Yesterday the field secretary of the West Africa Mission, Dr. W. Johnston, waited on me with two cables from the present board. They have practically refused to accept the resignation."

One cable indicated:

GENERAL COUNCIL ASSEMBLY AND BOARD MEMBERS AND OFFICERS . . . CANNOT ACCEPT WOODBRIDGE RESIGNATION.

They found it unacceptable he would leave his post to become secretary of the Independent Board for Presbyterian Foreign Missions because he "disregarded assembly constitutional authority." Moreover, they refused to authorize the treasurer of the Mission, he continued, "to advance me travel money; that if I persist in my determination to withdraw, it would mean my having to raise enough money on the field to take me home." Woodbridge indicated to Dr. Machen that he would raise the nearly $1000 for the boat passage on his own. He would sell his "car, bicycle, gun, ice-box, etc." Woodbridge added, "So someday there may be a 'Woodbridge case.' Dr. Johnston told me yesterday that he felt that such people as Machen and now of course, Woodbridge, should get out of the Presbyterian Church U.S.A. Needless to say, I took issue with him there. I have written Dr. Speer telling him very clearly just why I am resigning . . . I praise the Lord that he has called out men of God to take a stand for biblical Presbyterian foreign missions." He also noted to Dr. Machen, whereas before he had been subject to the intimidating treatment from the Presbyterian Mission Board in New York he had believed his working with the Independent Board was a "cause," he now deemed it a "crusade."[61]

---

61. Ibid.

In a cable, Professor Machen urged Woodbridge to accept an invitation to speak at a missions conference at Moody Bible Institute right after his return to the United States. Machen indicated that doing so would give Woodbridge a significant platform for advancing the cause of missions.[62] Machen did not hesitate to make this recommendation, even though Moody Bible Institute advocated dispensational theology. Though an orthodox Presbyterian, Machen felt quite comfortable supporting other Christians who upheld the fundamentals of the faith.[63]

Partnering with Professor Machen at the Independent Board for Presbyterian Foreign Missions

Under Professor Machen's wise tutelage, Charles Woodbridge began working as the general secretary for the Independent Board for Presbyterian Foreign Missions in room 1531 at 12 South Twelfth Street in Philadelphia. The two men regularly corresponded and talked in person. Woodbridge drafted for the board a "Statement as to Its Organization and Program": "The Independent Board for Presbyterian Foreign Missions is an agency established for the quickening of missionary zeal and the promotion of truly biblical and truly Presbyterian foreign missions throughout the world. It is independent in that it is not responsible, as an organization, to the General Assembly of the Presbyterian Church in the U.S.A. or to any other ecclesiastical body."

Woodbridge traveled widely, preaching the gospel and promoting the mission. When Woodbridge proposed overly ambitious promotional strategies, Professor Machen gently reined him in by suggesting other options. Woodbridge managed incoming correspondence, edited the *Independent Board Bulletin*, and wrote a regular column ("The Regions Beyond") for *The Presbyterian Guardian* focusing on news in world

---

62. Ibid.

63. Machen wrote, "We do not mean, in insisting upon the doctrinal basis of Christianity, that all points of doctrine are equally important. It is perfectly possible for Christian fellowship to be maintained despite differences of opinion" (*Christianity and Liberalism*, 40–41).

missions. Dr. Machen often wrote the journal's lead column, "The Changing Scene and the Unchanging Word."

Upon the invitation of Dr. James M. Gray, the president of Moody Bible Institute, Woodbridge spoke at the Founder's Week conference in 1934.[64] In his memoirs, he wrote, "Dr. Gray was fearless in the defense of the faith. Just before I spoke, he leaned over to me on the platform—a small man with his skullcap and big heart—and said, 'There are many Presbyterians here. Let them have it!' I readily complied with his presidential suggestion. There seemed to be a good audience response, although I suspect that not all the Presbyterians there were willing to abandon their respected Dr. Speer and his modernist program simply because the facts of the case were presented!"

Success almost immediately greeted the Independent Board for Presbyterian Foreign Missions in acquiring donations and in enlisting missionaries to go out under its auspices. Mr. Arthur Dieffenbacher, a friend of John Stam, was the first missionary. A man of remarkable evangelistic zeal, he served faithfully in China. During World War II, he lost his life as an army chaplain on July 4, 1944, soon after the Normandy invasion of France. On the transport ship to Europe, he and two other chaplains had led eighty-four men to the Lord.[65]

The success of the Independent Board for Presbyterian Foreign Missions did not go unnoticed by Robert E. Speer, the secretary of the Board of Foreign Missions of the Presbyterian Church in the U.S.A. In his memoirs, Woodbridge referred to the palpable spirit of distrust between Dr. Machen and Dr. Speer:

---

64. Dr. Gray was not a partisan for the use of the word *fundamentalist*: "I do not call myself a fundamentalist, not because I lack sympathy with the Bible truths for which that name now stands, but because I think the name itself is unnecessary and perhaps undesirable" (James M. Gray, "The Deadline of Doctrine around the Church," *Moody Monthly* [November 1922], 101). He worried that opponents might "speak of fundamentalism as something new, and not only new but divisive in the churches, which are said to be already 'sufficiently split and riven.'"

65. See "This Day in Presbyterian History: July 5: Arthur J. Dieffenbacher," July 5, 2013, www. thisday.pcahistory.org/2013/07/july-5-arthur-j-dieffenbacher (accessed May 15, 2017).

Dr. Machen's dealings with Dr. Speer were exasperating. When he challenged him with pure logic, Dr. Speer replied with bold but irrelevant assertions. I was lunching one day with Dr. Machen. He produced a letter he had just received from Dr. Speer. He had written Dr. Speer inquiring why the Presbyterian Mission Board could tolerate the unbiblical teachings of Miss Kirkland. Dr. Speer, dodging the question, replied to the effect that Miss Kirkland was an invalid and needed the prayers of Christians. Dr. Machen wrote again, expressing his sympathy for Miss Kirkland but pressing his point about the Presbyterians' acceptance of her heresy. To which inquiry Dr. Speer replied that Dr. Machen was clearly a bitter man, and that further correspondence with him would be to no avail.

In his column in *The Presbyterian Journal* (April 6, 1936), Professor Machen, apparently frustrated by the continuing "bitterness" charge, summarized his difficulty in interacting with supporters of the Board of Foreign Missions of the Presbyterian Church in the U.S.A. He observed that these supporters used the logic of caricature in their exchanges:

Machen: The Board of Foreign Missions has retained a
    signer of the Auburn Affirmation as candidate secretary.
Supporters of the board: Dr. Robert E. Speer is a splendid
    Christian gentleman.
Machen: You are wandering from the question. What I said
    was that the Board of Foreign Missions has retained a
    signer of the Auburn Affirmation as candidate secretary.
Supporters of the board: Dr. Machen, you are very bitter man.[66]

Earlier in 1934, the ecclesiastical roof had begun to cave in on the Independent Board. In that year, the General Assembly of the

---

66. J. Gresham Machen, "The Changing Scene and the Unchanging Word," *The Presbyterian Guardian* (April 6, 1936), 2.

Presbyterian Church in the U.S.A., in its meeting in Cleveland, Ohio, issued a "mandate" proclaiming that the Independent Board was unconstitutional. It ruled that a "church member or an individual church that will not give to promote the officially authorized missionary program of the Presbyterian Church is in exactly the same position with reference to the constitution of the church as a church member or an individual church that would refuse to take part in the celebration of the Lord's Supper."[67] This ultimatum appeared blasphemous to Charles Woodbridge. Like Dr. Machen, he thought it put institutional authority above the teachings of Scripture. In his memoirs, he wrote, "The Cleveland Assembly continued to apply its meat axe! It ordered the Independent Board's dissolution, demanded that all Presbyterian members of the board resign, and asked presbyteries to proceed to disciplinary action against any Presbyterian board members who proved recalcitrant! We were granted ninety days in which to comply with this iniquitous decree." Thereafter, multiple ecclesiastical trials ensued.

In his memoirs, Woodbridge described Dr. Machen's trial of February-March 1935 in considerable detail. He served as one of Dr. Machen's three defense lawyers. He also noted headlines from across the country referring to both men and women put on trial or otherwise disciplined. Dr. Machen was found guilty on six charges and "suspended" from the ministry. J. Oliver Buswell Jr., the president of Wheaton College; Carl McIntire; and others experienced the same fate.[68] Pages of Woodbridge's memoirs relate details about these happenings and his own trial.

On the evening of March 17, 1935, while under indictment by the Presbyterian Church in the U.S.A., Dr. Machen spoke at the First Presbyterian Church of Pittsburgh. His words capture well the reasons he opposed so vigorously the Auburn Affirmation:

---

67. Personal memoirs of Charles Woodbridge.
68. Accounts of these trials are scattered through *The Presbyterian Guardian*. The 1934 mandate was confirmed by the General Assembly of 1936.

My profession of faith is simply that I know nothing of the Christ proclaimed through the Auburn Affirmation . . . I know nothing of a Christ who is presented to us in a human book containing errors, but know only a Christ presented in a divine Book, the Bible, which is true from beginning to end. I know nothing of a Christ who possibly was and possibly was not born of a virgin, but know only a Christ who was truly conceived by the Holy Ghost and born of the Virgin Mary. I know nothing of a Christ who possibly did and possibly did not work miracles, but know only a Christ who said to the winds and the waves, with the sovereign voice of the Maker and Ruler of all nature, "Peace, be still." I know nothing of a Christ who possibly did and possibly did not come out of the tomb on the first Easter morning, but know only a Christ who triumphed over sin and the grave and is living now in His glorified body until He shall come again and I shall see Him with my very eyes. I know nothing of a Christ who possibly did and possibly did not die as my substitute on the cross, but know only a Christ who took on Himself the just punishment of my sins and died there in my stead to make me right with the holy God.[69]

Dr. Machen indicated he would "rather be condemned for an honest adherence to the Bible and to my solemn ordination pledge than enjoy the highest ecclesiastical honors and emoluments as the reward of dishonesty."[70]

Perhaps not surprisingly, in the same year 1935, Dr. Harry Emerson Fosdick declared that modernism had triumphed over fundamentalism. In a sermon titled "The Church Must Go Beyond Modernism," delivered at the Riverside Church in New York City, Fosdick declared,

---

69. "The Continuing Story: Dr. Machen's Profession of Faith," June 28, 2011, https://continuing .wordpress.com/2011/06/28/dr-machens-profession-of-faith (accessed May 15, 2017).

70. Ibid.

"We have already largely won the battle we started out to win; we have adjusted the Christian faith to the best intelligence of our day and have won the strongest minds and the best abilities of the church to our side. Fundamentalism is still with us but mostly in the backwaters. The future of the churches, if we will have it so, is in the hands of modernism."[71] But Dr. Fosdick surprised his listeners by confessing the principal weakness of modernism—that it is "no adequate religion to represent the Eternal and claim the allegiance of the soul. Let it be a modernist who says that to you!"[72] He added a great concession: "We cannot harmonize Christ himself with modern culture. What Christ does to modern culture is to challenge it."[73]

Woodbridge's memoirs describe his own suspension in May 1936:

I sat in the gallery of the Central High School of Syracuse, New York, when the Permanent Judicial Commission of the Presbyterian Church in the U.S.A. delivered its ultimate verdict . . . It found us "guilty" of all charges leveled at us [Judicial Case N. 1] . . . When the sound and fury of the Commission's diatribe had ceased and the audience, seemingly greatly impressed, was vacating the Central High School of Syracuse, a portly gentleman of florid countenance approached me and put his arm around my shoulder. He was Dr. J. Ross Stevenson, president of Princeton Theological Seminary. He had known me since my Princeton University days, but apparently he did not know me very well. He asked me, with a look of victorious satisfaction, "Why do you not give up all this foolishness? We'll be glad to give you a fresh start." To this helpful suggestion, I replied, "Only if you will discipline the Auburn Affirmationists in the church." Impatiently he dropped his arm,

---

71. Harry Emerson Fosdick, "The Church Must Go Beyond Modernism," *Riverside Sermons* (New York: Harper and Brothers, 1958), 362.

72. Ibid., 354–55.

73. Ibid., 362. Fosdick feared what would happen if Christianity adapted itself to "contemporary nationalism, contemporary imperialism, contemporary capitalism, contemporary racialism" (p. 361).

shook his ample double chin, shrugged his well-rounded shoulders, managed [a] sniff of disgust, and walked away in disdain. I have never seen Dr. Stevenson again. His ecumenical bias, he knew quite well, was permeating the Presbyterian Church with astonishing rapidity.[74]

During these very trying days of 1935–1936, Dr. Machen and Charles Woodbridge kept in close personal contact. In his memoirs, Woodbridge described Machen's visit to the family home after the birth of the Woodbridges' baby girl. Ever the gentleman, Machen asked Ruth and Charles for permission to touch the baby's cheek as if the baby were a little angel from heaven. Woodbridge noted that within a year, Dr. Machen would himself be in heaven.

Another significant glimpse of J. Gresham Machen in Woodbridge's memoirs concerned the founding of the new church, the Presbyterian Church of America. "Suspended" ministers like Machen and Woodbridge would soon have a new church home. In his memoirs, Woodbridge wrote:

We met in the New Century Club of Philadelphia on June 11, 1936—ministers, elders, and members of the Presbyterian Church in the U.S.A. The chairman asked how many in attendance desired to affiliate themselves as forming the new church. About two hundred people stood to their feet; and while they remained standing, the president officer declared the Presbyterian Church of America to be constituted. Ministers and elders who wished to be a part of the general assembly of the new church then stood, and that ecclesiastical organization was duly and legally constituted. The Presbyterian Church of America was now a going concern . . . To the great delight of all assembled, Dr. Machen

---

74. Regarding the Syracuse meetings, see "Syracuse Swan Song: The 148th General Assembly: A Description and an Interpretation," *The Presbyterian Guardian* (June 22, 1936), 112, 118–39.

was elected moderator of the new church. He was nominated by Dr. Gordon H. Clark, professor at the University of Pennsylvania, who described him as a scholar and a gentleman, a man who when reviled, reviled not again. Dr. Clark stated concerning his nominee, "He defended Christianity against his enemies, not by imitating their campaign of personal defamation, but by defending Christianity like a Christian gentleman." The protracted applause which greeted these elegant words revealed the confidence which we all felt in our hour of supreme joy and relief in the leadership of a great man of God who, in the opinion of us all, had been persecuted for righteousness' sake.[75]

Mourning the Sudden Death of Professor J. Gresham Machen

Not too many months later, deep sadness again gripped Charles Woodbridge. Dr. Machen was stripped of his presidency of the Independent Board for Presbyterian Foreign Missions. In a June 12, 1937, article in *The Presbyterian Guardian*, Woodbridge reflected retrospectively about this "tragedy," which had occurred in a November 1936 meeting of the board held in Philadelphia: "I shall never forget that meeting. It was one of the saddest sights that I have ever witnessed. Dr. Machen had been president of the Board ever since I had returned from Africa. But now on the part of certain persons on the Board a growing discontent with Dr. Machen's presidency had been developing. Weeks before the Board meeting, these persons had conferred and had decided to remove Dr. Machen from the presidency of the Board."

After hours of debate, an "independent" and non-Presbyterian

---

75. Personal memoirs of Charles Woodbridge. See also J. Gresham Machen, "The Church of God: A Sermon Preached at the Concluding Service of the General Assembly of the Presbyterian Church of America in the New Century Club, Philadelphia, Sunday Evening, June 14th, 1936," *The Presbyterian Guardian* (July 6, 1936), 152–56; see also Robert S. Marsden, "The First Ten Years: The Orthodox Presbyterian Church 1936–1946," https://opc.org/books/FirstTenYears.html (accessed May 15, 2017).

candidate favored by board member Carl McIntire was elected the new president of the board. Woodbridge continued: "Dr. Machen was greatly shocked. The evening of the Board meeting it was clear that he foresaw the collapse of the Independent Board as a Presbyterian agency. He said to me, with a note of tragedy in his voice, 'If it were not for our missionaries I would at once resign from the Board.'"[76]

In the last days of the next month, December 1937, Dr. Machen traveled to Bismarck, North Dakota, to fulfill a ministry assignment. He had a very bad cold. Some friends had advised him not to make the train trip. It was bitterly frigid in Bismarck. He was grieving the recent events of November, only to be stricken with pneumonia. Woodbridge reported that over and over again, Dr. Machen told Reverend Allen, his host in Bismarck, that "the Presbyterian Church of America would have to establish its own missionary agency if it desired to conduct truly Biblical and truly Presbyterian foreign missions."[77]

On December 30, 1936, Charles Woodbridge sent the following Western Union telegram to Dr. Machen at St. Alexius Hospital:

SO SORRY TO HEAR ABOUT YOUR ILLNESS STOP BY ALL MEANS BE IN NO HURRY TO LEAVE THE HOSPITAL STOP WE WILL DO ALL WE CAN TO PINCH-HIT FOR YOU STOP PRAYING FOR YOU STOP WITH REAL CHRISTIAN AFFECTION=CHARLIE WOODBRIDGE[78]

At 7:30 p.m. on January 1, 1937, J. Gresham Machen, the stalwart, orthodox Presbyterian, went to be with his Lord and Savior whom he had served so well in this life.[79]

---

76. Charles J. Woodbridge, "Why I Have Resigned as General Secretary of the Independent Board," *The Presbyterian Guardian* (June 12, 1937), 70, www.opc.org/cfh/guardian/Volume_4/1937-06-12.pdf (accessed May 15, 2017).

77. Ibid.

78. Archives of the Montgomery Library of Westminster Theological Seminary, Philadelphia, PA (Machen/Woodbridge correspondence, Box 1935–36).

79. For an account of Machen's death, see Stonehouse, *J. Gresham Machen*, 506–8.

Closing Reflections

Charles Woodbridge's largely behind-the-scenes glimpses and perceptions of Professors J. Gresham Machen and Adolph von Harnack are
just that—glimpses and perceptions. We need to consult perspectives
from additional primary sources and rich secondary literatures to gain
a fuller picture of the two men. We especially need to include the compelling concerns and arguments of well-respected Presbyterians such
as Pastor Clarence Edward Macartney and a number of Westminster
professors who believed Machen had seriously erred in establishing the
Independent Board for Presbyterian Foreign Missions.[80]

What might we learn from Charles Woodbridge's personal glimpses
of Machen and von Harnack? Perhaps our modest reception history of
Woodbridge's perceptions of these two iconic figures does felicitously
humanize them a bit more and fills in a number of gaps in our understanding. It reveals that Professors Machen and von Harnack admired
each other. It suggests that both men were on occasion subjected to
harsh criticisms. Moreover, it emphasizes the point that Machen was
motivated by a desire to remain faithful to the Lord both in his church
life and scholarship, no matter the cost. He combined a rare commitment to world-class Christian scholarship and to worldwide Christian
missions. He was deeply troubled by the fact that the herculean struggle
between Christianity and liberalism not only stirred the northern
Presbyterian Church in the United States, but also in the theatres of
the Presbyterian mission fields stretching from China (Pearl Buck) to
the French Cameroon in West Africa.[81]

A number of other observations might be salient:

---

80. See Stonehouse, *J. Gresham Machen*, 496–97; see also Nichols, *J. Gresham Machen*, 196–98;
James A. Patterson, "Robert E. Speer, J. Gresham Machen, and the Presbyterian Board of Foreign
Missions," *American Presbyterians* 64:1 (Spring 1986): 58–68. Several Westminster professors feared
the new mission board, among other things, might hinder the acceptance of Westminster graduates
as pastors in the Presbyterian Church in the U.S.A.

81. William Hocking's *Re-thinking Missions* provides an extensive report on Christian world
missions that is replete with modernist themes. For example, it reads, "The concept that God is a

1. Students at Princeton Theological Seminary in the years 1924–1927 apparently had scant knowledge of the struggle between Professor Machen and members of the administration regarding the direction of the school.

2. Newspaper reports sometimes portrayed Dr. Machen as "intolerant," "bitter," and "schismatic." Dr. Robert Speer also said as much. In fact, Dr. Machen was a gracious gentleman who generally refrained from personal attacks. Dr. Gordon Clark noted this trait in nominating Dr. Machen as moderator of the Presbyterian Church in the U.S.A. Upon hearing of Dr. Machen's death, Reverend Floyd Hamilton, a missionary in Korea, added his testimony:

> I can't put into words all that the friendship and teaching of Dr. Machen has meant to me personally. In all our close and intimate friendship I have never heard him enter upon a tirade against any man who was opposed to him in the theological fight. He never went into personal attacks against his foes, but always attacked the principles and practices of those who in any way deviated from the teaching of the Word of God. Vituperation he left to his enemies, and I suppose there has been no man of our generation more unjustly maligned and misrepresented by those who were supposed to be orthodox than he.[82]

3. Dr. Machen deemed individuals like Dr. Robert E. Speer—those he characterized as "evasive" tolerant moderates—as even more dangerous than Professor Adolph von Harnack, whom he viewed as a naturalist. Dr. Machen feared that "tolerant" evangelicals would prompt

---

loving father and that all men are brothers grips the imagination even though orientals realize that such concepts are rarely carried out in the lives of western people" (p. 246).

82. Reverend Hamilton knew Dr. Machen well. He received a ThB in 1919 and a ThM in 1926 from Princeton Theological Seminary. He served as a missionary in Korea with the Presbyterian Church in the U.S.A. and then with the Independent Board for Presbyterian Foreign Missions. In 1934, he delivered an important address to the League of Evangelical Students titled "Can a Christian Student Rationally Reject Evolution?"

Bible-believing evangelicals to trust modernists' teachings. Their alleged "indifferentism" toward those who did not affirm orthodox doctrines could imply that doctrines were not fundamental to the Christian faith after all. Machen wrote, "Indifferentism about doctrine makes no heroes of the faith."[83] Machen expressed feelings of frustration about modernists and moderates who were severely hampering Presbyterian Bible believers from being able to support evangelical missionaries overseas.

4. Dr. Machen was no obscurantist when it came to engagement with unbelieving world-class scholarship. He admired Professor von Harnack's writings. He recommended that Princeton students encounter unbelief in its "raw form." Whereas some fundamentalists like evangelist Billy Sunday did make outlandish statements critical of higher education, Machen extolled the merits of a first-class education, including the study of science.

5. Dr. Machen was quite reluctant to use the term *fundamentalist* to describe himself. Nonetheless, when he did employ the expression *fundamentalism*, he defined it carefully. In an article titled "What Fundamentalism Stands For Now," he wrote, "The term 'Fundamentalism' is distasteful to the present writer and to many persons who hold views similar to his. It seems to suggest that we are adherents of some strange new sect, whereas in point of fact we are conscious simply of maintaining the historic Christian faith and of moving in the great central current of Christian life. That does not mean that we desire to be out of touch with our own time, or that we live in a static world without variety and without zest."[84] In another article (1924), "Does Fundamentalism Obstruct Social Progress?" he observed, "The term 'Fundamentalism' in the title of our discussion is evidently to be taken in a broad sense, not to designate 'Premillennialists' but to include all those who definitely and polemically maintain a

---

83. Machen, *Christianity and Liberalism*, 42.
84. Quoted in Hart, ed., *J. Gresham Machen*, 116.

belief in supernatural Christianity as over against the Modernism of the present day. In what ways has 'Fundamentalism,' defined thus broadly to include men like ourselves, been held to be inimical to social progress?"[85]

6. Dr. Machen referred more generally to those "faithful" Presbyterians whose welfare he sought as "orthodox," "Bible-believing Christians," or "evangelicals." Dr. Machen viewed himself as an orthodox Presbyterian engaged in a struggle to defend Christianity against liberalism.[86] He saw himself as a faithful Calvinist defender of the Westminster Confession subjected to attacks by unfaithful churchmen—advocates of the Auburn Confession.[87] At the same time, he displayed great respect and appreciation for other conservative Christians ranging from Missouri Synod Lutherans and Methodists to dispensational premillennialists who upheld the "fundamentals" of the faith. Concerning candidates for the Presbyterian ministry, he wrote:

> Be it noticed that the candidates do not subscribe to the Reformed system of doctrine merely as one allowable system among many allowable systems. They do not even merely subscribe to it as the best system. But they subscribe to it as the system that is true.
>
> Being true, it is true for Methodists and Lutherans just as much as Presbyterians, and we cannot treat as of no moment the differences which separate us from Methodists and Lutherans without being unfaithful to the Word of God.

---

86. J. Gresham Machen, "What Is Orthodoxy?" in "The Changing Scene and the Unchanging Word," *The Presbyterian Guardian* (October 21, 1935): 38.

87. On February 1, 1935, Machen proposed to Woodbridge additions to his article "Sham Orthodoxy Versus Real Orthodoxy" destined for the *Independent Board Bulletin*: "What Sham Orthodoxy Says: Whether a man is a Modernist or not is determined by the kind of sermons he preaches; he is orthodox if he preaches orthodox sermons. What Real Orthodoxy Says: Whether a man is a Modernist or not is determined by the way he votes in presbytery and at the General Assembly; he is a Modernist, no matter what kind of sermons he preaches, if he votes with the Auburn Affirmationists in the great issues of the day" (archives of the Montgomery Library at Westminster Theological Seminary, Philadelphia, PA [Machen /Woodbridge Correspondence, Box 1935–36]).

Does that mean that we cannot have Christian fellowship with our Methodist or our Lutheran brethren?

It means nothing of the kind. On the contrary, we can have very precious fellowship with them.[88]

He continued by extolling the "Christian fellowship that I have enjoyed with many of my Lutheran brethren, especially those of the 'Missouri Synod.' How often when I have felt tempted to be discouraged, has some message come to me from them bidding me be of good courage and remember that the battle is the Lord's!"[89] Moreover, Charles Woodbridge was a premillennialist during the time he served as the general secretary for the Independent Board for Presbyterian Foreign Missions. Machen even lauded the Roman Catholic Church for its high view of the authority of Scripture.[90]

7. Dr. Machen faithfully upheld a very high view of the Bible's authority and emphasized Scripture's inerrancy. He sought to be faithful to the Lord and to biblical teaching whatever the cost. Delivering a sermon at Tenth Presbyterian Church of Philadelphia not long before his death, Dr. Machen declared:

The Bible is the Magna Charta of human liberty . . . When it is abandoned, tyranny stalks unchecked. When the Bible is no longer thought to be inerrant, the decisions of church assemblies are exalted above it. Thus the word of man is exalted above the Word of God.

What should be done when the machinery of the church thus pushed itself between the Christian and Christ? The Christian

---

88. J. Gresham Machen, "The Second Part of the Ordination Pledge," in "The Changing Scene and the Unchanging Word," *The Presbyterian Guardian* (December 2, 1935), 70.

89. Ibid.

90. Ibid. Machen observed, "The Roman Catholic Church, for example, holds to the full truthfulness of the Bible; yet no one would doubt but that its system of doctrine is widely different from ours."

must seek Christ again at any cost, and must yield implicit obedience to His command alone. We must allow nothing to stand between us and Christ—no ecumenical council, no presbytery, no synod, no general assembly.[91]

A witness of the service where Dr. Machen was preaching observed, "The edifice was crowded with a large number of eagerly listening worshippers obviously moved by the tenderness and sincerity of the sermon."[92]

Dr. Machen, the last major representative of "old Princeton," has much to teach us about our own discipleship as followers of Jesus Christ. He demonstrated exemplary courage despite daunting challenges. He sought to be faithful to the Lord and biblical teaching no matter the cost. He gives us an example of a person who lived all out for Christ. Little wonder his favorite hymn included these inspiring words he took very much to heart: "Were the whole realm of nature mine, that were a present far too small; love so amazing, so divine, demands my soul, my life, my all."

---

91. "Tenth Church Refuses to Cancel Invitation, Dr. Machen Preaches: Affirmationist Moderator Attempts to Intimidate Session," *The Presbyterian Guardian* (July 6, 1936): 163.

92. Machen's emphasis on the importance of biblical inerrancy in the cited statement and multiple others and in similar statements made by his close associates writing in *The Presbyterian Guardian* does not comport easily with Professor Daryl Hart's claim: "Machen did affirm inerrancy, but it was a side issue in his estimation" (D. G. Hart, *J. Gresham Machen*, 6.). Interestingly enough, cartoonist Phil Saint prominently placed clever cartoons criticizing evolution in *The Presbyterian Guardian*, October 21, 1935, 28; November 18, 1935, 63; February 17, 1936, 167.

Chapter 5

THE TOWER OF BABEL AND THE COVENANT

Rhetorical Strategy in Genesis Based on Theological and Comparative Analysis

JOHN H. WALTON

Thirty years ago, I wrote my dissertation on the Tower of Babel (Hebrew Union College-Jewish Institute of Religion) under the guidance of Chanan Brichto and Sam Greengus. Though it included some history of interpretation, it was primarily an exegetical and comparative study. In this essay, I will briefly summarize those findings and proceed to discussion of ideas that I have developed over the last thirty years, primarily from conversation with students as I have taught Genesis and from interaction with further studies. I am happy to dedicate this to Stan Gundry. I have worked with him throughout the decades represented in this paper and have found him a stimulating editor, a trustworthy confidant, and a good friend.

Summary of Early Work[1]

In terms of the technologies referred to in Genesis 11, I found that burnt brick technology was unique to Mesopotamia, where the alluvial

---

1. These matters were published in "The Mesopotamian Background of the Tower of Babel

plains location would have required stones to be imported at great expense. Bitumen mortar was commonly used with kiln-fired brick. This technology is first attested in the late Uruk period, but is more common in the Jamdat Nasr period and thus dates to the end of the fourth millennium. This technology was used in public buildings, and at the beginning of urbanization, cities were comprised solely of public buildings, primarily the temple complex.

The tower was a ziggurat whose architecture featured a brick structure filled with rubble; unlike a pyramid, there was no inside. These structures were the visible center of the temple complex, but served an ancillary function in sacred space, where the true center was the adjoining temple. The ziggurat and the temple served as a cosmic lynchpin bridging the gap between the realms. The names given to the ziggurats confirmed this ideology. In their cosmic role, they provided a convenience for the gods and invited them to descend into the temple to be worshiped. One is reminded of the executive elevator. Importantly, and against the history of interpretation, such a structure did not provide a way for humans to ascend, but for gods to descend, as Genesis 11 itself attests. Ziggurats were part of sacred space and inaccessible to the public. They were not temples per se because there were no rituals performed there and no image of deity resident there, but they were considered part of sacred space and thus their names were prefaced with the same Sumerian designations as the temples. The ziggurat was a stairway *from* heaven.

The main exegetical results concerned the making of a name and the desire not to scatter. Regarding the first, I proposed that making a name was naturally desirable and not intrinsically prideful. It is accomplished by anything that results in one being remembered. It could be motivated by pride, but was perhaps more importantly associated with the idea that one might find benefit in the afterlife by one's name being remembered. While conquests or great building

---

and Its Implications," *Bulletin for Biblical Research* 5 (1995): 155–75, and further citations can be found there.

projects could accomplish that end, so could having children.[2]

My findings also suggested that desiring not to scatter was natural. In Genesis 13, Abram and Lot did not want to separate, but circumstances demanded it. Scattered families bring discontinuity and disrupt relationship and traditions being passed on. The need for scattering was somewhat resolved through urbanization, which the building of a city addressed. No connection should be drawn to the creation mandate in Genesis 1 because "filling" is accomplished by reproduction, not by geographical dispersion.

At this point, it is obvious that my study had called into question all the main interpretations of the offense of the tower builders. They are not trying to ascend to heaven; they are not necessarily guilty of pride; and they are not disobeying a command to fill the earth. In fact, regarding the latter, the illocution of Genesis 1:28 is clearly indicated as being blessing, not command. Blessings cannot be disobeyed.

To conclude this summary, my dissertation then led me to posit an offense in place of those suggestions that had been refuted. I proposed that the offense was related to the religious system of Babylon that was focused on meeting the needs of the gods. The ziggurat was part of a system in which the gods descended to inhabit the image that had been prepared to contain their essence, and through that image the god would be cared for through rituals designed for that purpose. The text does not articulate this system, but I contended that it did not need to. The symbol of the ziggurat spoke clearly to Israelites familiar with its function. Jacob's dream in Genesis 28 is further evidence of their understanding.

Developments over the Last Thirty Years

In the thirty years since the completion of my dissertation, I have not abandoned any of those interpretations, though I have added much more

---

2. For a more recent affirmation of the same ideas, see K. Radner and Eleanor Robson, *Oxford Handbook of Cuneiform Culture* (Oxford: Oxford University Press, 2011), 113–14.

nuance to some of them, which has pushed the overall interpretation in somewhat different directions. My discussion of ziggurats has found support in studies such as those of A. R. George and Thorkild Jacobsen.[3] Most of my more recent study has focused on literary, rhetorical, and canonical issues, but they have been productive for exegetical results.

Offense

As I have continued to give attention to the nature of the offense, I have come to attach more significance to the making of the name than previously. The line of development starts with the original idea that the problem was in the Babylonian religious ideas. I have adopted the label "Great Symbiosis" to describe the system wherein the gods had created humanity to meet their needs, which was the goal of the rituals of the ancient world. In turn, the gods met the needs of humanity (provision and protection). This symbiosis results in codependence and is contrary to the biblical ideal, in which Yahweh has no needs. The Great Symbiosis thinking that pervaded the religious systems in the ancient world was based on mutual needs.

When Great Symbiosis thinking is brought to the context of Genesis 11, one can perceive an important nuance in the builders' desire to make a name for themselves. In the past, when this motivation was evaluated, it was often indicated that the builders' offense was in the fact that *they* were trying to make a name for themselves rather than allowing *God* to make a name for them. I propose instead that the contrast is not found in the verb (making a name rather than not making a name) nor in the subject (them making a name rather than God making a name for them), but in the indirect object (a name for *themselves* rather than for *God*). If sacred space is being constructed (as a ziggurat would suggest), it should be making a name for God. Note, for example, in

---

3. A. R. George, *House Most High: The Temples of Ancient Mesopotamia* (Winona Lake, IN: Eisenbrauns, 1993); Thorkild Jacobsen, "Notes on Ekur," *Eretz-Israel* 21 (1990): 40–47; see also Julian Reade and Irving Finkel, "The Ziggurat and Temples of Nimrud," *Iraq* 64 (2002): 135–216.

Enuma Elish VI.51: "Let us build a sanctuary whose name is famous." Great Symbiosis thinking, however, could easily lead to a motivation focused on their own success and well-being.[4] That is, their motivation for constructing sacred space was to bring benefits to themselves.

The ideal that construction of sacred space ought to make a name for deity is reflected both in the ancient Near Eastern literature, such as in the names of ziggurats or temples,[5] and in the biblical ideology.[6] Such an offense does not represent encroaching on divine boundaries (as has often been suggested as the offense of the builders) as much as diminishing divine attributes. The builders were attempting to establish sacred space, itself a commendable activity, but their motivations were flawed.

COHERENCE OF GENESIS 1–11

This understanding of the offense leads us to an understanding of the role of the tower-building account in the rhetorical strategy of Genesis 1–11. In Genesis 2, sacred space was constructed by God in the Garden of Eden. People were placed in sacred space with priestly duties (Genesis 2:15). Life and wisdom were available in the presence of God, represented by the trees.

When people, prompted by the serpent, sought to make themselves the center of wisdom and order ("you will be like gods"), they were cast out of sacred space and the presence of God. In Genesis 3, sacrificial gifts are being brought, and in Genesis 4:26, people began to call on the name of the Lord—but neither of these reestablish sacred space. Genesis 11:1–9 gives an account of the builders making a move to reinitiate sacred space through the abiding presence of God and to thereby regain a privilege lost at Eden.[7] The theme of Genesis 1–11 is not

---

4. Stimulated by an observation by Justin White.

5. See, for example, George, *House Most High*: "House of Fame" (*bit dalili*), #140 (p. 74); "House of the Exalted Name," #811 (p. 127); "House Chosen by Name," #812 (p. 127).

6. Psalm 34:3: "let us exalt [*rum*] his [the LORD's] name"; implied from Malachi 1:11–12 (if name can be defiled, it can theoretically be made great); building a temple for the name of the Lord (1 Kings 3:2; 5:3–5; 8:16–29).

7. Suggested by Eva Teague.

simply encroachment on divine prerogatives or violation of boundaries between divine and human identities, but the encroachment of disorder on the ordered realm. Adam and Eve brought disorder of sin and death (instigated by the chaos creature serpent). This trend continues in the following narratives:[8]

- Cain brought disorder in the family relationships.
- Sons of God brought disorder into the nature of humanity and society.
- Flood brought the resurgence of cosmic non-order as a response to societal disorder.
- Dry land emerged from cosmic waters in Genesis 8 as in Genesis 1; people and animals brought forth in both; blessing given in both; but God has not "rested" in his presence among his people.
- Renewed covenant after the flood does not repeat "subdue and rule"—expanding order based on sacred space no longer possible, but maintaining social order, which is still a responsibility (judging capital crimes).
- Babel introduced disorder into the divine and human inter-relationships and resulted in God's interruption of order by the confusion of languages.
- Tower builders likewise conceived of sacred space as focused on themselves (making a name for themselves)—a repetition of the Garden of Eden scenario—thus forming an inclusio to Genesis 1–11. Order determined by them and built around themselves.

Confusion of Tongues and Scattering

In this view of the offense and of the rhetorical strategy of Genesis 1–11, the confusion of tongues and the resultant scattering are not itself punishment. More precisely, it is a means, not an end in itself. The

---

8. For more detailed analysis and explanation, see John Walton and Tremper Longman III, *Lost World of the Flood* (Downers Grove, IL: InterVarsity Press, forthcoming 2018).

objective is for the city building to be stopped.[9] God indeed descends (11:5) as the builders intended, but he is not pleased at their initiative because of the premise on which it is founded. They have crossed a threshold (11:6) by seeking to establish order by means of sacred space and the institution of the Great Symbiosis that the sacred space facilitated.

The scattering by means of confusion of tongues sets the stage for the programmatic response that Yahweh intends. This began in Genesis 10, which describes the rise of the seventy nations; Genesis 11 describes the scattering of the nations. These nations can be recognized as being apportioned to the sons of God in Deuteronomy 32:8.[10] Then Genesis 12 initiates God's choice of the nation of Israel (again alluded to in Deuteronomy 32:8). Election (covenant) operates in the context of diversity. This then leads us to an examination of the rhetorical relationship of the two major sections of Genesis.

Linkage between Genesis 1–11 and Genesis 12–50[11]

The tower-building account has introduced a second theological problem that needs to be resolved. The first was the sin/disorder problem that was introduced at the fall and resulted in the loss of access to sacred space. Before those problems can be resolved, it is imperative that God takes the next step in his plans and purposes and institutes relationship so that sacred space can be reestablished on a proper basis.

In this way, the tower-building narrative is followed naturally by God's initiative to reestablish sacred space. This will happen after he has established a relationship (the covenant) through which he reveals himself (to the patriarchs and at Sinai) as prelude to the construction of sacred space (the tabernacle) on the corrected premise of a ritual system

---

9. Stimulated by an observation by Ashley Edewaard.

10. Stimulated by an observation by John Raines.

11. Mark A. Awabdy ("Babel, Suspense, and the Introduction to the Terah-Abram Narrative," *Journal for the Study of the Old Testament* 35 [2010]: 3–29) suggests the idea that Genesis 12 is a response to Genesis 11:1–9.

that does not presume a needy deity. He makes a place for *his* name to be honored. He rejected the builders' flawed strategy and embarks on his own initiative. The Babel problem must be resolved (through revelation) before the Eden problem can be resolved (through reconciliation). God's initiative is going to reestablish his presence, not on the strength of their unity, but in the midst of their diversity. In this way, Genesis 11 offers a bridge to Genesis 12: Genesis 11 is a failed human initiative to reestablish God's presence; Genesis 12 is God's initiative that will lead to his presence and sacred space.[12]

Intertextual Trajectories[13]

When we expand our view to include intertextual trajectories, we are immediately drawn to the account of the Day of Pentecost in Acts 2, which can be viewed as having an intertextual relationship to the Tower of Babel account, especially as it manifests the familiar motif of the languages. More precisely, we may identify several specific intertextual connections between Acts 2 and Genesis 11–12:

- Luke uses three terms from the Septuagint of Genesis 11: v. 4: γλώσσαις, "tongues"; v. 6: φωνῆς, "sound"; v. 6: συνεχύθη, "confound."
- Table of nations paralleled in Acts 2:9.
- After language confusion is reversed, covenant is announced as fulfilled ("The promise is for you and your children and for all who are far off" [Acts 2:39]).

On the basis of these explicit connections, we are invited to identify further points of comparison and contrast. The result is that Genesis 11–12 and Acts 2 can be seen to serve the function of a canonical/ theological inclusio.

---

12. Stimulated by an observation by Eva Teague.
13. Prompted by observations by Kelly Brady.

Contrasts include the following points:[14]

- The Spirit's descent represents the right establishment of God's presence in Acts 2, contrasted to Yahweh's descent to counteract a flawed initiative in Genesis.
- Essence of deity (represented in the Holy Spirit) does not come down to enter the image in the temple (Babylonian model), but to enter his image represented in people, particularly the church—the ultimate expression in New Testament theology of God in the midst of his people.
- Babel problem resolved (revelation completed; presence of God established) so differentiation of tongues is symbolically reversed, thus opening universal accessibility to relationship with God.
- Community disrupted in Genesis, but community is established at Pentecost as God begins regathering his people.
- Pentecost establishes the name of God/Christ through his people rather than establishing their name through what they gain.
- Tower was built to gain unity in divine presence; church is built by God for unity in divine presence.
- In Acts 2, as the people scatter with their own languages to their own homes, they take the presence of God with them rather than leaving a failed project behind.

In conclusion, we can identify some theological implications that may be drawn out, given the proposed understanding between Genesis 11–12 and Acts 2:

- Pentecost is seen in New Testament theology as (1) drawing a conclusion to the revelatory program God had initiated in Genesis

---

14. Many of these were identified by M. D. Goulder, *Type and History in Acts* (London: SPCK, 1964), 158–59.

12 through the covenant and (2) establishing the new covenant that had been announced in Jeremiah 31.

- Eden problem is seen in New Testament theology as having been resolved by Christ and reversed in new creation; Babel problem is seen as being resolved by the covenant and reversed at Pentecost, where order is brought in the midst of language diversity.
- God's intention through Pentecost is proclaimed by Peter as drawing all nations to himself—a further initiative in Divine Presence and sacred space reflected in the Pauline theology of believers as temple.

The Tower of Babel is a fascinating narrative that in its nine short verses poses a full array of questions: linguistic, comparative, rhetorical, literary, and theological. I have found it to be an inexhaustible mine for the insights of curious students and look forward to many more years of investigating its exegetical and theological depths.

Chapter 6

"What Was Said in All the Scriptures concerning Himself" (Luke 24:27)

Reading the Old Testament as a Christian

TREMPER LONGMAN III

C hristian scholars, pastors, and lay readers all in their own ways struggle with the question of the relationship between the two Testaments. There is obvious continuity between the Old and the New (Matthew 5:17–20), but how much and in what way? There is also obvious discontinuity (we neither offer animal sacrifices nor wage holy wars), but again, how much and in what way?

The history of interpretation and even contemporary hermeneutical approaches witness to many different answers to these questions from an emphasis on continuity, perhaps best illustrated by the now diminished theonomy movement and certain advocates of Messianic Judaism, to significant assertions of discontinuity, exemplified by traditional dispensationalist approaches.

This essay does not intend to resolve all the issues pertaining to this large and important question, nor will we weigh in on all the different answers presented through history and today.[1] We rather focus on an important element of the question of the relationship between the Old and New Testaments, namely, whether or not and in what way we might speak of Jesus in relationship to the Old Testament.

Jesus' Post-Resurrection Instruction in Hermeneutics

We begin with an examination of the most important passage that speaks to our inquiry into Christ's relationship to the Old Testament. Luke 24 tells us about Jesus' words and actions in the period between his resurrection and his ascension, a very brief period of time. Interestingly, at least for our question, he devotes all of his teaching during this time to the question of Old Testament hermeneutics. The significance of the subject is underlined by the fact that the gospel writer includes two encounters with disciples in which Jesus repeats essentially the same lesson.

The first occasion is on the famous walk on the road to Emmaus. Jesus, whose identity was kept from them (Luke 24:16), joins two of his followers and asks them about the subject of their conversation. They are amazed that he seems ignorant of the big news about Jesus, whose death has stunned them. Further, they have heard reports from some women disciples that they found his tomb empty.

Jesus' response is at the heart of our interest:

"How foolish you are, and how slow to believe all that the prophets have spoken! Did not the Messiah have to suffer these things and then enter his glory?" And beginning with Moses and all the

---

1. It is my intention to write a book-length treatment of this issue in the near future. Here I intend to lay out my basic approach to the question.

Prophets, he explained to them what was said in all the Scriptures concerning himself.

Luke 24:25–27

Before I comment on this passage, let me introduce the second example from the same chapter. In this case, Jesus is speaking to a broader group of disciples:

He said to them, "This is what I told you while I was still with you: Everything must be fulfilled that is written about me in the Law of Moses, the Prophets and the Psalms." Then he opened their minds so they could understand the Scriptures.

Luke 24:44–45

What is undeniable is Jesus' contention that the Scriptures the people of God possessed at the time and in some sense anticipated his coming and work. He refers to what Christians call the Old Testament, using nomenclature that was current among the Jewish people in the first century AD. In the first case, he uses the expression "Moses and all the Prophets," and in the second he uses the tripartite term, "the Law of Moses, the Prophets and the Psalms."[2] These are both variants referring to the same collection of books. The Law (*Torah*) of Moses, of course, is the first five books of the Old Testament. The Prophets (*Nebi'im*) refer to the books of Joshua, Judges, Samuel, and Kings (the Former Prophets), as well as Isaiah, Jeremiah, Ezekiel, and the Twelve Minor Prophets (the Latter Prophets). The Psalms is one way to refer to the third part of the Hebrew canon, which is more widely known as the Writings (*Ketubim*) and refers to a miscellaneous group of books too numerous to list here.[3]

---

2. See R. Beckwith, *The Old Testament Canon of the New Testament Church* (London: SPCK, 1985), 105–9.

3. But containing all the books found in the Protestant canon of the Old Testament that are not found in the first two sections. As we can see, the order of the books in the Hebrew Bible (known as the *Tanak* [an acronym based on the first letters of its three sections]) in our English translations is based on the Septuagint.

The bottom line of Jesus' two statements to his disciples is that the entire Hebrew Bible anticipated his coming and work, not just some isolated prophecies. Of course, Jesus does not say precisely how the Old Testament looks forward to his coming and this is a question we will take up shortly. His words also raise an interesting question in the light of the initial response to his crucifixion and resurrection.

To put it bluntly, from what we read in the gospel accounts, no one seemed to get it. We do not hear of people who were anticipating the crucifixion—far from it. After Jesus' death, when his followers visited the tomb, they were shocked to find it empty. From what we can tell about messianic expectation in the first century AD and in the centuries before it, no one was expecting a fully divine and fully human Messiah who would end up on a cross to die for people's sins. If anything, most expected a very human Messiah who would reestablish David's kingly line and cast off Israel's oppressors. There were variations, like the view that there would be two Messiahs, one kingly and one priestly. But again, nothing leads us to think that anyone had the slightest idea that the work of Jesus would take the course it did.[4]

This situation leads to the present debate as to whether Christ's presence in the Old Testament was something that could be discerned ahead of time or whether Christ's death and resurrection was prerequisite to seeing Christ in the Old Testament. We turn now to that subject.

Expected or Surprised?

Jesus tells his disciples that the whole Scripture (Hebrew Bible) anticipated his coming, but from what we read in the New Testament, no one seemed to have understood the message of what we call the Old

---

4. See S. E. Porter, ed., *The Messiah in the Old and New Testaments* (Grand Rapids: Eerdmans, 2007) for an excellent survey of what we know about messianic expectation at this time (in particular, see the chapter by L. Stuckenbruck, "Messianic Ideas in the Apocalyptic and Related Literature of Early Judaism," 90–116).

Testament to have looked forward to a Messiah who would die and be raised. Was Jesus' coming something that should have been expected, or was it a surprise that could only be understood after the fact?

This question has led to a sometimes bitter debate between the Christian scholars who believe the Old Testament anticipates Christ. On the one hand, some scholars insist that the message concerning the Messiah fulfilled in Christ must have been understood by the author and the original readers and others in advance of his life and work. This issue is connected to the question of how the New Testament cites texts from the Old Testament. Those who believe that the Christ-significance of the Old Testament should have been clear to the disciples at the time of Christ also tend to believe that the authors of the Old Testament themselves were aware of the messianic sense of their words. Gregory Beale, for instance, argues that the meaning ascribed to an Old Testament passage by the New Testament must have been at least in the "cognitive peripheral vision" of the Old Testament author.[5]

On the other hand, other scholars, such as Peter Enns and Richard Hays, point to the lack of awareness at the time of Jesus' death and resurrection, as well as the often surprising uses of Old Testament passages in the New Testament.[6] They suggest that the Old Testament could only be understood from a postresurrection vantage point.

The debate has generated its own terminology. The first school of thought labels their approach "christological interpretation," while at least some advocates of the second approach prefer the term "christotelic." Christological, combining Christ with *logos*, highlights the belief that Christ is an essential part of the Old Testament method. Christotelic, combing Christ with *telos* ("goal"), suggests that rather than Christ being an essential part of the Old Testament message, he

---

5. G. K. Beale, "The Cognitive Peripheral Vision of Biblical Authors," *Westminster Theological Journal* 76 (2014): 263–93.

6. Peter Enns, *Inspiration and Incarnation: Evangelicals and the Problem of the Old Testament*, 2nd ed. (Grand Rapids: Baker, 2015); Richard B. Hays, *Reading Backwards: Figural Christology and the Fourfold Gospel Witness* (Waco, TX: Baylor University Press, 2016).

is the goal of the Old Testament and not able to be seen until the goal is fulfilled.

Perhaps, however, we should not see these as two opposing viewpoints, but both as legitimate perspectives on the relationship between the Old and New Testaments. To say that Christ can only be seen in the New Testament after the fact makes ridiculous Jesus' statement to the two disciples on the road to Emmaus: "How foolish you are, and how slow to believe all that the prophets have spoken!" (Luke 24:25). In other words, they should have known. The Law and the Prophets spoke about his coming and the nature of his work.

On the other hand, again, especially when we look at the way the New Testament appropriates the Old Testament in reference to Christ and the fact that no one got it, we have to also say that Christ's presence in the Old Testament becomes clearer in the light of his death and resurrection. Even more, there are certainly many ways in which the New Testament uses the Old Testament that almost certainly were not in the mind of the original human author.[7] Beale's appeal to the *peripheral* cognitive vision of the Old Testament author is as desperate as it sounds. Explanations often given for how the Old Testament author could have understood the New Testament use are strained to the extreme.

Thus, in my opinion, both a christotelic and a christological approach to the Old Testament seem warranted for a Christian understanding of the Old Testament. I, accordingly, tend to use these terms interchangeably as I talk about the christocentric nature of the Old Testament.

The "Discrete Voice" of the Old Testament

Before proceeding, we need to address the charge that such an approach reads the New Testament into the Old Testament. We first

---

7. Which raises the question of divine author.

need to admit that such a distorting reading of the Old Testament is possible. There are many examples, both ancient and modern. For instance, for centuries and still among some today,[8] Song of Songs was interpreted by Christian readers as an allegory of the relationship between Jesus (the man in the Song) and the church or the individual Christian (the woman). During the Middle Ages, it was common to interpret Song of Songs 1:13 ("My beloved is to me a sachet of myrrh resting between my breasts") as referring to Jesus, who spans the Old and the New Testaments.[9] Though, as we will see below, there is a proper christotelic interpretation of Song of Songs, this common medieval interpretation not only ignores the Old Testament context of Song of Songs, but also presses the details of the story into service to relate the passage to Christ. A second example of too quickly reading the New Testament into the Old Testament may be seen in some interpretations of the tabernacle. Paul F. Kiene, for instance, suggests that the use of blue in the building of the tabernacle refers to Christ's royal status, while the large entrance to the tabernacle is like Christ's outstretched arms inviting us into relationship with him.[10] We will see that there is a proper christotelic interpretation, but Kiene and others like him do indeed impose the New Testament on the Old Testament. As a final example, we can also cite Ambrose's interpretation of Ecclesiastes 4:12, which speaks of the encouragement of relationships: "Though one may be overpowered, two can defend themselves. A cord of three strands is not quickly broken." Ambrose writes that this is a reference to the Trinity.[11] Even today, particularly at weddings, it is not unusual to hear a slight variation

---

8. A number of commentaries in the Brazos Theological Commentary on the Old Testament are examples of ignoring the "discrete witness" of the Old Testament. For examples, see F. A. Murphy, *1 Samuel* (Grand Rapids: Brazos, 2010); P. J. Griffiths, *Song of Songs* (Grand Rapids: Brazos, 2011).

9. Marvin H. Pope, *Song of Songs* (Garden City, NY: Doubleday, 1977), 114.

10. Paul F. Kiene, *The Tabernacle of God in the Wilderness of Sinai* (Grand Rapids: Zondervan, 1977).

11. See M. M. Beyenka, trans., *Saint Ambrose: Letters*, vol. 26 of *The Fathers of the Church: A New Translation* (Washington D.C.: Catholic University of America Press, 1954), 319.

of this approach that suggests a marriage is much stronger if it is grounded in God. While there is a proper christotelic interpretation of Ecclesiastes (see below), Ambrose and those who follow him in this interpretation are imposing a New Testament meaning on an Old Testament text.

How do we protect ourselves from such fanciful readings that impose meaning on an Old Testament text? We must begin by listening to what Brevard S. Childs, an interpreter who practices christological interpretation himself, calls the "discrete voice" or "discrete witness" of the Old Testament.[12] We must first read any passage of the Old Testament from the vantage point of its original authors as they address the first intended audience, also known as the implied readers. Here we see the benefits of what we might call a historical-grammatical, or historical-critical, approach. Only after we interpret the text from the perspective of the original author and first readers should we then do a second reading from the perspective provided by the New Testament.

Reading the Old Testament as a Christian is analogous to watching a movie or reading a book or piece of literature a second time. One's first interpretation of a passage must be based on how the text would have been understood by its original audience. In this way, we honor the fact that the books of the Old Testament were not written to us but to an ancient audience, and in this way, we preserve the "discrete voice" of the Old Testament witness to God. However, a Christian cannot stop at that point, but must read the text a second time from the full perspective of the New Testament. While some believe that such a reading entails a problematic Christian appropriation of Jewish literature, we agree with the Jewish scholar Jon Levenson of Harvard University, who

---

12. Brevard S. Childs, *Biblical Theology of the Old and New Testaments: Theological Reflection on the Christian Bible* (Minneapolis: Fortress, 1993), 76. Walter Brueggemann also calls for a reading of the Old Testament apart from the New Testament in order to preserve the "wild and untamed'... theological witness of the Old Testament" (Walter Brueggemann, *Theology of the Old Testament: Testimony, Dispute, Advocacy* [Minneapolis: Fortress, 1977], 107).

recognizes that "Christian exegesis requires that the Hebrew Bible be read ultimately in a literary context that includes the New Testament. To read it only on its own would be like reading the first three acts of Hamlet as if the last two had never been written."[13]

Three Case Studies

Ultimately, christotelic interpretation needs to be supported and illustrated by examples. Thus, I have chosen to provide three christotelic interpretations corresponding to the faulty examples cited above. My hope is that readers will see a respect for the discrete voice of the Old Testament and then a christotelic interpretation that organically connects the Old Testament with the New Testament.

READING ECCLESIASTES IN THE LIGHT OF CHRIST

First Reading: The book of Ecclesiastes presents the voices of two different individuals. The long, middle portion (1:12–12:7) contains the first-person reflections of someone who goes by the name Qohelet (traditionally, "the Preacher"; more recent translations, "the Teacher"). The prologue (1:1–11) and epilogue (12:8–14) frame Qohelet's speech and come from a second wisdom teacher, who talks about Qohelet in the third person ("he, Qohelet") to his son (see 12:12).[14]

Qohelet's message is that life is hard and then you die. He looks for meaning in the world in areas like work (2:18–23; 4:4–6), pleasure (2:1–11), wealth (5:10–6:9), and even wisdom (2:12–17), but comes up empty. Death (3:16–22; 12:1–7), injustice (7:15–18; 8:10–15), and the inability to discern the proper time (3:1–15) lead him to conclude that life is meaningless. The best anyone can do is to enjoy whatever pleasure

---

13. Jon D. Levenson, *The Hebrew Bible, the Old Testament, and Historical Criticism: Jews and Christians in Biblical Studies* (Louisville: Westminster John Knox, 1993), 9.

14. For a full presentation of this view, see Tremper Longman III, *Ecclesiastes* (New International Commentary on the Old Testament; Grand Rapids: Eerdmans, 1998).

one can during his life (*carpe diem*; 2:24–26; 3:12–14, 22; 5:18–20; 8:15; 9:7–10) in order to distract oneself from the harsh reality that life is meaningless and then one dies.

The second wisdom teacher sometimes goes by the name of the frame narrator since his words frame the words of Qohelet in 1:1–11 and 12:8–14.[15] In the epilogue, the frame narrator evaluates Qohelet's thought for his son, who is mentioned in 12:12. To summarize, he tells his son that Qohelet wrote "honest words of truth" (12:10).[16] After all, it is true that life has no ultimate meaning when one tries to find it "under the sun,"[17] as Qohelet's failed attempt demonstrates.

The frame narrator does not stop with his respectful critique of Qohelet's perspective on life, but goes beyond his message, offering what we might call an "above the sun" view of life:

> Now all has been heard; here is the conclusion of the matter:
> Fear God and keep his commandments, for this is the duty of all
> mankind. For God will bring every deed into judgment, including
> every hidden thing, whether it is good or evil.
>
> *Ecclesiastes 12:13–14*

I unpack these brief, but rich words in more detail elsewhere,[18] but we should here notice the main point. While Qohelet tried to find the meaning of life in such things as wisdom, pleasure, work, and wealth, the frame narrator urges his son (and thus readers of the book) to find the meaning of life in a proper relationship with God characterized by fear and also to maintain that relationship by living

---

15. Michael V. Fox ("Frame-Narrative and Composition in the Book of Qohelet," *Hebrew Union College Annual* 48 [1977]: 83–106) was the first, to my knowledge, to introduce this term into the discussion.

16. Fox, "Frame-Narrative and Composition," 97.

17. An expression Qohelet uses twenty-nine times (1:3, 9; 2:11, 17, 18, 19, 20; 22; 3:16; 4:1, 3, 7, 15; 5:14, 19; 6:1, 12; 7:11; 8:9, 15 [twice], 17; 9:3, 6, 9 [twice], 11, 13; 10:5).

18. See Tremper Longman III, *The Fear of the Lord Is Wisdom: A Theological Introduction to Wisdom in Israel* (Grand Rapids: Baker, 2017), 38–41.

in obedience to God's commandments, as well as in the light of the coming judgment.[19]

Our first reading of Ecclesiastes recognizes two voices in the book, Qohelet's and the frame narrator's. Since the latter's words frame and provide an evaluation of the former's words, we should take the message of the frame narrator as the message of the book. That message is that the meaning and purpose of life can only be found in a relationship with God. Trying to find the meaning of life in anything or anyone else will ultimately fail.

In a phrase, it is appropriate to understand the book of Ecclesiastes as an idol buster—an idol being anything or anyone besides God that is occupying the most important place in one's life. Ecclesiastes urges its readers to put God first in order to live a meaningful life.

Second Reading: Only after completing our first reading of the book to discover its distinctive message to its readers do we proceed to a second reading that interprets the book in the light of the coming of Christ and the fuller revelation that follows in the New Testament.

We begin at the only place where there is a quotation of or allusion to the book of Ecclesiastes in the New Testament, namely, Romans 8:18–21:[20]

> I consider that our present sufferings are not worth comparing with the glory that will be revealed in us. For the creation waits in eager expectation for the children of God to be revealed. For the creation was subjected to *frustration*, not by its own choice, but by the will of the one who subjected it, in hope that the creation itself will be liberated from its bondage to decay and brought into the freedom and glory of the children of God.

---

19. See Tremper Longman III, "'Meaningless, Meaningless, Says Qohelet': Finding the Meaning of Life in the Book of Ecclesiastes," in *God and Meaning: New Essays*, ed. Joshua W. Seachris and Stewart Goetz (New York: Bloomsbury Academic, 2016), 231–50.

20. Emphasis added. The broader context extends to 8:30, but this shorter passage is sufficient to make my point.

Paul describes the present state of the creation as in "bondage to decay" and acknowledges that God's human creatures experience suffering. He explains this situation by appealing back to the story in Genesis 3, when human experience led God (notice the use of the so-called divine passive "the creation was subjected") to "subject" the creation to frustration. "Frustration" translates the Greek word *mataiotēs*, which is the Greek word used in the Septuagint to render the Hebrew *hebel* ("meaningless"). Thus, Paul agrees with Qohelet that the world "under the sun" is frustrating or meaningless.

Paul, however, does not stop with that observation, as Qohelet himself does. Rather, he speaks of a future "glory that will be revealed in us" and a future "freedom . . . of the children of God." In other words, rather than sharing Qohelet's rather depressing conclusion about life, Paul invites his readers to share his hope and "eager expectation for the children of God to be revealed."

And where does Paul's hope come from? Jesus, "who, being in very nature God, did not consider equality with God something to be used to his own advantage; rather, he made nothing by taking the very nature of a servant, being made in human likeness. And being found in appearance as a man, he humbled himself by becoming obedient to death—even death on a cross!" (Philippians 2:6–8).

Jesus subjected himself to the *mataiotēs/hebel* of the fallen world in order to free us from the sting of death ("Christ redeemed us from the curse of the law by becoming a curse for us" [Galatians 3:13]). A Christian reading of the book of Ecclesiastes leads us to understand that it is the work of Jesus—his death and resurrection—that makes our lives meaningful.

READING THE TABERNACLE (EXODUS 25–40) IN THE LIGHT OF CHRIST

First Reading: In Exodus 25:1–9, God tells Moses to build a tabernacle for him so he can "dwell among" the Israelites and to make it "exactly like the pattern" that he will show him. The tabernacle thus is the place where God will make his presence palpable to the Israelites during this time. For six chapters (chaps. 25–30), God gives Moses the pattern for building the tabernacle and its furniture, and then later there are six chapters (chaps. 35–40) detailing the execution of those instructions.[21]

What exactly is the tabernacle? It is a tent, a quite ornate tent to be sure. After all, the tabernacle is the place where God will make his presence known among his people, and during this period, his people are themselves living in tents since they have not yet become established in the land.

A close look at the structure of the tabernacle and its furniture reveals that there is indeed symbolic significance to its various parts. However, rather than the kind of arbitrary connections we observed Paul Kiene make above, the tabernacle's symbolism revolves around one central idea: that God, the King, makes his presence known in the tabernacle and in particular in the back portion of the tabernacle. We will not provide an exhaustive description here, but just point out a few salient points.[22]

First, we note the description of the innermost curtain of the tabernacle, the one that would be seen as the ceiling within the building. This curtain is made from "finely twisted linen and blue, purple and scarlet yarn, with cherubim woven into them" (Exodus 26:1). This deep blue curtain with the powerful angelic beings known as the cherubim depicted on it would make people realize that the tabernacle is heaven on earth.

The ark of the covenant was in the back part of the tabernacle and served as God's footstool (1 Chronicles 28:2; Psalm 99:5). God

---

21. The chapters between these two parts (32–34; chap. 31 describes the commissioning of the workers) narrate the sin with the golden calf, which raises a threat to proper worship in contrast to the worship of God at the tabernacle.

22. Menahem Haran's *Temples and Temple Service in Ancient Israel: An Inquiry into Biblical Cult Phenomena and the Historical Setting of the Priestly School* (Winona Lake, IN: Eisenbrauns, 1985) is particularly helpful.

was imagined to be enthroned above the ark, which explains why the cherubim figures that were on top of the ark cover had their heads down, because not even these mighty heavenly creatures could stand to gaze on God's great glory (Exodus 25:20).

The presence of God in this place explains the placement of metals in the construction of the tabernacle. As one moves from the outer edges of the courtyard toward the innermost chamber of the tabernacle, there is a general move from less precious to more precious metals, showing that as one moves toward the throne room of God, the levels of holiness become increasingly intense. Specifically, we note that bronze is used on the outside, and then as one moves closer to the ark, bronze gives way to silver and then silver to gold, and finally there is fine gold, a higher quality of gold.

These gradations of holiness also explain the increasing levels of restricted access as one moves from outside the Israelite camp toward the most holy part of the tabernacle. Outside the camp is the realm of the Gentile and the ritually unclean Israelite. Only ritually clean Israelites may enter the camp. Only the Levites may dwell in the vicinity of the tabernacle, and only "righteous" Israelites can go there to offer sacrifices (see the entrance liturgies found in Psalms 15 and 24). Famously, only the high priest, and he only once a year, may go into "the Most Holy Place" (Leviticus 16:2).

We will end with a comment on the lampstand. Of course, the lampstand serves the very practical purpose of illuminating what would otherwise be a rather dark interior. In terms of its symbolic value, however, we should note all of the tree imagery associated with it. As described in Exodus 25:31–39, we see that it has "flowerlike cups, buds and blossoms," as well as "branches." In other words, the lampstand represents a tree, and the purpose of such a representation can only be to recall the Garden of Eden, the place and time when humans dwelt without problem in the presence of God.

Thus, the tabernacle and its furniture were built in order to communicate the idea that God made his presence known among his people. Accordingly, it was heaven on earth and recalls the Garden of Eden.

Second Reading: How does the tabernacle anticipate Christ then? We will be suggestive rather than exhaustive again. First, we will place the tabernacle within the context of the Old Testament. The need for a special holy place where God would make his presence known only arose after Adam and Eve were expelled from the garden. Sin erected a barrier to easy access to the holy God. At first, holy places were marked by altars, but then when the people of God grew from an extended family to a nation-state, a more public and larger structure was needed that incorporated the altar, and that was to be the tabernacle. When Israel was firmly established in the land, the tabernacle, which was appropriate until Israel was established in the land,[23] was replaced by the temple, whose very architecture represents establishment in the land.

When Jesus lived, the second temple was standing, a building Jesus himself honored. He drove the money changers from its courts because they were turning his "Father's house into a market!" (John 2:16). On another occasion, however, when his disciples marveled at the grandeur of the temple, he replied, "Do you see all these great buildings? . . . Not one stone here will be left on another; every one will be thrown down" (Mark 13:2).

With the coming of Jesus, the temple in which God made his presence known was no longer needed. Why? The opening of John's gospel explains:

> In the beginning was the Word, and the Word was with God, and the Word was God. He was with God in the beginning . . . The Word became flesh and made his dwelling known among us. We

---

23. David is represented as the one who completes the conquest by subduing the last of Israel's internal enemies, and thus the law of centralization (Deuteronomy 12) becomes relevant. It is David's son, Solomon, whose name means "peaceful one," who builds the temple to symbolize Israel's "rest from all your enemies around you" (Deuteronomy 12:10).

have seen his glory, the glory of the one and only Son, who came from the Father, full of grace and truth.

John 1:1–2, 14[24]

Jesus is God and makes God's glory manifest. Indeed, the verb "made his dwelling" comes from a Greek verb related to the noun *skēnē* ("tabernacle"). Jesus tabernacled among us. When Jesus died, the curtain of the temple "was torn in two from top to bottom" (Matthew 27:51). This curtain separating the Most Holy Place from the rest of the temple, indeed from the rest of the world, ripped, most likely signifying that God's holy presence is no longer limited to this particular location, but now extends throughout the world. Thus, as Jesus commissions his disciples to carry the good news throughout the world, he promises them that he will surely be with them (Matthew 28:20). He also promises to send the Spirit (John 14:15–31), thus making the church and individual Christians "temples of the Holy Spirit" (1 Corinthians 6:19; see 2 Corinthians 6:16).

The tabernacle was the place where God made his presence known on earth. In this way, it anticipates the coming of Christ, who is the very presence of God himself.

Reading Song of Songs in the Light of Christ

First Reading: Though read as an allegory of the relationship between God and Israel by Jewish interpreters and as an allegory of the relationship between Christ and the church by Christians in the past, today most recognize that the Song of Songs is a love poem about the intimacy between a man and a woman.[25]

The debate continues about the precise nature of this love poetry,

---

24. John reports that Jesus himself drew an analogy between himself and the temple in 2:19. In response to the Jewish leaders' request for a sign, Jesus said, "Destroy this temple, and I will raise it again in three days." John notes that "the temple he had spoken of was his body" (2:21).

25. For a full presentation of this view, see Tremper Longman III, *Song of Songs* (Grand Rapids: Eerdmans, 2001).

but my own view is that the Song is a collection of about twenty love poems. Most of these poems celebrate sexual intimacy (for example, 4:1–5:1) or else warn that such intimacy is difficult to achieve (for example, 5:2–6:3). The purpose of this poetry is to show God's approval of sexual pleasure within the context of marriage.

Phyllis Trible rightly points out that the Song fits into a powerful biblical theology of sexuality.[26] She observes that the poems of the Song depict intimacy in garden settings reminding the reader of the Garden of Eden. After all, at the end of Genesis 2, Adam and Eve are said to be naked and feeling no shame. However, because of sin, in Genesis 3 they feel the need to cover their nakedness. Sin creates a barrier not only between God and humans but between humans as well. Trible points out that the Song speaks to the redemption of sexuality. I would only add, based on the poems of warning (see above), that this redemption is not perfect.

Second Reading: The canonical setting of the Song also suggests that the allegorists were not incorrect to see an important theological dimension to the book. Their problem was that they dismissed the connection to human relationships. After all, one of the most fertile biblical metaphors of the relationship between God and humans is marriage. Only rarely in the Old Testament do we see this image used positively (Jeremiah 2:1; Hosea 2:14–15), but even its negative use (Israel has prostituted itself in her relationship with God [see, for example, Ezekiel 23; 25; Hosea 1]). In the New Testament, Paul likens the relationship between Jesus and the church to the relationship between a husband and a wife (Ephesians 5:25–33). As we read about the passion, intimacy, enjoyment, and exclusivity of the relationship between the man and the woman in the Song, it teaches us about the passion, intimacy, enjoyment, and exclusivity of our relationship with God. As the Song admits that the physical relationship between the man and the woman

---

26. See Phyllis Trible, *God and the Rhetoric of Sexuality* (Philadelphia: Fortress, 1978).

is not easily achieved, we also remember that our redemption in Christ is not yet consummated and won't be until we enter the new Jerusalem.

Conclusion

My intention in this essay is to make a case for a christological/telic interpretation of the Old Testament. A responsible reading must begin by recovering the "discrete voice" of the Old Testament witness to God (First Reading), but must continue by asking how this passage anticipates Christ (Second Reading; see Luke 24). But this must be done in a way that respects the integrity of the Old Testament text and the organic relationship between the two Testaments rather than imposing a meaning on the text. This does not mean the Old Testament human author always would recognize the way in which his text would be used in the New or interpreted by Christian interpreters, but it does mean one can make sense of a literary and/or theological consistency between them.

It is my great joy to write this chapter in a volume that honors Stan Gundry, who has worked with me as my editor and publisher over the past three decades. In connection with this topic, I particularly thank him for supporting the new Story of God Bible Commentary, which is the first series to my knowledge where all the volumes will provide a christological/telic interpretation of all the books of the Old Testament.

Chapter 7

"IT IS WRITTEN"

The Septuagint and Evangelical
Doctrine of Scripture[1]

KAREN H. JOBES

The intersection of the topics of the Septuagint (LXX) and doctrine of Scripture often focuses on issues of canon, such as whether the apocryphal books sometimes found bound within manuscripts of the Greek Old Testament should be considered canonical today.[2] This essay will instead focus on the implications for evangelical doctrine of Scripture where the New Testament writers quote the Greek Old Testament as authoritative, especially in those places where the quotation does not match the corresponding extant Hebrew Masoretic Text (MT). The literature on the use of the Old Testament (OT) in the New Testament (NT) is vast, and the doctrine of inspiration and inerrancy is today in some circles irrelevant and in others contentious.[3] Therefore, some definition of the limits of this essay is needed. This discussion is about the quotation specifically of the *Greek* Old

1. Presented in honor and appreciation of Stan Gundry, whose collegiality and encouragement have supported my academic career through the years.
2. I think they should not. For further discussion of that topic, see my "When God Spoke Greek: The Place of the Greek Bible in Evangelical Scholarship," *Bulletin of Biblical Research* 16 (2006): 219–36.
3. For example, the Peter Enns controversy; see also Robert C. Kurka, "Has 'Inerrancy' Outlived Its Usefulness?" *Stone-Campbell Journal* 18 (Fall 2015): 187–204.

Testament in the New Testament (as opposed to any and all quotations of the Old in the New)—and, especially where the quotation does not agree with the extant Hebrew Masoretic Text, how this disagreement engages the evangelical doctrine of the inspiration and inerrancy of Scripture. I will not address the larger debates about whether the term *inerrancy* is still useful—I personally am not ready to dispense with the term—and whether a "literal" hermeneutic is necessary when reading the inerrant word (whatever "literal" might mean in that context). Nor will I engage the controversies about christological readings of the OT. But I do hope to encourage reflection on what are the entailments of believing in an inspired and inerrant Bible when (1) the vast number of Christians throughout history have read their Bibles in translation, not in the original languages, much less the autographic forms on which the concept of the doctrine of Scripture is based; and when (2) the evident use of the Greek OT in the NT seems to raise tensions about how to understand inspiration and inerrancy.

When I was a new Christian reading the Bible for the first time through, I would often flip from the NT quotation back to read the OT source text, and I was disturbed that so often the two did not agree. At the time, I thought it was some kind of copyediting problem, but of course you know that the underlying reason is that our English OT is translated from the Hebrew text, but our English NT is translated from the Greek NT, which naturally quotes the OT from a Greek translation that was then in circulation. In some ways, this is no more mysterious than if you were writing a letter in Spanish to a friend and wanted to quote Scripture, you'd most likely quote from a Spanish Bible. But the intrigue deepens when an inspired NT writer quotes a Greek translation of the OT as authoritative—and one that doesn't match the surviving Hebrew source text we have, the Masoretic Text, at that! This discovery can bring our ideas about inspiration and inerrancy into tension with our reverence for the MT.

The Doctrine of Scripture
among Evangelicals

We should here remind ourselves of how the doctrine of Scripture has been articulated in evangelical settings familiar to the likely readers of this article. The statement that all Evangelical Theological Society (ETS) members must affirm reads, "The Bible alone, and the Bible in its entirety, is the Word of God written and is therefore inerrant in the autographs."

Wheaton College faculty sign a statement of faith that includes the declaration that "the Scriptures of the Old and New Testaments are verbally inspired by God and inerrant in the original writing, so that they are fully trustworthy and of supreme and final authority in all they say."

The Chicago Statement on Biblical Inerrancy was formulated in 1978 by more than two hundred evangelical leaders. An extensive document, its "Short Statement" includes these points about the nature of Scripture, among others:

- God, who . . . speaks truth only, has inspired Holy Scripture in order thereby to reveal Himself . . .
- Holy Scripture, being God's own Word, written by men prepared and superintended by His Spirit, is of infallible divine authority in all matters upon which it touches . . .
- Being wholly and verbally God-given, Scripture is without error or fault in all its teaching . . .[4]

Our doctrines rightly influence how we read Scripture and what we think is entailed concerning such topics as the use of the Old in the New, but sometimes we bring *unnecessary*, and often unconscious,

---

4. "Chicago Statement on Inerrancy with Exposition: A Short Statement," www.bible -researcher.com/chicago1.html (accessed on May 22, 2017).

assumptions to these considerations. For instance, consider the intriguing discussion I've had with students in the classroom about the entailments of the phrase "it is written" as found in the NT, and especially how assumptions derived from an evangelical doctrine of Scripture color their understanding of that phrase. The formula "it is written" (γέγραπται, a third person perfect passive form of the verb γράφω) introduces a quotation from the OT sixty-seven times in the NT.[5] Several students throughout the years interpreted that formula in combination with their doctrine of inspired and inerrant Scripture to mean that the quotation that followed presented in the NT, through the inspiration of the NT author, a translation of the very words of the Hebrew autograph of the OT text! This would mean the form of the quotation in the NT, perhaps after textual critical evaluation, should be accepted as a preservation of the original Hebrew text, even if it disagrees with the MT Hebrew manuscript evidence extant today. Such a "literal" understanding of the formula γέγραπται is undoubtedly wrongheaded—and it leaves the many remaining quotations not introduced by that or any formula unaddressed—but it was a certain understanding of *verbal* plenary inspiration that led to their erroneous conclusion.

In contrast, a nineteenth-century British writer, George Warington, who also believed in the inspiration of Scripture, came to the exact opposite conclusion. After examining the quotations of the Old in the New, he concluded that the words of the NT writers were inspired everywhere *except* in what he judged to be their distorted and erroneous quotations of the OT. Warington lists many discrepancies between the Old Testament and its quotation in the New, describing the quotations as "partial, inaccurate, and, at times, even misleading."[6] He then concludes:

---

5. According to Accordance version 11.1.0 (2015).
6. George Warington, *The Inspiration of Scripture: Its Limits and Effects* (London: Skeffington, 1867), 106.

For these alterations and omissions the *human authors only* are responsible; in other words, that in regard to the *letter* of their quotations from the Old Testament, the Apostles and Evangelists were not in any way directed or controlled by the Holy Spirit, but were left entirely to their own memories, habits, and ordinary sources of information, no matter what mistakes and defects might as a consequence arise . . . The evidence considered merely proves that this inspiration, whatever else it did, did not affect or control the *letter* of quotations made from the Old Testament by New Testament writers.[7]

So the doctrine of inerrancy and verbal plenary inspiration is thought by some to entail the preservation of the Hebrew autograph, for at least those quotations introduced with γέγραπται, and yet for others it is thought to entail the conclusion that the Holy Spirit had nothing to do with the differences found between the NT quotations and their source texts, evidence counting against inspiration of those sections of the NT. Although these two views seem at first glance to be at opposite ends of the spectrum, both share the same mistaken inference derived from the doctrine of inspiration, namely, that the NT writers must have or should have used the inspired, and perhaps autographic, form of the Hebrew OT text, and used it to make the same point the OT text made.

Differences between the quotations and their source texts led Samuel Davidson, a nineteenth-century Irish biblical scholar, to reject the doctrine of inspiration completely, for "the terms and phrases of the Old Testament, if literally inspired, were the best that could have been adopted," and, therefore, the New Testament writers "should have adhered to the *ipsissima verba* of the Holy Spirit (seeing they were the best) as closely as the genius of the Hebrew and Greek languages allowed."[8] For him, the doctrine of verbal inspiration (perhaps informed

---

7. Warington, *Inspiration of Scripture*, 107, italics original.
8. Samuel Davidson, *Sacred Hermeneutics Developed and Applied; including A History of Biblical*

by a dictation theory of the mode of inspiration) meant that no other words could have communicated what the Spirit intended to say. This comes close to arguing that Scripture cannot be restated or paraphrased, much less translated, in spite of the biblical mandate to do so (see discussion below).

Davidson argues that the fact the NT writers "cite the Septuagint translation much more frequently than the Old Testament original itself, is a presumption against the theory [of verbal inspiration]."[9] Both Davidson and Warington attempted to salvage the authority of Scripture by arguing that the sense of the quotations even where their form presented "discrepancies" nevertheless carried the divine message and its authority. But the doctrine of verbal inspiration means that the Spirit inspired not only the words of the Hebrew text, but also the Greek words employed in the NT to "quote" it.

The differences between NT quotations of the Old in Greek and their presumed source texts in Hebrew are undeniable, and the issues raised are presented by the biblical text itself. If the prima facie differences don't compel reflection on what this means for an evangelical doctrine of Scripture, a deeper look at just one example, the notorious example of the quotation of Amos 9:11–12 in Acts 15:16–18, will highlight the issues. Luke, the author of Acts, reports the words of James at the Jerusalem Council, by putting the Septuagint of Amos 9:11–12 into the mouth of the half brother of Jesus. Did Luke do so intentionally or because he could not read Hebrew and therefore quoted the only version accessible to him and to the majority of his original readers? Or did James, leader of the presumably Aramaic-speaking *Jerusalem* church, speak Greek at the Council, perhaps in consideration of the visitors from Antioch, and therefore quoted from the Septuagint? The decision of the Jerusalem Council was momentous—nothing less than the basis on which Gentiles were to be accepted into the infant Christian church.

Interpretation from the Earliest of the Fathers to the Reformation (Edinburgh: Clark, 1843), 513.
    9. Davidson, *Sacred Hermeneutics*, 513.

And yet the Greek Scripture used to ground this decision, as reported by Luke, differs significantly from the canonical Hebrew text. Moreover, the difference could very well be due to an error in the textual transmission of the Amos text.

The Hebrew of Amos 9:12 reads, "so that they [God's people] may possess the remnant of Edom and all the nations that bear my name." Its quotation in Acts 15:17 reads, "that the rest of mankind may seek the Lord, even all the Gentiles who bear my name." Luke is quoting the Septuagint translation of Amos, for which two of its differences from the Hebrew text depend on just one letter in the Hebrew: "possess" (יִירְשׁוּ) versus "seek" (יִדְרְשׁוּ), the difference between a yod (י) and a daleth (ד). Textual critics most often attribute a difference of this kind to a misreading of the Hebrew word either by a scribe producing an errant copy of the Hebrew that was later translated into Greek or by the translator who rendered the word into Greek. The second difference is one of pointing the Hebrew word as אֱדוֹם (Edom) or אָדָם ("adam" or mankind), depending on the vowel supplied by the reader to the unvocalized word as written. That kind of difference could be either due to an inadvertent misreading of the text or an intentional interpretation of the word for a Greek audience, broadening "possessing Edom," an ancient pagan nation, to mean "all nations will seek God."

Since this quotation is prefaced by "it is written" (γέγραπται), the students I mentioned above would have argued that, in fact, the reading found in Acts 15:17 preserves what the original Hebrew autograph of Amos 9:12 must have read. It happens there is a theory that the Septuagint reading does in fact preserve a version of the Hebrew text earlier than the MT reading.[10] Barry Alan Jones argues that after the Greek translation of Amos was made, changes in the Hebrew text of Amos resulted from a subsequent redaction of the Minor Prophets that has come down to us in the extant MT. While we may never know how

---

10. Barry Alan Jones, *The Formation of the Book of the Twelve: A Study in Text and Canon* (Atlanta: Scholars Press, 1995), 186–91.

to account with certainty for how the two texts came to differ, what is undeniable is that the Holy Spirit quoted through Luke's agency a verse of Scripture that differs from the extant Hebrew, presenting to readers of Acts the decision of the Jerusalem Council based on a text that may have arisen either from a misreading of the Hebrew text or the uninspired interpretation of an ancient Jewish translator. Clearly examples such as this one raise some interesting questions about how modern evangelical doctrines of inerrancy and inspiration are to be squared with the reality of the ancient textual data presented by the Bible itself.

The Use of a Translation in the Inspired Text

The fact that the inspired writers of the NT apparently did not hesitate to quote a *translation* of their Hebrew Scriptures as God's authoritative word indicates Christianity has embraced translation of the gospel since its foundational years. The gospel writers recorded Jesus' words in Greek, even though he very likely spoke in Aramaic most of the time. And it indicates how differently the apostles viewed their Scriptures than, for instance, Orthodox Jews and Muslims do today, who consider any translation of their sacred texts to be mere commentary on God's word.

We must recognize that God implicitly mandated translation of his word. We read in Revelation 14:6, "Then I saw another angel flying in midair, and he had the eternal gospel to proclaim to those who live on the earth—to every nation, tribe, *language* and people" (italics added). Since God chose to introduce linguistic diversity into the world at the Tower of Babel as narrated in Genesis 11, and he expects his gospel to be proclaimed in every language, translation is necessarily entailed. Since God apparently had confidence that his word could be translated and still adequately fulfill its purpose, we should not in theological principle find the use of a translated OT in the NT problematic. So from its very beginning, Christianity has embraced the practice of translation and expressed confidence in a translation's efficacy to function as God's word.

But Bible translation is often controversial and has been ever since the first translation of Scripture, the Septuagint, was made by order of the Greek king Ptolemy (285–247 BC). In the Talmud's tractate *Sefer Torah*, the Greek translation was compared to idolatry: "Seventy sages translated the Torah into Greek for King Ptolemy. That day was as difficult for the people of Israel as the day on which the [Golden] Calf was made; for the Torah could not be fully translated" (*Sefer Torah*, 1:8).

But an opposing view is found in *Midrash Tanhuma*, which says more than a thousand years before King Ptolemy ordered the translation of the Torah into Greek, Moses had already, by divine command, translated the Torah into seventy languages.[11]

Although Christianity has no objection to Bible translation and holds up Bible translations to be the word of God, Protestantism does not accept any translation as an inspired text. Since the time of the Reformation, Protestants have rejected Augustine's argument that the Septuagint—and only the Septuagint among the ancient Greek versions—was inspired along with the Hebrew.

But if the Spirit does not inspire any translation of Scripture, how do we understand the authoritative use of an uninspired translation of God's word in the inspired text of the New Testament?

To address this question, we must first be clear about where differences in quotations possibly enter the text. There are issues arising from the translation of the Hebrew source text into Greek by the Jewish translators long before the production of the NT. And there are issues arising from subsequent use of a source text within the same language, i.e., the NT writers quoting a Greek version of the OT while writing in Greek. The distinction is crucial for NT exegesis, as those modifications

---

11. See Samuel Berman, ed., *Midrash Tanhuma-Yelammedenu* (Hoboken, NJ: KTAV, 1996), 106.

intentionally introduced by the NT writer are most likely to be exegetically significant. In modern studies, it is sometimes not possible to know with certainty whether a NT writer simply repeated the text of the Greek OT he happened to have before him or whether he modified, paraphrased, or otherwise changed the "quotation" for his own purposes.[12] And so, apart from textual corruptions introduced during transmission, we observe "quotations" of the OT in the NT that disagree with the corresponding MT either because (1) the Hebrew *Vorlage* (the text from which a translator worked) of the Greek translation used was different from the text that has come to us as the MT; (2) the Jewish Greek translator modified his translation to contextualize the Hebrew before him for a new target audience (Hellenistic, polytheistic diaspora) that was quite unlike the audience of the original Hebrew (Hebrew, monotheistic theocracy); or (3) because the NT writer changed the form of the source text for his own purposes.

Given the various ways differences between a NT quotation and its OT source text could arise, a seminal article written in 1881 by Archibald Hodge and Benjamin Warfield is helpful.[13] About the same time that George Warington and Samuel Davidson were raising objections to the doctrines of inspiration and inerrancy, the Old Princeton scholars Hodge and Warfield defended plenary verbal inspiration in their article. Since we are not the first generation to have questions about the origin of Scripture, it is often beneficial to look at the thoughts of a previous generation. Writings of the nineteenth century discuss many of the issues still current today among evangelicals about the use of the Septuagint in the NT. Addressing Davidson's conclusion against the doctrine of inspiration based on his inference that the NT

---

12. For one notorious example involving the question of whether σῶμα ("body") was already present in LXX Psalm 39:7 or added by the NT writer when the verse was quoted in Hebrews 10:5, see Karen H. Jobes, "The Function of Paronomasia in Hebrews 10:5–7," *Trinity Journal* 13NS (1992): 181–91.

13. Archibald Hodge and Benjamin Warfield, "Inspiration," *Presbyterian Review* 6 (1881): 225–60, www.bible-researcher.com/warfield4.html (accessed May 22, 2017).

writers "should have adhered to the *ipsissima verba* of the Holy Spirit (seeing they were the best [possible words]) as closely as the genius of the Hebrew and Greek languages allowed" (see discussion above),[14] Hodge and Warfield caution against erroneous inferences from the doctrine and counter, "Here . . . a false view of inspiration is presupposed, and also a false view of the nature and laws of quotation."[15] And so attention to their arguments here will be instructive.

Since ancient use and practices regarding quotations are quite different from the rigid specificity of the standards set in modern publishing, it is helpful to critique our own assumptions by the principles offered by Hodge and Warfield. They insist "that in ancient quotation, any amount of deviation from the original *in form* is thoroughly allowable, so long as the sense of the original is adhered to; provided only that the quoter is not professing to give the exact form."[16]

And so when NT writers use the verbal form "it is written" sixty-seven times in the NT, is it their intention to give us the autographic text form? A survey of usage shows that this phrase in Christian, Jewish, and secular writers is used to appeal to a written authority that presumably would be known to the reader, but not with reference to the particularities of the text form.[17] The NT writers are not claiming to give us the autograph or any other specific text form of the quotation; they are referencing a version of the text readily known to them and their readers.

And as Hodge and Warfield point out, "There is a vast difference between exactness of statement, which includes an exhaustive rendering of details, an absolute literalness, which the Scriptures never profess, and accuracy, on the other hand, which secures a correct statement of facts or principles intended to be affirmed."[18]

---

14. Davidson, *Sacred Hermeneutics*, 513.

15. Hodge and Warfield, "Inspiration," 236.

16. Ibid., 256–57.

17. For a good collection of the data and a survey of its use, see Michael P. Theophilos, "New Light from the Papyri: The Legal Background of "καθὼς γέγραπται" in Matthew 26:24," paper presented at the Annual Meeting of the Society of Biblical Literature, Atlanta, GA, November 2015.

18. Hodge and Warfield, "Inspiration," 238.

But if a NT writer is appealing to the sense of the OT quotation, and perhaps to only one aspect of that sense, surely there is evidence that must be considered on that point as well. Hodge and Warfield argue that "any adaptation of the original to the purpose in hand is allowable, so long as it proceeds by a true exegesis, and thus does not falsify the original [and] that any neglect of the context of the original is allowable so long as the purpose for which the quotation is adduced does not imply the context, and no falsification of sense is involved."[19]

Now these principles should give us pause. What about the many places in the NT where an OT statement that applied to ancient Israel is applied directly to Jesus or the Christian church? One can think of the notorious reference in Matthew 2:15, "Out of Egypt I called my son," which was in its original context a reference to ancient Israel in the exodus.[20] Or the references to Isaiah in Revelation 3:9, where Jewish persecutors of Christians will submit to the church, when the Isaiah prophecy specified it would be pagans who bowed to Israel? Or to the statement of Psalm 16:10 of not being abandoned to Sheol applied in Acts (2:22–32; 13:35) as a prophecy of Jesus' resurrection? Or what about Paul's tour de force reversal of the promises made to Israel through Abraham and Sarah, when Paul aligns the Jews with Hagar in Galatians 4 in apparent contradiction of the OT? Numerous other such examples could be listed. Do they not falsify or contradict the OT source?

The NT writers clearly do not use many of their OT quotations in the same context as the source text. Rather, they are using the quotation in a new context to make a new point *that is organically related to the original OT context.* There is latent meaning in the OT that could only be understood after the resurrection of Christ (cf. Luke 24:25–31; John 2:22; 8:27–28; 13:7; 14:26; 16:12–13). The resurrection is not only an historical event; it is also a *hermeneutical* event apart from which

---

19. Ibid., 257.
20. For an excellent discussion of this quotation, see G. K. Beale, "The Use of Hosea 11:1 in Matthew 2:15: One More Time," *Journal of the Evangelical Theological Society* 55.4 (2012): 697–715.

the Scriptures cannot be understood. As Michael Graves explains, the key to understanding the many apparent discrepancies and issues raised by the NT quotation of the OT is to "find the theological link that connects the Old Testament citation with the point that the New Testament writer is trying to make."[21] In other words, the NT writers are doing what might be called theological exegesis of the OT driven by the new context of the resurrection of Jesus Christ (see Luke 24:36–45). The thought that the quotation is legitimate as long as it does not *falsify* its OT source seems to be a very helpful way to think about it, though the definition of *falsify* must be sought within the context of Christianity and even so leaves room for hermeneutical debate over what would constitute a falsification. Jewish and Christian interpreters would undoubtedly disagree on this very point.

The issues raised by the presence of the Septuagint version in the NT that seem to trip us up have to do with what we believe, consciously or subconsciously, about what the evangelical doctrine of Scripture entails. As Graves points out, "the term 'entailment' refers to the relationship between two statements, where the second is necessarily true in logical consequence of the first being true."[22] This is why so many people with varying views can affirm the inspiration of Scripture and yet explain the issues raised by the use of the Old in the New in various, and sometimes conflicting, ways. And so we each need to think more deeply and deliberately about what our view of Scripture *entails*. As Hodge and Warfield write, "The Inspiration of the Scriptures is true, and being true is a principle fundamental to the adequate interpretation of Scripture."[23] Therefore, taking as our starting point the inspiration of Scripture as true means we must let the character and features of Scripture define for us what inspiration entails, not insist on bringing our own entailments to the text.

For instance, while a difference of textual form does not necessarily

---

21. Michael Graves, *The Inspiration and Interpretation of Scripture: What the Early Church Can Teach Us* (Grand Rapids: Eerdmans, 2014), 8.

22. Graves, *Inspiration and Interpretation*, 3.

23. Hodge and Warfield, "Inspiration," 237.

entail a difference of meaning, it seems to me evangelicals err if we try to make the NT quotation of the Septuagint mean the same as the corresponding extant Hebrew out of reverence for the MT. To do so violates respect for the words of the NT writer. And may God forbid NT translators from harmonizing the words of the NT quotation to the Hebrew source text, in total disregard for the words written by the NT author. Because of the resurrection of Jesus, the NT authors were not writing within the same religious context as the OT writer, and therefore may be trying to highlight an aspect of the meaning of the OT that becomes particularly important or interesting in the new postresurrection context. Thus to simply ignore difference in textual form of the quotations may hinder NT exegesis and impoverish our understanding of what the NT author is trying to tell us. For this reason, the adoption of the language of the OT does not necessarily bind the NT author to the original sense. But neither does it allow readers to see in the different text forms a sense that would falsify the sense of the meaning of the OT text in its own context. Paul's use of Hagar and Sarah in Galatians 4 is an excellent example of a new sense in a new context that does not falsify the sense of the text in its original context, though a prima facie reading may seem that Paul contradicts his OT source.[24] Let the inspired NT text stand, for its writer is making a different, related point in his use of the OT quotation than the original OT author made, though not incompatible or contrary.

The Authority of the Septuagint

Now to the question of the authority of the Septuagint and other quoted Greek versions of the OT, especially where the LXX text does not agree

---

24. For a full discussion of the Galatians 4 passage, see Karen H. Jobes, "Jerusalem, Our Mother: Metalepsis and Intertextuality in Galatians 4:21–31," *Westminster Theological Journal* 55 (1993): 299–320.

with the extant MT. We have the interesting case of a NT writer quoting a not-inspired Bible translation as nevertheless authoritative. Now we know that the NT writers use many sources that are not inspired, e.g., Paul in Acts 17:28 quotes the Cretan philosopher Epimenides and the Cilician Stoic philosopher Aratus. But in distinction from OT quotations, the NT writers don't introduce such sources in the same way as OT canonical texts, such as with the phrase "it is written" that was used to refer to a written source known to be authoritative.

If inspired writers cited verses from the Septuagint as authoritative, was Augustine right that we should therefore consider the text of the Septuagint inspired? Augustine believed that God inspired the translators of the Septuagint—and only the Septuagint (not Aquila, Theodotion, or Symmachus or any other)—in anticipation of the advent of Christ during the Hellenistic era, a view Jerome also shared early in his life but later abandoned.[25] Augustine argued with Jerome while he was producing the Vulgate that where the Septuagint was known to deviate from the Hebrew text extant at that time the Holy Spirit had either restored the true meaning of the Hebrew or he was providing a more congenial interpretation of the OT text in anticipation of the gospel of Jesus Christ.[26] But even if we were to adopt Augustine's view, it is now known that the Septuagint version is not the only Greek version cited by the NT. So Augustine's view does not completely relieve doctrinal tensions.

Should we consider the differences between the extant MT and the ancient Greek translation of its ancestor to be revealing the true meaning of the Hebrew, or providing additional revelation within the OT text? If we do, we should probably become Eastern Orthodox or Roman Catholic and argue for the Septuagint to be the canonical text for the Christian church, as, for instance, Mogens Müller has.[27]

---

25. See Jerome, *The Letters of St. Jerome*, vol. 1, trans. Charles Christopher Mierow, no. 33 in *Ancient Christian Writers*, ed. Johannes Quasten and Walter J. Burghardt (New York: Newman, 1963), 186 n.17.

26. Augustine, *City of God* 18.44 (NPNF1 2:387).

27. See Mogens Müller, *The First Bible of the Church: A Plea for the Septuagint* (Sheffield: Sheffield Academic Press, 1996).

But consider that the NT writers citing as God's authoritative word a Greek version of the OT that was commonly available is not unlike the church today that preaches, teaches, and points to modern language Bible translations as the authoritative word of God. Evangelical doctrine does not hold to the divine inspiration of any translation (though one might wonder given the ferocity of debates over the various English versions). The doctrine of verbal, plenary inspiration pertains to only the original language of the original manuscripts. We can rightfully have confidence in the critically reconstructed texts from which our translations are made, but we don't ascribe inspiration to either the Nestle-Aland Greek New Testament (28th ed.; NA28) or the Biblia Hebraica Quinta (BHS/Q). And there certainly is a place for the evaluation of various translations in terms of accuracy and clarity. But that does not stop us—nor should it—from pointing to the Bible in an accessible language as the word of God. The evangelical church has been especially active in producing Bible translations around the world and offering them as God's word. The Septuagint and the other ancient Greek versions may or may not have been up to the standards of modern Bible translation, but they were God's word to the early church, including the NT writers. And so while we can affirm the Septuagint as God's word for those people in those times, we need not conclude that it is divinely inspired because of its use in the NT. Neither should we ignore, neglect, or anathematize it.

We are, of course, not the first Bible readers to notice that the NT writers cite the Septuagint as authoritative Scripture and to ponder the theological implications of those citations. The rejection of the Septuagint as the canonical text of the church at the time of the Reformation gave opportunity for the Reformers to ponder these same questions. The eminent Lutheran Reformer Johann Gerhard (1582–1637) provides an extensive discussion of Scripture translations and especially of the Septuagint.[28] After affirming the necessity of translated Scripture,

---

28. See Johann Gerhard, *On the Nature of Theology and Scripture*, vol. 1 of *Theological Commonplaces*, trans. Richard J. Dinda (St. Louis: Concordia, 2006), 459–502.

Gerhard states that "we cannot attribute authentic authority, however, to that Greek translation nor equate it with the Hebrew text. First, it is a translation and, therefore, is not authentic nor does it have the same authority as the Hebrew text."[29] And yet, in God's providence (but not by his inspiration), a Greek translation was made in the centuries immediately prior to the advent of Christ, contextualizing the OT story of God's redemptive history for a Greek, diaspora audience. Adolf Deissmann once commented that Greek Judaism had with the Septuagint "ploughed the furrows for the gospel seed in the Western world."[30] F. F. Bruce added that it was the Christian preachers quoting the Septuagint who sowed that seed of the gospel.[31] Bruce notes several places "in which the Septuagint translators used a form of words which (without their being able to foresee it, naturally) lent itself to the purposes of the New Testament writers better than the Hebrew text would have done" (e.g., Matthew 1:23, quoting Isaiah 7:14; Acts 15:15–18, quoting Amos 9:11–12).[32] When the apostles set out to write how God's redemptive work culminated in Jesus Christ during the Greco-Roman era, it was natural for them to cite the Greek version of the OT because it was preeminently known among and accessible to the Greeks.

Johann Gerhard, picking up the centuries-earlier view of Jerome, represents how one stream of the Reformation tradition handled these citations, especially where the wording disagrees with the inspired Hebrew text: "Whenever the prophets and apostles quote testimonies from the Old Testament, one must note quite carefully that they did not follow the words but the sense. Wherever the Septuagint differs from the Hebrew, one must note that they have expressed *the Hebrew sense in their own words*."[33]

---

29. Gerhard, *On the Nature of Theology and Scripture*, 459, 470.

30. Adolf Deissmann, *New Light on the New Testament: From Records of the Graeco-Roman Period* (Edinburgh: T&T Clark, 1908), 95.

31. See F. F. Bruce, *The Canon of Scripture* (Downers Grove, IL: InterVarsity, 1988), 50.

32. Bruce, *Canon of Scripture*, 53.

33. Gerhard, *On the Nature of Theology and Scripture*, 472, italics added (citing Jerome's Letter 151 to Algasia).

Jaroslav Pelikan elaborates that the Reformers' defense of the correctness of the Septuagint as employed by the New Testament did not extend to the version as a whole, but only to those renderings that had been "approved and sanctified by the Holy Spirit" in inspiring the New Testament writers.[34]

And so does this mean the OT verses quoted in the NT are little inspired nuggets embedded in the otherwise uninspired Septuagint text, like diamonds in rock? Not at all. Divine inspiration applies only to the semantic contribution specifically made by the Septuagint quotations *by virtue of becoming part of* the inspired New Testament text as used in their specific New Testament context. As Hodge and Warfield remind us, any adaptation of the original text to the purpose of the inspired NT authors is allowable, so long as it proceeds by a true exegesis, and does not falsify the original, and any neglect of the original context is allowable so long as the purpose for which the quotation is used does not falsify its sense in the particular aspect needed for the purpose in hand.[35]

Two points must be noted. First, the NT writers by inspiration of the Holy Spirit may amplify and highlight some sense of the OT text that was only latent in the text until the postresurrection era. And second, this understanding of the use of the OT in the NT reduces or eliminates the tension of how the Greek OT text came to be (recalling the example of Amos 9:11–12 in Acts 15:16–18, with its possibility that the LXX text was created by an error in the Hebrew *Vorlage* or a misreading of the Hebrew).

Rather than being rattled when we observe a "problem" with the text form or with the sense of a NT quotation of the Old, it is at just that place we may have a clue as to what theological point the NT writer is attempting to make. Where we see differences in the text form of quotations—especially those that were probably introduced by the NT

---

34. Jaroslav Pelikan, *Reformation of Church and Dogma (1300–1700)*, vol. 4 of *The Christian Tradition. A History of the Development of Doctrine* (Chicago: University of Chicago Press, 1984), 345.
35. Hodge and Warfield, "Inspiration," 257.

writer himself—or where the use of the OT source text in the New does not seem to agree with the OT usage in its original context (e.g., Sarah and Hagar in Galatians 4:21–31), it is there we should think more deeply about what theological point the NT is making, for, in fact, it is there that the NT presents God's interpretation of the OT source text in light of Christ's resurrection.

Chapter 8

DOES THE QUEST FOR THE HISTORICAL JESUS STILL HOLD ANY PROMISE?

CRAIG L. BLOMBERG

Albert Schweitzer famously demonstrated how classic nineteenth-century German liberalism consistently created a historical Jesus made in the image of the philosophical school of thought to which each author already belonged.[1] Today various critics still charge historical Jesus scholars with writing more autobiography than biography.[2] The plethora of competing perspectives on Jesus would at first glance seem to support this charge.[3] In the century and a bit since Schweitzer, however, detailed reflections on criteria of authenticity have developed. Much of the diversity in Jesus portraits today can be traced to the use of competing criteria and to the inconsistent use of acknowledged criteria.[4] N. T. Wright, in his landmark *Jesus and the Victory of God*, discussed

---

1. Albert Schweitzer, *The Quest of the Historical Jesus* (London: Macmillan, 1906).
2. For example, John Dominic Crossan, *The Historical Jesus: The Life of a Mediterranean Jewish Peasant* (San Francisco: HarperSanFrancisco, 1991), xxviii.
3. See, e.g., David B. Gowler, *What Are They Saying about the Historical Jesus?* (New York: Paulist, 2007).
4. See Rafael Rodríguez, "Authenticating Criteria: The Use and Misuse of a Critical Method," *Journal for the Study of the Historical Jesus* 7.2 (2009): 152–67.

both of these trends and denied that his portrait of Jesus was completely consistent with the images he had before he began his research.[5]

Wright himself powerfully demonstrated that holistic historical methods and valid criteria of authenticity support the reliability of the major contours of the Jesus of the Synoptic tradition, reflecting what the historical Jesus actually did and said. Wright also concludes that the heart of Jesus' message was the announcement of the end of exile, spiritually speaking, for the people of Israel, if they allied themselves with him and his mission. Not all scholars, including those otherwise sympathetic to Wright's overall approach, are as convinced that as much fits well into the "end of exile" summary as Wright thinks,[6] but his overall methods make a substantial contribution to the discipline.

Of course, it has often been pointed out that many of the competing pictures of the historical Jesus are not mutually exclusive; it is simply a question of which sides of the many-faceted depictions in the Gospels one chooses to emphasize and in what fashion. Is Jesus a charismatic holy man, an Oriental guru, a laconic sage, an apocalyptic seer, a herald of the kingdom, a marginalized Messiah, or Wisdom incarnate? The answer just might be yes! Ben Witherington's very detailed and helpful taxonomy of the varying portraits of Jesus the Third Quest has produced, from which these labels are largely lifted, does not demonstrate hopeless contradiction among the scholars involved, but recognizes that all of them have their key starting points, portions of the Gospels they privilege, and differing syntheses of the details they find credible.[7] There is actually a fair amount of agreement, however, as to the basic elements, especially within the Synoptic tradition, that are most likely to be authentic.[8]

---

5. N. T. Wright, *Jesus and the Victory of God* (Minneapolis: Fortress, 1996), 13–78, 657–62.

6. See esp. throughout Carey C. Newman, ed., *Jesus and the Restoration of Israel: A Critical Assessment of N. T. Wright's* Jesus and the Victory of God (Downers Grove, IL: InterVarsity, 1999).

7. See Ben Witherington III, *The Jesus Quest: The Third Search for the Jew of Nazareth* (Downers Grove, IL: InterVarsity 1995).

8. Nicely summarized in much of James H. Charlesworth, *The Historical Jesus: An Essential Guide* (Nashville: Abingdon, 2008). More recently, compare how similar the portraits are by Gerhard

Rethinking the Criteria of Authenticity

The question of the criteria of authenticity, however, remains crucial. In surveys of the three quests of the historical Jesus, development of the criteria tends to be assigned to the second, or "New Quest." Rudolf Bultmann's *History of the Synoptic Tradition* became the springboard for numerous subsequent applications, while the 1970s brought the new quest to a close with a flurry of studies, including two particularly important ones by Morna Hooker on the right and wrong uses of the standard criteria that had developed.[9] The 1980s and 1990s saw far less methodological reflection of this nature as the Third Quest turned in different directions. Nevertheless, in 2000, Stanley Porter offered a book-length study of the criteria, half of which was a summary of past scholarship and half of which presented three new criteria that he wanted to include in the mix.[10]

Porter's work did not receive the attention it deserved at the time, possibly because much of what it analyzed involved returning to earlier periods of questing, although one of his major points was that the conventional divisions among the periods of historical Jesus research were to some degree artificial. But today additional voices are calling for a rethinking of the value of the criteria. On the one hand, James Dunn has spearheaded a movement in which he argues that it is better to speak merely of how Jesus was remembered.[11] Dunn appeals to Kenneth Bailey's studies on informal controlled oral tradition to suggest that there

Lohfink, *Jesus of Nazareth: What He Wanted, Who He Was* (Collegeville, MN: Liturgical, 2012); Gerald L. Borchert, *Jesus of Nazareth: Background, Witnesses, and Significance* (Macon, GA: Mercer University Press, 2011); Armand Puig i Tàrrech, *Jesus: A Biography* (Waco, TX: Baylor University Press, 2011); José Antonio Pagola, *Jesus, an Historical Approximation* (Miami: Convivium, 2009); and Michael F. Bird, *Are You the One Who Is to Come? The Historical Jesus and the Messianic Question* (Grand Rapids: Baker, 2009).

9. Morna Hooker, "Christology and Methodology," *New Testament Studies* 17 (1971): 480–87; "On Using the Wrong Tool," *Theology* 75 (1972): 570–81.

10. Stanley E. Porter, *The Criteria for Authenticity in Historical-Jesus Research: Previous Discussion and New Proposals* (Sheffield: Sheffield Academic Press, 2000).

11. See James D. G. Dunn, *Jesus Remembered* (Grand Rapids: Eerdmans, 2003); *The Oral Gospel Tradition* (Grand Rapids: Eerdmans, 2013).

is not a huge distance between the Jesus of history and the remembered Jesus.[12] Dunn still employs various authenticity criteria; he just insists methodologically that all we can hope to get back to are the earliest ways in which Jesus was recalled and portrayed by his followers. On the other hand, Chris Keith finds no use for the criteria of authenticity at all.[13] In a volume he and Anthony Le Donne coedited, an all-star cast of scholars either criticizes the standard criteria of authenticity severely or rejects them altogether.[14] As often happens, the title of the collection is a bit more provocative than its contents warrant—*Jesus, Criteria, and the Demise of Authenticity*—but we get the point.

There is no question that a number of scholars have been arguing for a long time that double dissimilarity, multiple attestation, Palestinian environment, coherence, embarrassment, and the like have serious shortcomings. Double dissimilarity (from both Judaism and the early church), to rehearse Hooker's memorable words, can only disclose that which was "distinctive" about the historical Jesus, not that which was "characteristic."[15] We would expect Jesus in many ways to have been a Jew of his time, and we certainly hope that the rest of the New Testament and early Christianity had significant points of continuity with Jesus himself. Scholars employing multiple attestation must make sure they are utilizing independent sources; something that occurs in all three Synoptic Gospels is still only singly attested because of the literary relationships among them. More helpful may be to find something in multiple layers of the tradition (e.g., Mark, Q, and L) or in multiple

---

12. See Kenneth E. Bailey, "Informal Controlled Oral Tradition and the Synoptic Gospels," *Themelios* 20.2 (1995): 4–11; "Middle Eastern Oral Tradition and the Synoptic Gospels," *Expository Times* 106 (1995): 263–67.

13. Chris Keith, "The Indebtedness of the Criteria Approach to Form Criticism and Recent Attempts to Rehabilitate the Search for an Authentic Jesus," in *Jesus, Criteria, and the Demise of Authenticity*, ed. Chris Keith and Anthony Le Donne (New York: T&T Clark, 2012), 25–48.

14. Le Donne does not tip his hand in his chapters in *Jesus, Criteria, and the Demise of Authenticity*, but more clearly shares Keith's rejection of the standard criteria in favor of what he calls "refracted memory" in Anthony Le Donne, *The Historiographical Jesus: Memory, Typology, and the Son of David* (Waco, TX: Baylor University Press, 2009); *Historical Jesus: What Can We Know and How Can We Know It?* (Grand Rapids: Eerdmans, 2011).

15. Hooker, "Christology and Methodology," 481–86; "On Using the Wrong Tool," 577–81.

literary forms, both inside and outside of the Gospels.[16] And single attestation need not be a sign of inauthenticity; the criterion of multiple attestation works well only positively, not negatively.

Coherence is a secondary or derivative criterion and only as useful as the material that a part of the tradition coheres with. The criterion of Palestinian environment remains in an uneasy tension with the criterion of dissimilarity from Judaism. The criterion of embarrassment has some value positively, but not negatively, and like the principle of the harder reading in textual criticism, something can be too hard or, by analogy, too embarrassing to be credible. John Meier added the criterion of necessary explanation into the mix, especially for Jesus' rejection and crucifixion,[17] but a lively debate still surrounds which factors actually contributed to these events and to what degree each contributed.

Other criteria of authenticity that have popped up from time to time include the criterion of Aramaic linguistic phenomena, the tendencies of the developing tradition, and divergent patterns from redaction.[18] Demonstrating Aramaic underlying the Greek sayings of Jesus in the Gospels is fraught with difficulty, since the more we study the breadth of Hellenistic Greek, the more we learn that some of what we thought were Aramaisms have turned out to be used elsewhere in non-translation Greek. Or they reflect Septuagintalisms that not only Jesus might have used. Indeed, any suggested Aramaism, even if it could be proven to be such, would at best take us back to a Palestinian Jewish speaker, but not necessarily Jesus. Appealing to the tendencies of the developing tradition proves even more subjective, because just about every alleged tendency (expansion, embellishment, addition of personal names, adding the miraculous, etc.) can be countered by an

---

16. Robert H. Stein, "The Criteria of Authenticity," in *Studies of History and Tradition in the Four Gospels*, vol. 1 of *Gospel Perspectives*, ed. R. T. France and David Wenham (Sheffield: JSOT Press, 1980), 232–33.

17. John P. Meier, *A Marginal Jew: Rethinking the Historical Jesus*, vol. 1 (New York: Doubleday, 1991), 177.

18. See Stein, "Criteria of Authenticity," 233–36, 238–40, 247–48.

equally prevalent tendency to do the opposite.[19] Divergent patterns from redaction is a criterion that proves more helpful, but again only if used positively, not if it is used to argue automatically that something which appears redactional cannot be historical.

Stanley Porter's additional three criteria are the criterion of Greek language and its context, the criterion of Greek textual variance, and the criterion of discourse features. Porter stresses in his monograph, as he has done elsewhere, the probability of Jesus knowing enough Greek to use it in conversation with individuals who likely did not speak Aramaic.[20] The primary value of this criterion, as he acknowledges, is to give us reason not to summarily dismiss a small number of specific episodes in the Gospels as inauthentic, in which Jesus could have actually spoken in Greek with a given conversation partner.[21] Textual variance posits that with two independent sources, the greater the variation between the wordings in the sources, the further one is likely to be from the original tradition. The criterion of discourse features looks for self-contained passages distinct in vocabulary, style, and rhetoric from their immediate contexts, which hang together and could therefore go back to Jesus in unified form. Little has been done with these final two criteria in the years since Porter proposed them to determine if they are valuable on any widespread basis.[22]

In a series of studies, Tom Holmén has defended what he calls a continuum approach to the historical Jesus.[23] Instead of relying heavily

---

19. As demonstrated as far back as in E. P. Sanders, *The Tendencies of the Synoptic Tradition* (Cambridge: Cambridge University Press, 1969).

20. See Stanley E. Porter, "Did Jesus Ever Teach in Greek?" *Tyndale Bulletin* 44 (1993): 199–235; "Jesus and the Use of Greek in Galilee," in *Studying the Historical Jesus: Evaluations of the State of Current Research*, ed. Bruce D. Chilton and Craig A. Evans (Leiden: Brill, 1994), 123–54.

21. See Porter, *Criteria for Authenticity*, 158, for a preliminary list. For a critique of this criterion, see Michael F. Bird, "The Criterion of Greek Language and Context: A Response to Stanley Porter," *Journal for the Study of the Historical Jesus* 4.1 (2006): 55–67.

22. Porter himself has updated the state of the discussion in his "The Role of Greek Language Criteria in Historical Jesus Research," in *How to Study the Historical Jesus*, vol. 1 of *Handbook for the Study of the Historical Jesus*, ed. Tom Holmén and Stanley E. Porter (Leiden: Brill, 2011), 361–404; see also Brian J. Wright, "Greek Syntax as a Criterion of Authenticity: A New Discussion and Proposal," *Catholic Biblical Quarterly* 74.1 (2012): 84–100.

23. See Tom Holmén, "Doubts about Double Dissimilarity: Restructuring the Main Criterion

on double dissimilarity as Rudolf Bultmann and many of his followers did, Holmén argues that double *similarity* proves far more significant. Where a feature was a crucial part of the Judaism Jesus inherited and the early church continued to be characterized by that feature, even as it moved into an increasingly less Jewish milieu, the only reasonable explanation for the continuity is that Jesus promoted it. Holmén uses his criterion to authenticate Jesus' approach to the new covenant; contributors to anthologies he has edited have used it for topics as diverse as Jesus' approach to sexuality and holiness, Jesus and his "servant community," and attitudes to the Jewish priesthood.[24] Dale Allison has employed something very much along these lines to once again defend an apocalyptic Jesus announcing an imminent kingdom. He notes how central this approach was to John the Baptist and various other sign-prophets of the first century in Judaism and how it continues as a central element in the writings of Paul, James, Peter, and John, even as it is partially muted in various Hellenistic contexts. Therefore, Allison determines that the historical Jesus must be the mediating figure who kept apocalyptic central even as he diverged from John the Baptist in other important respects.[25]

Finding a Way Forward

What are we to make of this methodological potluck of approaches? Is there any place left for any of the New Quest's criteria of authenticity? In the late 1990s, Darrell Bock and Robert Webb believed there was, and

of Jesus-of-History Research," in *Authenticating the Words of Jesus*, ed. Bruce Chilton and Craig A. Evans (Leiden: Brill, 2002), 47–80; *Jesus in Jewish Covenant Thinking* (Leiden: Brill, 2001).

24. For these and other applications, see Tom Holmén, ed., *Jesus from Judaism to Christianity: Continuum Approaches to the Historical Jesus* (New York: T&T Clark, 2007); *Jesus in Continuum* (Tübingen: Mohr Siebeck, 2012). Also strongly stressing the continuity between Jesus and Judaism are André LaCocque, *Jesus the Central Jew: His Times and His People* (Atlanta: SBL Press, 2015); Amy-Jill Levine, *The Misunderstood Jew: The Church and the Scandal of the Jewish Jesus* (San Francisco: HarperSanFrancisco, 2006).

25. See Dale C. Allison Jr., *Constructing Jesus: Memory, Imagination, and History* (Grand Rapids: Baker, 2010), 31–220.

they convened a team of scholars from the Institute for Biblical Research who met annually for a decade, producing the meticulously researched volume published first by Mohr Siebeck and then by Eerdmans titled *Key Events in the Life of the Historical Jesus.*[26] Twelve prominent and significant events were shown to be historically credible, providing crucial links between the historical Jesus and the Christ of faith, by means of patient, careful application of the criteria and appeal to carefully scrutinized primary sources. The twelve events were the prophetic ministry of John the Baptist, the choosing of the Twelve, Jesus' meals with sinners, Jesus' conflicts over the Sabbath, Jesus as exorcist, Peter's declaration of Jesus' identity on the road to Caesarea Philippi, the triumphal entry, the clearing of the temple, the Last Supper, Jesus' examination by the Sanhedrin, his examination by Pilate and crucifixion, and the women's discovery of an empty tomb.

Very similar to Martin Hengel and Anna Maria Schwemer in their magisterial *Jesus und das Judentum,*[27] the IBR Historical Jesus Study Group determined there was enough evidence from the probable authenticity of these twelve events, interpreted in light of each other, to understand Jesus as having made a messianic claim that was vindicated by his resurrection. Unfortunately, the anthology edited by Chris Keith and Anthony Le Donne proceeded in complete ignorance of this major work. A similarly painstaking study using standard historical criteria was Craig Keener's book on *The Historical Jesus of the Gospels,* produced independently of the IBR group's volume but with strikingly similar conclusions and with an unprecedented grasp of the ancient Jewish and Hellenistic sources.[28] Jens Schröter does refer to Keener's book in his article in the Keith and Le Donne volume, but only to dismiss

---

26. Darrell L. Bock and Robert L. Webb, eds., *Key Events in the Life of the Historical Jesus: A Collaborative Exploration of Context and Coherence* (Tübingen: Mohr Siebeck, 2009). A simplified and drastically abbreviated version of the book appears as Darrell L. Bock, *Who Is Jesus? Linking the Historical Jesus with the Christ of Faith* (New York: Howard, 2012).

27. Martin Hengel and Anna Maria Schwemer, *Jesus und das Judentum* (Tübingen: Mohr Siebeck, 2007).

28. Craig Keener, *The Historical Jesus of the Gospels* (Grand Rapids: Eerdmans, 2009).

the appropriateness of its title without any actual interaction with the book's contents![29]

When Scot McKnight called for an end to all the historical Jesus quests, he referred to Hengel and Schwemer only as a book that recently crossed his desk.[30] He complained of the diversity of portraits in historical Jesus studies and appealed for a return to the orthodox church's Jesus,[31] but that hardly settles the question that swirls around the diversity of approaches. *Which* church's Jesus? Does he want Anabaptism's pacifist Jesus, pietistic Lutheranism's individualistic Jesus, classic Calvinism's world-reforming Jesus, ancient Greek Orthodoxy's mystical Jesus, or Messianic Judaism's kosher Jesus? And if McKnight wants to go back to the earliest church, as depicted in the New Testament, then we are still left with the question of diversity—not the diversity of scholars' views or denominations' views of the historical Jesus, but the diversity of the biblical authors' portraits of him.[32] Any synthesis is necessarily of human manufacture and humans will disagree. But that does not mean there are never certain syntheses that are more persuasive than their rivals. Lost in all of this discussion, moreover, are the striking similarities between Hengel and Schwemer, Keener, the IBR Study Group, numerous other scholars like those listed in note 8 above, and even John Meier's more minimalist reconstruction, which painstakingly applies all the criteria while trying to set his own faith commitments to one side and imagine what Protestant, Catholic, Jew, and Muslim scholars might rightfully agree on.[33] In every instance,

---

29. Jens Schröter, "The Criteria of Authenticity in Jesus Research and Historiographical Method," in *Jesus, Criteria, and the Demise of Authenticity*, 53.

30. Scot McKnight, "Why the Authentic Jesus Is of No Use for the Church," in *Jesus, Criteria, and the Demise of Authenticity*, 174, n. 6.

31. Keith and Le Donne, eds., *Jesus, Criteria, and the Demise of Authenticity*, 176.

32. See, e.g., Mark Allan Powell and David R. Bauer, eds., *Who Do You Say That I Am? Essays on Christology* (Louisville: Westminster John Knox, 1999). The same problem of diversity vitiates F. David Farnell's tirade against evangelicals who participate in the historical Jesus quest, along with his misunderstanding of their goals in doing so ("Three Searches for the 'Historical Jesus' but No Biblical Christ [Part 2]: Evangelical Participation in the Search for the 'Historical Jesus,'" *Master's Seminary Journal* 24 [2013]: 25–67).

33. Meier, *A Marginal Jew*, 5 vols. to date (1991–2015).

something along the lines of what Meier calls a marginalized Messiah emerges.

So perhaps the situation isn't quite so bleak. Is there a way forward? Can we salvage any criteria for the Third Quest? Some have turned to the upsurge in interest in social memory theory.[34] Others have reminded us that the somewhat negative response to the guarded tradition hypothesis of Birger Gerhardsson often didn't pay close enough attention to the amount of flexibility he allowed for in the transmission of tradition.[35] Indeed, if we put Gerhardsson's emphasis on memorization,[36] Bailey's focus on informal controlled oral tradition,[37] and the most relevant insights of social memory theory, especially as illustrated by Richard Bauckham and Robert McIver,[38] we have three areas of study that all combine to create a general presumption in favor of the Jesus tradition being transmitted with considerable care. But as Paul Foster has rightly stressed, these general trends do not produce criteria of authenticity. In other words, they do not allow us to pinpoint specific parts of the Gospel tradition that we can affirm as most likely historical.[39]

In his *Jesus and the Victory of God*, N. T. Wright proposed a four-part criterion he called the criterion of double similarity and double

---

34. See esp. Rafael Rodríguez, *Structuring Early Christian Memory: Jesus in Tradition, Performance and Text* (New York: T&T Clark, 2010); see also Le Donne, *Historiographical Jesus*; as well as several of the chapters in Tom Thatcher, ed., *Jesus, the Voice, and the Text: Beyond the Oral and the Written Gospel* (Waco, TX: Baylor University Press, 2008).

35. See esp. Werner Kelber and Samuel Byrskog, eds., *Jesus in Memory: Tradition in Oral and Scribal Perspectives* (Waco, TX: Baylor University Press, 2009); cf. Birger Gerhardsson, *The Reliability of the Gospel Tradition* (Grand Rapids: Baker, 2001).

36. Birger Gerhardsson, *Memory and Manuscript: Oral Tradition and Written Transmission in Rabbinic Judaism and Early Christianity* (Lund: Gleerup, 1961); cf. Rainer Riesner, *Jesus als Lehrer: Eine Untersuchung zum Ursprung der Evangelienüberlieferung* (Tübingen: Mohr, 1981).

37. See n. 12 above; see also Alan Kirk and Tom Thatcher, eds., *Memory, Tradition, and Text: Uses of the Past in Early Christianity* (Atlanta: SBL, 2005).

38. Richard Bauckham, *Jesus and the Eyewitnesses: The Gospels as Eyewitness Testimony* (Grand Rapids: Eerdmans, 2006), 319–57; Robert K. McIver, *Memories, Jesus, and the Synoptic Gospels* (Atlanta: SBL, 2011).

39. See Paul Foster, "Memory, Orality, and the Fourth Gospel: Three Dead-Ends in Historical Jesus Research," *Journal for the Study of the Historical Jesus* 10.3 (2012): esp. 193–202.

dissimilarity.[40] If an element of the Gospel tradition fit well into an early first-century Jewish milieu but had some distinctive twist not known to us from any other ancient Jewish source, and if that same element likewise showed significant points of continuity with the Christianity that grew from the Jesus movement while again containing something different or surprising than what we know of from later Christians, then we could reasonably infer it was most likely authentic. The strengths of the classic dissimilarity criterion were combined with the strengths of the continuum approach. Gerd Theissen, Annette Merz, and especially Dagmar Winter almost simultaneously were proposing what they dubbed in German *die Plausibilitätskriterium*.[41] This criterion has four parts to it that closely correspond to the four parts of Wright's double similarity and double dissimilarity criterion. Two of them come under the heading of "plausibility of influence," and two under "plausibility of context." One of the two in each category represents "coherence and agreement," the other "incoherence and disagreement." Specifically, then, the four parts of the *Plausibilitätskriterium* are labeled "plausible coherence of influence," "plausible influence contrary to the tendency," "correspondence of context," and "individuality of context."[42] These four items clearly mesh well with Wright's similarity with early Christianity, dissimilarity with early Christianity, similarity with Judaism, and dissimilarity with Judaism, respectively, while nuancing what is meant in each instance and putting various limitations on how similar or dissimilar something can be and still be credible. Interestingly, Winter herself writes one of the chapters for *Jesus, Criteria, and the Demise of Authenticity*, which suggests that she sees what she is doing as sufficiently new so that her complex criterion cannot simply be dismissed with the criticisms leveled against

---

40. Ibid., 131–33.

41. Gerd Theissen and Dagmar Winter, *The Quest for the Plausible Jesus: The Question of Criteria* (Louisville: Westminster John Knox, 2002).

42. Gerd Theissen and Annette Merz, *The Historical Jesus: A Comprehensive Guide* (Minneapolis: Fortress, 1998), 118.

the older criteria.[43] By including her chapter in their volume, Keith and LaDonne apparently agree.

Relatively noncontroversial applications to the Synoptic tradition can illustrate how Wright's and Winter's approach works. Consider the expression "kingdom of God/kingdom of heaven." Although God as King permeates Old Testament and Second Temple Jewish thought, the expression itself is absent from the Hebrew Scriptures and rare in the period between the Testaments. Yet it is pervasive and characteristic of the Synoptic Gospels and the Jesus tradition, appearing more than eighty times. It does appear occasionally in several subsequent New Testament authors, but with not nearly the same frequency. Paul has it fourteen times; the rest of the New Testament authors only six, probably because of their increasingly Hellenistic environment. So it is probably authentic and a bedrock core of the historical Jesus' teachings.[44] Or consider Jesus' exorcisms. There are traditions of other Jewish exorcists, even within the Gospels (Luke 11:19; cf. Acts 19:13), though they do not seem to have been common. Paul performs an exorcism in Acts 16:18, but such activity is rare outside of the Synoptics, again no doubt due to the magical dimensions the Greco-Roman world often perceived in them. And in no instances do we hear of an individual simply performing an exorcism by commanding the demon to leave, without at least praying to God first, and in the non-Jewish realm, usually utilizing incantations and various magical paraphernalia.[45]

A third example turns to the conflicts with the Jewish authorities Jesus had over the interpretation of Torah. The debates fit flawlessly into the context of pre-Christian Judaism—issues about Sabbath keeping, the dietary laws, *korban*, Jesus' lack of fasting while feasting with

---

43. Dagmar Winter, "Saving the Quest for Authenticity from the Criterion of Dissimilarity: History and Plausibility," in *Jesus, Criteria, and the Demise of Authenticity*, 115–31.

44. See, already, via the older criteria, George R. Beasley-Murray, *Jesus and the Kingdom of God* (Grand Rapids: Eerdmans, 1986).

45. See Graham H. Twelftree, *Jesus the Exorcist: A Contribution to the Study of the Historical Jesus* (Tübingen: Mohr, 1993).

"sinners," and claiming to be able to pronounce God's forgiveness of sins apart from the authority of the temple establishment and the prescribed animal sacrifices. Yet in every case, Jesus took unparalleled liberties with traditional interpretations. One finds the very occasional reference to these topics in the rest of the New Testament and some continual struggles, but for the most part, Christians came within a generation to the same convictions as their Lord. Again the double elements of similarity and dissimilarity with Judaism and similarity and dissimilarity with emerging Christianity appear.[46]

For a final example, consider the calling of the Twelve. The number is clearly rooted in the history of Israel, with its twelve patriarchs and the territories allotted to them. Yet Jesus claims that in them is constituted the nucleus of a new, true, freed Israel. Peter sees fit to preserve the number twelve after Judas takes his life (Acts 1:15–26), but the next time an apostle dies—James, the brother of John—not a word is spoken about replacing him (Acts 12:1–2). As the Jewishness of the Jesus movement recedes, continuity with the twelve tribes appears less important.[47] Even a term like "disciple" (*mathētēs*) nicely illustrates our four-part criterion. Prophets like Elijah and rabbis before, during, and after Jesus' time regularly had followers in training, yet no one else we know of chose twelve to replicate the number of tribes in Israel. Paul regularly traveled with less experienced coworkers whom he was discipling, but stunningly, the actual word *mathētēs* appears nowhere outside of the Gospels, despite occurring 262 times within them. Did the first Christians recognize something irreproducible about the relationship Jesus had with his closest followers while he was still alive?[48]

The positive value of the *Plausibilitätskriterium* is seen when one compares the extent to which Theissen and Merz, like Wright

---

46. See even Chris Keith, *Jesus against the Scribal Ethic: The Origins of the Conflict* (Grand Rapids: Baker, 2014).

47. See James D. G. Dunn, *Beginning from Jerusalem* (Grand Rapids: Eerdmans, 2009), 152.

48. See Michael J. Wilkins, *Discipleship in the Ancient World and Matthew's Gospel*, 2nd ed. (Grand Rapids: Baker, 1995).

independently of them, find the major contours of the Synoptic tradition to a large extent historically credible. Their works show far more confidence in what can be retrieved from the Gospels than do the Jesus Seminar or Robert Funk, John Dominic Crossan, and Marcus Borg in their individual Jesus books. A flurry of even more recent publications, with and without the methodological self-consciousness of these authors, shows that the Third Quest has proved extremely productive. Stanley Porter and Tom Holmén coedited an astonishing 3,600 pages of 111 articles on the historical Jesus in four volumes of what they ineptly titled a "handbook" of research on the topic.[49] James Charlesworth and Petr Pokorný have edited two large volumes of fifty papers from the two Princeton-Prague seminars on Jesus research, with cutting-edge scholarship demonstrating just how much historical methods can help us in recovering who Jesus really was and what he did and taught.[50] To implicitly write off all of this and similar research as simply leading to a cul-de-sac by saying that the quest(s) for the historical Jesus have played themselves out and have no more significant contributions to make represents a simplistic generalization of astonishing proportions.

Conclusion

Jesus research has hardly reached a dead end, even if select scholars grow weary of it and announce its demise to justify their fatigue. Each of the three established quests has produced more substantial and lasting results than its predecessor. It may indeed be time to shift from the standard approaches of the Third Quest. But that does not mean falling back into some type of unfalsifiable (and therefore ultimately

---

49. Tom Holmén and Stanley E. Porter, eds., *Handbook for the Study of the Historical Jesus*, 4 vols. (Leiden: Brill, 2011).

50. James H. Charlesworth and Petr Pokorný, *Jesus Research: An International Perspective* (Grand Rapids: Eerdmans, 2009); James H. Charlesworth, ed., with Brian Rhea and Petr Pokorný, *Jesus Research: New Methodologies and Perceptions* (Grand Rapids: Eerdmans, 2014).

indefensible) fideism. It may mean inaugurating the Fourth Quest with the Fourth Gospel as the exciting new equal partner with the Synoptics for scholarly scrutiny.[51] The new look on John is no longer new. Even if scholars in other areas of New Testament studies, with the myopia caused by their increasingly narrow specializations, are unfamiliar with this look, that does not justify business as usual with respect to either suspicion about the trustworthiness of John or the lack of use of the Fourth Gospel for historical-Jesus research. It is time to re-Johannify the historical Jesus and re-historicize the gospel of John. The results will almost inevitably reprioritize which themes were truly central to Jesus of Nazareth compared to the standard lists that emerge almost exclusively from the Synoptics.[52] If scholars are willing to take this step, and it will probably have to be evangelicals who take the lead in the undertaking, the field of historical Jesus research will have an exciting and valuable future indeed.[53]

---

51. As repeatedly called for by Paul N. Anderson; see esp. his *The Fourth Gospel and the Quest for Jesus* (New York: T&T Clark, 2006). I have sketched out one possible way of moving forward in this arena in Craig L. Blomberg, "The Historical Jesus from the Synoptics and the Fourth Gospel? Jesus the Purifier," in *The Message of Jesus: John Dominic Crossan and Ben Witherington III in Dialogue*, ed. Robert B. Stewart (Minneapolis: Fortress, 2013), 163–79.

52. See Paul N. Anderson and Felix Just, eds., *John, Jesus and History*, 3 vols. (Atlanta: SBL, 2007–2016).

53. This essay is offered in gratitude for Stan Gundry's friendship and support over the years and his remarkable ability to balance faithfulness to valuable traditions with an eagerness to adopt important, cutting-edge developments in the publishing industry.

Chapter 9

ON WOMEN REMAINING SILENT IN THE CHURCHES

A Text-Critical Approach to 1 Corinthians 14:34–35

GORDON D. FEE

It was with considerable pleasure that I received the kind invitation to submit a chapter for this Festschrift honoring Stan Gundry, with whom I worked closely for more than two decades. But when I read further that the contributions were to focus on history, this understandably gave me a moment of pause, since that is an area in which I read, not write. So I sent off a word of acceptance to my friends at Zondervan, noting that New Testament textual criticism was my first field of expertise, and what could be more historical than getting it right regarding the biblical text itself. So when I suggested my topic, it was warmly received.

I begin by noting that one of the more radical things to appear in the second edition of my 1 Corinthians commentary,[1] and the one destined to be noted in every review, whether applauding or damning, was the removal of the three non-Pauline sentences that appear in our Bibles in 1 Corinthians 14 as verses 34–35. However, and significantly

---

1. Gordon D. Fee, *The First Epistle to the Corinthians*, 2nd ed. (Grand Rapids: Eerdmans, 2014).

for our present purposes, in every preserved manuscript west of Italy, these sentences appear at the end of the chapter. In the current NIV, and as a paragraph of their own, the sentences themselves read (with the non-Pauline moments underlined):

> Women should remain silent in the churches. They are not allowed to speak, but must be in submission, as the law says. If they want to inquire about something, they should ask their own husbands at home; for it is disgraceful for a woman to speak in the church.

To be sure, full comment on the three sentences does appear in my commentary, but now at the end of the chapter, where they are carefully examined in eleven pages of smaller print. There it is demonstrated in considerable detail that they are altogether spurious, in the double sense that from a text-critical perspective they could not possibly have been written by the apostle Paul, while at the same time they contradict much that he has said elsewhere in this same letter. What appears there in full detail has here been condensed and rewritten for a broader readership.

For the sake of those not fully acquainted with the context in which these unusual sentences appear, an overview of the whole letter is perhaps the best way to begin. In what turned out to be his second (but first preserved) letter to the sometimes poorly behaved believers in Corinth, the apostle first takes up in turn four matters that had been reported to him: a church divided by favoritism regarding its leaders (chaps. 1–4), a case of incest (chap. 5), a case of lawsuits among believers (6:1–11), and a case of sexual immorality (6:12–20). The rest of the letter responds to issues they raised with him by way of a letter, in which it is quite clear that for the most part they were challenging Paul regarding certain behavioral issues where they believed themselves to be right and the apostle to be wrong: their right to eat meals in the pagan temples, since those gods do not really exist (chaps. 8–10); resistance by some women regarding either head coverings or letting down hair in worship

(11:2–16); the more well-to-do abusing the poor regarding the Lord's Supper (11:12–24); the use and abuse of gifts of the Spirit (chaps. 12–14); and correcting some misunderstandings about the bodily resurrection of the dead (chap. 15). It is of some further interest that the majority of these issues, including the present one, are most often responded to in an A-B-A' pattern of argumentation, where the first A introduces the subject in a more general way, followed by an interlude of some sort, while the final A' deals with the issue in a more specific way.

The non-Pauline sentences that are the subject of this study occur as unrelated intrusions in the second A' (thus part 3) of his corrections of their abuse of the gifts of the Spirit, where Paul basically addresses two concerns, correctly identified by the headings in the current NIV: Intelligibility in Worship (verses 1–25) and Good Order in Worship (verses 26–40). All of this has been set up, typically so in this letter, by what has preceded in chapter 12 (A), where Paul eases his way into the issue by pressing first of all for a large variety of Spirit manifestations in the worshiping community, so that they will regularly experience both diversity and unity. That is followed in chapter 13 (B) by what is probably the best-known passage in the Pauline corpus, making clear that love, as a many-splendored reality that is not self-seeking, is the key to everything. That in turn brings him to our chapter 14 (A'), which is where the present argument has been going right along. Here he reasons with them at some length, first of all establishing the need for *intelligibility in worship* (verses 1–25), apparently over against their enthrallment with speaking in tongues, which is then followed by a considerable appeal for *good order in worship* (verses 26–40), so that, as he concludes, "everything should be done in a fitting and orderly way."

For reasons that will be forever unknown in terms of the details, the three sentences being examined in this study appear as a totally non sequitur interruption in the middle of his final concern. Thus right where Paul segues from explanation (verse 33, "for God is not a God of disorder but of peace—as in all the congregations of the Lord's people") to application (verses 36–40 = A' in the long passage), he does so with two certainly intentional in-your-face questions: "Or did the word of God originate with you? Or are you the only people it has reached?" He then concludes with two "if anyone" sentences: "If anyone thinks they are a prophet or otherwise gifted by the Spirit, let them acknowledge that what I am writing to you is the Lord's command. But if anyone ignores this, they will themselves be ignored" (verses 37–38). It is these latter two clearly Pauline moments that were interrupted by the spurious sentences that are the subject of this study.

It should be noted at the outset that the only concern that is actually viable in this inquiry is singularly a matter of textual criticism, which happens also to be my own first field of expertise. And in this instance, the issue at hand is one of twofold jeopardy: the matter of placement itself and the matter of their considerably non-Pauline content.

So I begin this inquiry with some words about the technical language of our discipline known as Bengel's first principle, namely, that the form of the text that best explains all the others is most likely the original. Regarding these bizarre sentences, one has three options: that (1) Paul wrote them in their present setting, as they appear in all Greek manuscripts east of Rome; or (2) he wrote them at the end of the chapter, as in all the Greek manuscripts west of Rome; or (3) they began as a marginal gloss that Paul did not write at all, since they are so obviously out of place here and otherwise have too many non-Pauline moments in them to be authentic. In terms of Bengel's first principle, only option three is in fact able to explain all the data.

What is intended in the rest of this essay is to demonstrate that in terms of the discipline of textual criticism itself, these three sentences fail altogether regarding the two primary criteria of intrinsic and transcriptional probability. The former has to do with what the author himself is most likely to have written when one or more of the extant manuscripts differ from each other; the latter has to do with what a later scribe, who is basically a copyist, was most likely to have done. It should come as no surprise to note that as a matter of textual criticism, option 3 above is the only viable one historically.

Text Displacement Concerns

We begin this study with the matter of the dislocation of these sentences, which is the first text-critical concern that needs to be taken up in some detail. Indeed, contrary to those few who have either brushed it aside or disregarded it altogether, and without fear of viable contradiction, this altogether unique text-critical phenomenon in itself calls these sentences into question. Scribes, after all, were basically copyists, who, to be sure, occasionally tended to "help the author out" by adding or clarifying, or slightly rearranging some of the author's words. Significantly, in terms of text-critical history, the displacement of sentences of this kind is altogether unique, since there is nothing even remotely comparable to it in the entire Bible or in the Apocrypha. Either to assume or to suggest otherwise simply amounts to abandoning history while displaying almost no knowledge of New Testament textual criticism.

To be sure, and at first blush understandably so, some have argued that since there are no manuscripts that do not have these sentences in one of these two places, this in itself supports their authenticity. The problem with such an assertion, however, is that the exact opposite is, in fact, the historical reality. Indeed, the closest thing that is even marginally similar elsewhere in the New Testament is the reversal in Matthew's gospel of the first two beatitudes in a few manuscripts of the early Western tradition. But in that case, what appears to have happened seems quite clear, namely, that the scribe caught his own error and corrected himself by putting the first beatitude now as the second.

However, as to the misplacement of the text in the present case, the promoters of its having validity seem quite unable to come to terms with the primary text-critical question itself, the "how" question. How, as a simple matter of historical reality, is it possible that these three totally unrelated sentences to the argument that began in chapter 12 could appear in two quite different places in the manuscript tradition—at the end of the chapter in all manuscripts west of Rome and as verses 34–35 in all the other manuscripts?

Indeed, the only other "displacement" that might legitimately be brought into this discussion, but in fact one of an altogether different kind, is the narrative of Jesus and the woman caught in adultery, which found its way into most manuscripts at the beginning of chapter 8 in John's gospel, where it appears in the NIV in italics. The historical reality in terms of textual transmission, however, is that it appears in no less than four other places in various manuscripts of the Gospels (John 7:36; 21:25; Luke 21:38; 24:53).

One can be quite sure that this present most unusual phenomenon, the only one of its kind in the entire Bible, can only be the result of its also being the singular narrative of its kind, namely, an almost certainly authentic event that simply never made its way into the four-gospel canon. To be sure, the reason for such a phenomenon in this instance seems plain enough—that the story itself has all the markings of historical veracity, a genuine Jesus-story simply too good not to have been included at some point in the Gospels but in fact not found in any of them.

But the present text-critical issue is of a different kind altogether. The only historically viable way this unique phenomenon could have happened is that someone from a much later time, probably in the late second or early third century, wrote these spurious words in the margin of his manuscript. In turn, that manuscript was apparently used by two later copyists, who then presented us with the misfortune of the spurious sentences finding their way into this chapter in two quite different places in two different manuscripts.

It is of some interest here to note that those who have taken exception to this understanding of the three sentences have, to a person, carefully avoided the text-critical issue, which, to be sure, is something of an arcane "science" appreciated by many but understood by few. But in this case, they have regularly done so by asserting that since these sentences are found in one of these two places in all surviving manuscripts, they must therefore be authentic. However, both the historical and pragmatic unlikelihood of such a view simply outweighs any and all arguments to the contrary. After all, the manuscript with the words at the earlier place would have looked something like this (put in English caps for the sake of the majority of contemporary readers):

FORGODISNOTAGODOFDISORDERBUTOFPEACEASIN
ALLTHECHURCHESOFTHELORDSPEOPLEWOMENSHO
ULDREMAINSILENTINTHECHURCHESTHEYARENOTA
LLOWEDTOSPEAKBUTMUSTBEINSUBMISSIONASTHE
LAWSAYSIFTHEYWANTTOINQUIREABOUTSOMETHIN
GTHEYSHOULDASKTHEIROWNHUSBANDSATHOMEFO
RITISADISGRACEFORAWOMANTOSPEAKINTHECHURC
HORDIDTHEWORDOFGODORIGINATEWITHYOUORWE
REYOUTHEONLYPEOPLEITREACHED

What simply defies probability, in terms of textual criticism, is that someone could pull out the last eight letters in the second line through to the first letter of the eighth line and place them at the end of the chapter, especially so since there was no such thing as chapter breaks either. That is, in any manuscript of this period, there would be no signal as to where a scribe should put what is clearly out of place here. The reality that needs to be noted is that there is, in fact, nothing elsewhere in the entire Bible or in the Apocrypha that comes anywhere close to such a textual displacement.

All of this, then, to say that on text-critical grounds alone, it is altogether doubtful, bordering on impossible, that Paul could have had anything to do with these spurious sentences in 1 Corinthians 14. To be sure, there has been a considerable reluctance on the part of a few to accept, and at times even an animosity toward, this affirmation. So the rest of this presentation will offer in some detail the several contextual and linguistic reasons, having to do with what is actually promoted in these sentences, that Paul could not have written them. It is the text critic in me that proposes to set forth the several reasons these three sentences stand in stark contrast to what the apostle affirmed in several ways earlier in this letter and elsewhere in other letters. In so doing, we will begin by pointing out that Paul's own sentences throughout chapter 14 make especially good sense without these words—indeed, quite the opposite, they are a total intrusion into what Paul is here arguing with the believers in Corinth.

Pauline Argument

First, and significantly, these strange sentences have nothing at all to do with what the apostle was doing in chapter 14. While an ordinary reader may only wonder how this intrusion could have happened, an overview of the argument to this point should help one to see how completely unrelated they are to what Paul has been arguing since chapter 12. There he begins by setting forth what comes next in this very long letter: "Now about the gifts of the Spirit, brothers and sisters, I do not want you to be uninformed." Although for a later reader, this may appear as something of a circuitous way to get where he wants to go, it very soon becomes quite clear that at issue throughout chapters 12–14 is the verbal expression of Spirit gifting in the gathered community. Apparently some of the more influential members had become enamored with the gift of tongues—speaking praise or adoration in a language unknown to the rest of the community.

So as an introduction almost certainly intended to help the Corinthian believers come to terms with his real concern, Paul begins by emphasizing the need for diversity of such Spirit manifestations in their times of worship. In rather typical fashion, he begins on a lower "key," identified correctly by the NIV headings for chapter 12: "Concerning Spiritual Gifts," followed by "Unity and Diversity in the Body." This is followed, in the A-B-A' pattern of argument noted earlier, with the eloquent, probably best-known and best-loved passage in all of Paul's letters, that "Love Is Indispensable." As elsewhere, this B portion of the argument is intended to be the glue that holds the introductory affirmations in chapter 12, which themselves border on correction, together with the elaborations that follow in chapter 14.

What comes next, then, by way of conclusion to the whole, is a long discourse regarding "Intelligibility in Worship" (verses 1–25), almost certainly as a way of contrasting with what appears to have been something close to cacophony in the Corinthians' gathered assembly. He then concludes with an appeal to "Good Order in Worship" (verses 26–40 = the second part A in the long passage). Thus the argument that began on the lower notes of chapter 12 now moves toward conclusion in a very Pauline style, that "everything should be done in a fitting and orderly way" (verse 40). Right where he segues from explanation (verse 33, "for God is not a God of disorder but of peace—as in all the congregations of the Lord's people") to application (verses 36–40 = the second part A in the long passage), he begins with two certainly intentional in-your-face questions: "Or did the word of God originate with you? Or are you the only people it has reached?"

He then concludes with two "if anyone" sentences that call the Corinthian believers back to the apostle's own role in all of this: "If anyone thinks they are a prophet or otherwise gifted by the Spirit, let them acknowledge that what I am writing to you is the Lord's command. But if anyone ignores this, they will themselves be ignored" (verses 37–38). These latter two, somewhat typical moments for Paul, are what has been totally interrupted by the spurious sentences of this study—sentences so obviously quite unrelated to the subject at hand. So just before those last two questions, surely intended to catch the Corinthian believers' attention, a scribe somewhere in the east inserted from the margin the three spurious sentences that became our verses 34 and 35. In all manuscripts west of Italy, however, another scribe at another time chose to put these words at the end of our chapter 14.

Whatever else, the plain meaning of the evidence from Paul's own letters elsewhere further makes it quite clear that he could not have been the author of these interruptive, rather thoroughly un-Pauline moments. A prime example that would seem to make this certain is the apostle's mention of his friends Priscilla and Aquila in three different letters (Romans 16:3; 1 Corinthians 16:19; 2 Timothy 4:19), who are twice referred to in this order (1 Corinthians being the exception). It would take a considerable stretch of the imagination for one to think that when the community of faith came together in their domicile, Priscilla would be expected to be silent!

The Non-Pauline Moments in Detail

All of this should be evidence enough that the apostle could not possibly be responsible for these spurious sentences that are so totally unrelated to the matter at hand. What remains to be spelled out at the end is a more detailed look at the several singularly non-Pauline moments in them, which we noted at the beginning:

> Women should <u>remain silent</u> in the <u>churches</u>. <u>They are not allowed to speak</u>, but <u>must be in submission, as the law says</u>. If they want to inquire about something, <u>they should ask their own husbands at home</u>; for it is <u>disgraceful for a woman to speak in the church</u>.

By taking a detailed look, it is my hope that we can put these sentences to rest as altogether foreign matter with which the apostle himself could simply have had nothing at all to do. The sentences will be taken up in their order of appearance in the Greek text.

1. The first contradictory issue appears at the end of the first sentence: "Women should remain silent in the *churches*." The problem here is with the word "churches" in the plural. Why, any good reader should ask, would Paul suddenly abandon his normal way of speaking in this letter, where he consistently refers to the local community of faith in Corinth as "the church." Especially is this so since there was only one such community of believers in the city. Thus throughout the letter, Paul regularly refers to these believers in the singular (see 1:2; 6:4; 10:32; 11:18; 12:28; 14:4–5, 19, 23, 28; 15:9). One of these (12:28) is especially noteworthy: "God has placed in the church first of all apostles, second prophets, third teachers." Here, in fact, the plural would be especially fitting, but it was not so for the apostle in this particular letter. In fact, the only times he uses the plural are precisely when he is referring to other believing communities beyond Corinth.

But the second- or third-century male reader responsible for this marginal gloss was not concerned with Corinth at all, but with the many "churches" of his time, a century or more later—and perhaps (probably?) none of which were actually located in Corinth. This plural in itself is the first certain giveaway that what is being asserted here could not have come from the apostle Paul.

2. The second contradictory issue is even more telling—and equally impossible to have been written by Paul—namely, the elaboration regarding their silence, that women "are not allowed to speak." The problem here, of course, is that this so totally contradicts what Paul has affirmed just three issues earlier in chapter 11, where he states as something clearly to be understood as a straightforward fact that a woman "prays or prophesies" (verse 5). These two verbs in this instance are almost certainly intended to cover the entire range of verbalization in the gathered community at worship, some that is directed toward God and some toward people. Whatever else, it is simply impossible to prophesy silently!

3. The above contradictory moment is further reinforced when 1 Corinthians 14:34 is compared with the matter of head coverings

referred to in 11:5. The issue is not whether or not the woman "prays or prophecies," but rather *assuming* she does, the woman must be properly attired—and the academic community is nearly evenly divided as to whether this had to do with an external covering of some kind or with her hair properly "put up".

4. The third considerably non-Pauline moment comes with the words "but [they] must be in submission." The problem here is that such a requirement stands in rather total opposition to earlier moments in this letter, beginning with what is implied in chapter 7, where the husband, in sexual relations, "does not have authority over his own body but yields it to his wife" (verse 4). Here the husband is understood as engaging in co-submission with his wife. The interpolator responsible for this marginal gloss could scarcely imagine such a thing!

5. The fourth equally non-Pauline moment, which in this case stands in double jeopardy to the rest of the New Testament as well, is the phrase that women "must be in submission, as the law says." The double jeopardy lies first in the reality that, try as its proponents have done, there is not a single moment anywhere in the law that such a thing is even hinted at. But second, and more improbable still, is for anyone even to imagine that the apostle would appeal to the law as somehow binding on followers of Christ. It is a matter of total wonder as to how this misogynist could have dreamed this up. Indeed, one can only wonder whether this man had ever read Galatians, or especially Romans 4, 7, and 8.

In the new era inaugurated by our Lord and continued by the Spirit, God's newly formed people live not in keeping with the law but, through the power of the Spirit, in keeping with the likeness of Christ, which is the *primary* work of the Spirit in our lives. Requiring a woman to be singularly in submission to her husband thus lies totally outside Christlikeness. For Paul, it is both husband and wife being in submission to the other (1 Corinthians 7:4) that demonstrates living in/by the Spirit, which is the newly formed "law" of life in the Spirit.

6. The sixth item, that women "should ask their own husbands at home," is especially off center and totally non-Pauline in that it puts single women quite outside the community of faith. Without husbands, how are they to "inquire about something," as this misogynist would have us believe as something with which God had anything to do? The poor widow or unmarried woman is apparently simply told to keep her mouth shut.

7. The seventh and final matter, and certainly the most damning of all, is to return at the end to the text-critical question noted earlier. As defining as the preceding six items are in terms of improbability bordering on impossibility as to Pauline authorship, the singularly real issue is the "how" question, having to do first of all with how these spurious sentences came to exist at all. This, after all, is only and altogether a matter of textual criticism, despite how often that fact has been brushed aside by those who have argued otherwise. Furthermore, and understandably so, this is the question that is absolutely avoided when anyone writes in favor of their validity. Put simply, the only legitimate question has to do with *how* these three sentences happened to appear in two quite different places in the later copying tradition of this letter.

The singular matter at issue is how these sentences, totally unrelated to the concern at hand, could be found in this place in all manuscripts east of Rome, but be found at the end of the chapter in all manuscripts west of Rome. The only viable answer to this question is that they began as a marginal gloss from a much later time that eventually found their way into the text at two different places and in two different moments in history. Moreover, and to put it strongly, anyone who thinks otherwise can only be accused of knowing very little at all about textual criticism.

As noted earlier, all handwritten manuscripts up to the invention of the printing press appear in capital letters, without breaks between words and usually with very little or no sense of syllables in the words themselves. The text-critical question at this point is how these sentences could have been lifted out of the text, had they been original here, and placed at the end of the chapter, since for the early copyists there were no sentences or paragraphs, or spaces between words, not to mention the convenient numbering of chapters and verses. For any person well versed in text-critical matters, there is only one viable answer: these words first appeared much later than the apostle Paul's day as a marginal gloss by someone in the second or third century who was opposed to women having a voice in the assembled community at worship. And in time, that marginal gloss made its way into the text at two quite different places.

Paul's own concern in this chapter, of course, and especially so at this point in his argument, has nothing at all to do with "all the churches" or with women speaking in the gathered assembly or with wives being in submission to their husbands. Moreover, neither do these matters appear in any shape or form elsewhere in his many letters. In the present case, his concern is singularly with "Intelligibility in Worship" (verses 1–25) and "Good Order in Worship" (verses 26–40). And it is consistently either asserted or assumed throughout the passage that both men and women verbalized in the context of corporate worship.

But for reasons now past finding out, someone in the second or third century thought it unchristian for a woman to speak openly in the community of faith. So in the margin he put the three spurious sentences about women remaining silent in the churches, words that eventually found their way into the Greek text in these two different places. Those who wish to contend with me and others on this matter must show evidence of any kind, either that a scribe could have taken these words out at this point and put them at the end of this passage or the reverse of that, namely, to choose to move them from the end and put them at an earlier spot.

So when one removes these spurious words that stand so openly over against what the apostle affirmed earlier about women in the worshiping community, the whole passage reads rather smoothly. "For God," Paul affirms, "is not a God of disorder, but of peace, as in all the churches of the Lord's people. Or did the word of God originate with you? Or are you the only people it has reached?" And since the entire chapter is devoted to intelligibility and good order in the worshiping community, let the women pray or prophesy to be sure, but let them, along with the men, do all things "in a fitting and orderly way" (verse 40).

I might add as a footnote to the discussion that I am a member of the committee of fifteen Old and New Testament scholars who are responsible for the current NIV. And I also remember well our discussion of this passage in the committee. All but one agreed that these words could not have been written by the apostle himself. But I also agreed with the majority that we dare not take them out, spurious as they are, because there is an element in the evangelical community—people who are greatly troubled that a lifelong Pentecostal scholar sits on the committee—that would damn the whole translation were we to have taken these sentences out. So they were included as a paragraph of their own, and thus let the reader be astounded at such nonsense and wonder why they appear at all in a chapter where everything has to do singularly with intelligibility and good order in worship.

Nor should anyone be surprised that I believe we humans are a fallen people desperately in need of divine redemption, which is what the "good news" is ultimately all about. So being good historians should tell us that, whatever else, we should let Paul be Paul and not burden him with nonsense that he could not have written. To do otherwise surely points to history gone off the rails.

Chapter 10

EVE, JEZEBEL, AND THE WOMAN AT THE WELL

Biblical Women Hijacked in the Fight against Equality

RUTH A. TUCKER

If I were to identify one incident that transformed me into a biblical feminist, it would be a Sunday morning adult education class at Whitneyville Bible Church in the early 1980s. In a series on Philippians, the teacher suggested that the reason Paul appealed to Euodia and Syntyche to get along was that they were having a catfight over the color of tile to install in the women's restroom. Really? I was taken aback. While it is true that Paul does not identify the nature of the problem, why should we assume their argument was trivial? Who knows, they may have been having a manly quarrel over supralapsarianism and the problem of evil or subordinationism and male headship.

In this paper, we will discuss the frequently utilized tactic of hijacking biblical women in the fight against equality. But there is an equally pernicious attitude that occurs unconsciously and often without malice. In fact, I do not believe this teacher intentionally sought to slur more than half the students in his class. He was a nice guy, unaware that his comment was saturated with sexism. No doubt his listeners were unaware as well—that is, until I lit a fuse to an otherwise sluggish Sunday school class.

If a biblical woman can be sufficiently shamed and diminished, she becomes a serviceable tool in the ongoing headship debate. And such tools extend far beyond Euodia and Syntyche. In the first section, we briefly review Eve, recognizing that she stands alone on this account. She is the *First Lady* of the Bible, the *Mother of all the living.* Yet biblical scholars and theologians have too often stripped her of good qualities and seen her as the *Mother of all evil*—in some cases the original foul feminist. And not Eve alone. Throughout history *Daughters of Eve* are similarly charged with getting out of line in a male-dominated world.

In the second section, we move on to Jezebel. We know from Scripture that she had serious issues, though some might point out that Elijah had some of his own. In fact, if we were to pit them against each other today in light of calls for religious tolerance and the popularity of the cosmetics industry, her beauty might dazzle us as much as, dare we say, her Constitutional demand for freedom of religion. But to be called a *Jezebel*, whether in the first century or the twenty-first, is the worst insult one can fire at a woman. Indeed, we will see that name-calling throughout history has been an incredibly creative literary genre, at least when women are the subject.

In the third section, the Woman at the Well represents biblical women more generally, demonstrating how they have been denied their rightful place in the Hall of Faith. If space permitted, this focus could extend not only to the Samaritan woman, but also to dozens of biblical women, including Job's wife, Lot's wife, Deborah, Bathsheba, Huldah, Mary Magdalene, and Junia—those and many more who have been hijacked by patriarchalists.

Deceived about Eve

It all started with the apostle Paul. Nowhere in the Hebrew Bible after the familiar Genesis story is Eve even mentioned—not even once. But then Paul, in a letter to Timothy, lets loose: "And Adam was not the one deceived; it was the woman who was deceived and became a sinner" (1 Timothy 2:14). That she alone became a sinner appears to be seriously inconsistent with Paul's statement in Romans 5:12 that "sin entered the world through one man."

Paul's confusing comments in 1 Timothy 2 and the surrounding passage have been endlessly exegeted, and here is not the place to enter the fray. In 2 Corinthians 11:3, however, Paul again references Eve, and here his assertion is perfectly clear and applicable to all Christians: "But I am afraid that just as Eve was deceived by the serpent's cunning, your minds may somehow be led astray from your sincere and pure devotion to Christ."

Here I propose that anyone who claims to make perfect sense of Paul in 1 Timothy 2:14 has most certainly been deceived by the serpent's cunning. Nevertheless, most Bible commentators have not been able to resist interpreting Paul in a way that supports their own efforts to revile Eve, and through her, all womanhood.

The most quotable of the Latin Fathers was Tertullian (d. 245), who piled invective on Eve with literary ease: devil's gateway, unsealer of forbidden fruit, first deserter of divine law, destroyer of God's image (that image being man). And not Eve alone. All women should be walking about in mourning and repentance for each of you, he declared, is an Eve.

John Chrysostom (d. 407) was equally disparaging of Eve. "The woman taught once, and ruined all," he wrote. "On this account therefore he [Paul] says, let her not teach."[1] Jerome (d. 420) made a similar case, arguing that the first woman was the root of all evil. In Paradise, she was a virgin (as presumably was Adam); thus virginity is natural, and marriage and sexual intercourse are unnatural—a result of Eve's sin.[2] Augustine (d. 430) laid the blame on Eve for the banishment from

---

1. John Chrysostom, "Homily 9 on First Timothy," *New Advent*, www.newadvent.org/fathers/230609.htm (accessed May 22, 2017).

2. See Jerome, "To Eustochium: Letter 22," *New Advent*, www.newadvent.org/fathers/3001022.htm (accessed May 22, 2017).

the garden and took the argument a step further, tying Adam's superiority not only to Eve's God-ordained subjection, but also to her "small intelligence."

> That a man endowed with a spiritual mind could have believed this [the lie of the serpent] is astonishing. And just because it is impossible to believe it, woman was given to man, woman who was of small intelligence and who perhaps still lives more in accordance with the promptings of the inferior flesh than by the superior reason.[3]

To claim that Eve was less intelligent than Adam is a stretch, though it may be fair to argue that she was the first ever to strike a Faustian bargain—selling her soul to the devil for sure knowledge. But unintelligent? Certainly not.

While Paul emphasized that, like Eve, all—male and female—are prone to be led astray by the serpent's cunning, the church fathers, and most biblical commentators who followed them, focused on women only. And then without a shred of biblical evidence, they expounded on Eve's potent infection of her "daughters." Although never named in connection with any other biblical woman, Eve's nature is claimed to be evident among certain Old Testament "daughters of Eve," as Maureen Fries observes:

> While Adam is assigned equal blame with Eve in the Genesis text of the Fall, biblical exegesis in the hands of the celibate Fathers of the Church tended to excuse Adam and to make Eve the sole source and symbol of Original Sin. Like her successors such as Delilah, Bathsheba, and Potiphar's wife, she represented lust and dangers of the Flesh to man, while Adam represented Reason

---

3. Augustine, *Literal Commentary on Genesis 11.42*, cited in Elizabeth A. Clark, *Women in the Early Church*, vol. 13 of *Message of the Fathers of the Church* (Wilmington, DE: Glazier, 1983), 40.

drawn awry by her influence . . . As daughters of Eve, women were said to tend naturally to disobedience, vanity, *cupiditas*, indeed to all sin. Because of Adam's failure properly to guide his (properly) weak and inferior wife, all women should be obedient and submissive.[4]

Pope Gregory I (d. 604), the highest-ranking monk of his day, warned fellow monks about the snares of Satan, most particularly the "daughters of Eve" who had brought down great men ever since the days of Adam:

> For, my beloved, our adversary is skilful . . . For it was through Eve that he came in upon Adam . . . David was victorious in all his battles, yet through means of a daughter of Eve there was found a blemish in him . . . Furthermore, the adversary tempted Job . . . and he came, bringing with him a daughter of Eve, who had caused Adam to sink, and through her mouth he said to Job, her righteous husband:—*Curse God* . . . John was greater than all the prophets, yet Herod slew him because of the dancing of a daughter of Eve.[5]

While Gregory warned monks, Bernard of Clairvaux in a sermon consoled women by cheering them on. "Hasten, ye mothers! Press forward, ye daughters of Eve!" We can almost hear him applauding from the sidelines. "Come quickly, all you who, on account of Eve's fall, bring forth in sorrow!" Even in sorrow he cheers them on, pausing only to revile Eve: "O Eve, from whom the evil first originated, and whose

---

4. Maureen Fries, "Feminae Populi: Popular Images of Women in Medieval Literature," in *Popular Culture in the Middle Ages*, ed. Josie P. Campbell (Bowling Green, OH: Bowling Green State University Popular Press, 1986), 49.

5. Gregory the Great, "*Demonstration VI.*—Of Monks," in *A Select Library of the Nicene and Post-Nicene Fathers of the Christian Church*, 2nd series, vol. 8, Christian Classics Ethereal Library, 880–84, www.ccel.org/ccel/schaff/npnf213.iii.ix.v.html (accessed May 22, 2017).

reproach passed as a disgraceful legacy to womanhood." It is a disgraceful legacy that is not without hope—hope in awaiting the return of Christ: "The time is at hand when that reproach shall be taken away."[6]

In the medieval Catholic Church, negative references to "daughters of Eve" were balanced by the cult of the saints, crowned by the Virgin herself—an unfallen radiant goddess in Paradise. She was illuminated and elevated so high on the pedestal of sainthood that women were blinded in her presence, while at the same time they were ever reminded of their own sin inherited from the fallen Eve. "Eve became the mother of woman's fraudulent character, bodily seduction, and desire for usurpation."[7] In fact, in the high Middle Ages, Bibles "often contained pictorial genealogies of the evil daughters of Eve, such as Jezebel, Athaliah, the daughters of Lot, Tamar, Potiphar, Delilah, Bathsheba, Solomon's foreign wives, Job's wife, Mary Magdalene, and Herodias, all of whom inherited Eve's sinful nature."[8] Such women, in varying degrees of fallenness, were representative of womanhood.

The only way a woman could hope to forsake the sinfulness of Eve in this life was to follow the example of Mary and, like her, remain forever a virgin. Jerome had summed up the choices in numerical terms. Virginity ranked one hundred; widowhood, sixty; and marriage, a mere thirty. But how could he even concede a thirty to marriage that had its foundation in Eve's sin? Here Jerome does a little dance of circular reasoning. "To show that virginity is natural while wedlock only follows guilt, what is born of wedlock is virgin flesh," Jerome wrote. "I praise wedlock, I praise marriage, but it is because they give me virgins."[9]

Augustine's words also spoke for many churchmen during medieval times. To a young man who apparently was having issues with his

---

6. J. C. Hedley, ed., *Sermons of Saint Bernard on Advent & Christmas* (1909; repr., London: Aeterna, 2014).

7. Haruko Nawata Ward, *Women Religious Leaders in Japan's Christian Century, 1549–1650* (Burlington, VT: Ashgate, 2009), 112.

8. Ward, *Women Religious Leaders*, 112.

9. Jerome, "To Eustochium: Letter 22."

mother, he wrote, "What is the difference whether it is in a wife or a mother, it is still Eve the temptress that we must beware of in any woman. I fail to see what use woman can be to man, if one excludes the function of bearing children."[10]

"Eve's independence and curiosity, her so-called lack of submissiveness and obedience was projected upon all of Europe's women" during the Middle Ages, writes Cherel Olive. "Only though virginity, obedience, poverty and outstanding moral fortitude could a woman be redeemed from the burden she bore as a daughter of Eve. Only then could she be considered of equal value to a man."[11]

It should not surprise us that in the sixteenth century an outspoken woman Reformer would be dubbed a "daughter of Eve." Argula von Grumbach, a Bavarian noblewoman and staunch defender of Luther, risked her wealth and family status for the cause. In one instance, she ably defended a student who had been secretly absorbing Luther's writings at the Catholic University of Ingolstadt. So outraged was one Professor Hauer that he attacked her mercilessly. In one single sermon, he let loose, calling her, among other things, a "female devil," a "wretched and pathetic daughter of Eve," a "heretical bitch," and a "shameless whore."[12]

But Catholics did not have a monopoly on misogyny. The Scottish cleric John Knox (d. 1572) was notorious for his sexist verbiage. His *First Blast of the Trumpet Against the Monstrous Regiment of Women* has had a long shelf life. That the rule of women (in this case the English Queen Mary I, Mary of Guise, and Mary, Queen of Scots) was more monstrous than that of many men was less a concern than the fact that

---

10. Augustine, "Epistle 243.10," cited in P. Brown, *Augustine of Hippo: A Biography* (London: Faber & Faber, 1967), 63.

11. Cherel Jane Ellsworth Olive, "Self-Actualization in the Lives of Medieval Female Mystics: An Ethnohistorical Approach," doctoral dissertation (2009), *UNLV Theses, Dissertations, Professional Papers, and Capstones*, 1113 (Las Vegas: University of Nevada, 2009), 189, http://digitalscholarship .unlv.edu/thesesdissertations/1113 (accessed May 22, 2017).

12. Quoted in Bobby Valentine, "Argula von Grumbach: Courageous Debater, Theologian, Female Voice in the Reformation," September 11, 2007, *Wineskins.org*, http://stonedcampbelldisciple .com/2007/09/11/argula-von-grumbach-courageous-debater-theologian-female-voice-in-the -reformation-a-woman-on-the-family-tree (accessed May 22, 2017).

they were women. Knox tells Eve that before she sinned, her obedience was voluntary, but since the Fall such freedom has been revoked "by constraint and by necessity." And for good reason: "because you have deceived your man, you shall therefore be no longer mistress over your own appetites, over your own will or desires." While the man retains his own will, hers is taken away. "He shall be lord and governor, not only over your body, but even over your appetites and will." John Calvin did not approve of the *Blast*, but why did he not challenge such heresy? Nowhere does Scripture suggest that man governs woman's will, and Knox made it clear that he was not speaking of Eve only. "This sentence, I say, did God pronounce against Eve and her daughters, as the rest of the scriptures do evidently witness."[13] An odd claim considering such willful patriarchal wives as Sarah, Rebekah, and Rachel—and most of the biblical queens.

Anglican Hugh Latimer (d. 1555) would have surely agreed with Knox that the Catholic Queen Mary I was part of a monstrous regiment of women rulers. He had been the Catholic bishop of Worcester, who called for reform and then served as an Anglican chaplain to King Edward VI. Less than two years after she ascended the throne, Queen Mary ordered Latimer burned at the stake. Women, he had argued, brought men to destruction. And queens were not exempted: "For a woman is frail, and proclive unto all evils; a woman is a very weak vessel, and may soon deceive a man and bring him unto evil. Many examples we have in holy scripture. Adam had but one wife, called Eve, and how soon had she brought him to evil, and to come to destruction."[14]

John Knox would have wholeheartedly agreed, but agreement between Anglicans and Presbyterians went only so far. Indeed, Henry Leslie, "a violent and bigoted Episcopalian," in the words of

---

13. John Knox, *The First Blast of the Trumpet Against the Monstrous Regiment of Women* (1558), in *Selected Writings of John Knox* (Dallas: Presbyterian Heritage, 1995), 42, www.swrb.com/newslett/actualNLs/firblast.htm (accessed May 22, 2017).

14. Cited in Else L. Hambleton, *Daughters of Eve: Pregnant Brides and Unwed Mothers in Seventeenth-Century Massachusetts* (New York: Routledge, 2004), 7.

a religious adversary, became the bishop of Down in Ireland in 1635. Soon thereafter, he began his attacks on the Presbyterian "Gospellers" who appealed particularly to "the weaker sexe in whom there is least ability of judgment." It all started with Eve: "By this means the serpent overcame mankind; he first tempted the woman . . . By this means the Philistines overcame Sampson . . . And this indeed hath been the common practise of all hereticks . . . These new Gospellers make use of such instruments . . . [for] it is naturall unto the daughters of Eve to desire knowledge."[15]

Yes, it was natural for Eve (and her daughters) to desire knowledge. The abbreviated story in Genesis is too captivating to pass over without creative embellishment. Literary giants, including John Milton (d. 1674), have enhanced the story with relish. Milton's account is truly memorable.

Eve, as we pick up the story, has already plucked and eaten. "Back to the Thicket slunk the guiltie Serpent." No "such delight till then . . . In Fruit she never tasted." But also there was "expectation high of knowledg." So "greedily she ingorg'd without restraint . . . And hight'nd as with Wine." She does not know, however, that she is "eating Death." But she does wonder: "what sort shall I appeer" to Adam? Should she inform him "and give him to partake full happiness with mee"? Or should she keep secret the "Knowledge in my power," which will add to her "Femal Sex," causing him to love her more and, she hopes, "render me more equal, and perhaps, a thing not undesireable, somtime superior: for inferior who is free?"[16]

No one does Eve better than John Milton. Here she is, gorging on the sweet taste of knowledge, tempted to keep it all for herself. Any objection to his not making Eve Adam's equal to begin with is countered

---

15. James Seaton Reid, *History of the Presbyterian Church in Ireland*, vol. 1 (Edinburgh: Waugh and Innes, 1834), 191.

16. John Milton, *Paradise Lost*, book 9, "The Argument, The John Milton Reading Room," lines 780–795, www.dartmouth.edu/~milton/reading_room/pl/book_9/text.shtml (accessed May 22, 2017).

by her desire and determination to be his equal, indeed, sometimes his superior. Yes, "for inferior who is free"? Was Eve here perhaps anticipating a future book title, *Woman Be Free!* by Patricia Gundry?

Milton's Eve was too secularized for Presbyterians, Puritans, Pilgrims, Reformers, and all those who came before. Their Eve was not only easily deceived, but the Mother of all evil. And they gave no slack to gullible daughters of Eve, that "weaker sexe." John Robinson (d. 1625), pastor to the Plymouth Pilgrims in the Bay Colony, spoke for all those who were wont to demean this "sexe." He enjoined wives to offer their husbands a "reverend subjection." Indeed, they dare not "shake off the bond of submission, but must bear patiently the burden, which God hath laid upon the daughters of Eve."[17]

But there is a paradox in the thinking regarding women particularly within the American experience. Women were regarded as easily deceived daughters of Eve who were under subjection to their husbands and forbidden to teach and preach, but as Puritanism melded into Victorianism, women became the keepers of the faith in the *cult of true womanhood* and were seen as morally superior to their male counterparts. Among Catholics, the cult of Mary served as an antidote to the evil Eve. A book by Nicholas L. Gregoris sums up this contradiction in the title *"The Daughter of Eve Unfallen": Mary in the Theology and Spirituality of John Henry Newman.*[18]

Lest we imagine that today the phrase "daughters of Eve" has gone the way of the Maytag wringer washer, we would be wrong. Writing on *The Peaceful Wife* blog in the spring of 2016, Shannon Popkin shares her laundry room experience: "Then one day, I was painting my laundry room and listening to John Piper preach a sermon on the curse of Genesis 3 . . . God was telling the woman that she would be cursed with a desire to control her husband . . . With paintbrush in hand, I realized

---

17. Robert Ashton, ed., *The Works of John Robinson: Pastor of the Pilgrim Fathers*, vol. 1 (London: Snow, 1851), 240.

18. Nicholas L. Gregoris, *"The Daughter of Eve Unfallen": Mary in the Theology and Spirituality of John Henry Newman* (Mount Pocono, PA: Newman House, 2003).

that I, too, as a daughter of Eve, am cursed with the desire to control my husband . . . As a daughter of Eve, I am infected with a desire to control him."[19] Name-calling: *cursed daughter of Eve*. Shannon is not offended by the label.

The Jezebel Label

Is there any other name so easily hissed at a woman? John Piper can easily convince Shannon Popkin and other women that due to their rebelliousness they are each a daughter of Eve, but a Jezebel? Here we ratchet up the name-calling, a common sport among men in every era and culture.

In fact, it is interesting to call forth English language terms used to disparage women in comparison to terms reflecting on men (unless the man is gay). The woman through the generations has been called a bitch, a bawd, a broad, a battle-axe, a crone, a floozy, a gossip, a henpecker, a harridan, a harpy, a hoe, a hussy, a hag, a nag, a slut, a skank, a shrew, a termagant, a tart, a whore, and many more—some too disgusting to reference. Should it surprise us that the worst slurs against a man calls forth his contemptible mother: a bastard, a son of a bitch?

And if we assume only Shakespeare and other men would label an unpleasant woman a shrew, we would be mistaken. Mary Kassian, author, speaker, and proponent of male headship, asks women who come to her blog to take a quiz: "Are You a Shrew?"[20] We can only wonder how Shannon would score, since the entire quiz relates to a woman controlling "her man." Nothing, of course, about a man who controls "his woman," nor is there a shrewish name for such a man.

---

19. Shannon Popkin, "When 'Submit' Feels like a Dirty Word," *The Peaceful Wife*, April 14, 2016, https://peacefulwife.com/2016/04/14/when-submit-feels-like-a-dirty-word-by-shannon -popkin (accessed May 22, 2017).

20. Mary Kassian, "Are You a Shrew? Take This Quiz," April 22, 2014, *Girls Gone Wise*, http:// girlsgonewise.com/are-you-a-shrew-take-this-quiz-to-find-out/ (accessed May 22, 2017).

The terms used in this quiz are common "code words" employed against women: nag, badger, harangue, scold, tongue-lash, and others. Indeed, gender code words are easy to spot. Women are manipulating, domineering, bossy, headstrong, and overbearing, while men are strong, confident, self-assured, and in charge. A woman who marries up financially is a *gold digger*; an assertive woman has *hair on her chest*; and an argument between women is a *catfight*, while men's arguments are high-minded. But here we focus on women who have been called a Jezebel (with no comparable Ahab slur against a man).

Throughout history, the name Jezebel has been hurled at uppity, meddling women, and students of church history should not be surprised that John Chrysostom flung that label at Empress Eudoxia. "The fragmentary version of a sermon he [Chrysostom] delivered before going into exile," writes historian J. H. W. G. Liebeschuetz, "has some violent attacks on Eudoxia. He compares her to Jezebel, to Job's wife, to Herodias, and to the wife of Potiphar." Truly, it sounds just like old John, but sadly for historians the claim, made by an enemy, is probably not true. Golden-mouthed John's archives are rich in sermons, but alas such a Jezebel sermon is not well documented.[21]

Documentation for countless other women on the receiving end of Jezebel slurs are considerably more substantial. In the fifteenth century, when Cardinal Nicholas of Cusa, the bishop of Brixen, sought to reform the well-endowed convent of Sonnenburg, the wealthy noblewoman and abbess Verena von Stuben rebelled. She scorned him as no more than a "bourgeois Rhinelander" and for some six years held her ground, protected by loyal militia. But in the end, with the power of the Catholic Church behind him, Cusa successfully installed another abbess. Verena, however, held onto her own land and her independence while being smeared publicly as a "true Jezebel."[22]

---

21. J. H. W. G. Liebeschuetz, *Ambrose and John Chrysostom: Clerics Between Desert and Empire* (New York: Oxford University Press, 2011), 232.

22. Cited in Jo Ann McNamara, *Sisters in Arms: Catholic Nuns Through Two Millennia* (Cambridge: Harvard University Press, 1996), 394.

Cusa was not the only well-known cleric of the era to sting an abbess with a Jezebel dart. In 1524, Martin Luther published a tract titled *A Story of How God Rescued an Honorable Nun*, her name Florentina von Oberweimar. After having been incarcerated for five years at the Neu-Helfta convent near Eisleben, Germany, the eleven-year-old Florentina was forced to "take the veil." After unsuccessfully attempting to escape, she was flogged and held captive by the abbess. When she finally broke loose, she fled to Wittenberg. Her cruel abbess was a Jezebel, Luther thundered, and her escape was guided by the hand of God.[23]

It should come as no surprise that John Knox would employ the J-word, calling Mary I "Cursed Jezebel" and "that horrible monster Jezebel of England."[24] Nor should we be surprised that New England Puritans labeled Anne Hutchinson an "American Jezebel," not to be confused with a German or English one.[25] John Wesley was married to an English one. He told a friend that "if Mrs. Wesley had been a better wife, he might have been unfaithful to the great work to which God had called him, and might have too much sought to please her according to her own views."[26] Such a view was not uncommon among early Methodists preachers. John Berridge confessed that like Wesley, he had been tempted by a "Jezebel" but God's "divine intelligence" had saved him.[27] Speaking of both Wesley and Whitefield, Berridge again gave God credit for bad marriages, observing that their ministries might have been ruined if "a wise Master had not graciously sent them a brace [pair] of ferrets."[28] Here Berridge graciously offers us an alternative to *shrew* for our name-calling file.

---

23. Martin Brecht, *Martin Luther: Shaping and Defining the Reformation*, 1521–1532, trans. James L. Schaaf (Minneapolis: Fortress, 1990), 101.

24. Knox, *First Blast of the Trumpet*, 88, 147.

25. Cited in Eve LaPlante, *American Jezebel: The Uncommon Life of Anne Hutchinson, the Woman Who Defied the Puritans* (San Francisco: HarperOne, 2005), xvii.

26. Cited in Bufford W. Coe, *John Wesley and Marriage* (London: Lehigh University Press, 1996), 71.

27. Coe, *John Wesley and Marriage*, 71.

28. Quoted in Bruce Hurt, "John Berridge: The Countryside Pedlar of the Gospel (February, 1716-January 22, 1793)," http://preceptaustin.org/john_berridge_biography.htm (accessed May 22, 2017).

Another Englishman who used the J-word was C. H. Spurgeon (d. 1892), longtime popular pastor of the Metropolitan Tabernacle in London. In his case, however, in a sermon on "Ladies' Dress," he employed the name to reign in women's ideals of beauty. "A forgiven sinner decked out in the flaunting garments of a worlding," he bellowed, "casts suspicion upon her own pardon; if she had ever been renewed in heart, would she, could she, adorn herself after the manner of a Jezebel?"[29] If that was not clear enough, he explained elsewhere: "The fair maid of truth does not paint her cheeks and [at]tire her head like Jezebel."[30]

Whether or not they decked out in flaunting garments, painted their cheeks, and attired their heads, women Pentecostal preachers were fair game for the J-word. Maria Woodworth-Etter, in the words of Alexander Dowie, was "a regular Jezebel."[31] A Methodist minister took aim at a woman preacher a generation later: "This Aimee Semple McPherson is a modern Jezebel, that's the kind of woman she is."[32]

One of the most curious cases of Jezebelism relates to Jessie Penn-Lewis (d. 1927),[33] an internationally known writer and speaker associated with such notables as Andrew Murray, Oswald Chambers, F. B. Meyer, A. B. Simpson, and D. L. Moody. Her most controversial association was with Evan Roberts, who is regarded by many as the preacher behind the Welsh Revival of 1904–1905 that sparked the spread of Pentecostalism around the world, culminating in Azusa Street. Penn-Lewis has been featured in *Priscilla Papers*, with Mimi Haddad (citing David Bebbington) noting favorably that she was a prominent leader in both the "Welsh and Keswick revivals in Great Britain at the turn of the Twentieth Century."[34]

---

29. Henry Davenport Northrop, ed., *Life and Works of Rev. Charles H. Spurgeon* (Washington D.C.: Jones, 1892), 353–54.

30. Charles H. Spurgeon, *Second Series of Lectures to My Students* (New York: Carter, 1889), 51.

31. John Alexander Dowie, "Elijah's Restoration Messages" in *Leaves of Healing*, vol. 13 (Zion City, IL: Zion, 1903), 374.

32. Quoted in Chas H. Barfoot, *Aimee Semple McPherson and the Making of Modern Pentecostalism, 1890–1926* (New York: Routledge, 2014), 337.

33. Writers also spell her name Jesse.

34. Mimi Haddad, "Jessie Penn-Lewis: Revival and God's Word on Women," *Priscilla Papers* 13.2 (Spring 1999), www.cbeinternational.org/resources/article/priscilla-papers/jessie-penn-lewis.

More recently, however, Penn-Lewis has been the center of a tug-of-war in *Charisma* magazine. In the summer of 2013, Felicity Dale wrote an article titled "Heroine of the Faith: Jessie Penn Lewis."[35] Two years later, in the summer of 2015, Jennifer LeClaire weighed in on "How Jezebel Killed One of the Greatest Revivals Ever." Referring to the Welsh Revival of 1904, LeClaire writes that "the spirit of Jezebel cut off the voice of Evan Roberts, a young man God used to set a nation on fire for God." But the revival "finally fizzled out in 1905 when the spirit of Jezebel operating through Jesse Penn-Lewis . . . seduced and deceived the revivalist in the prime of his anointing."[36] Here the J-word is hurled by a woman against another woman; and while competing assessments of Penn-Lewis are appropriate, "the spirit of Jezebel" does seem extreme.

Interestingly, the usage "spirit of Jezebel" is far more common today than it was when, as far as I can discern, John Knox first coined the term.[37] Google the phrase with quotes, and you'll get nearly 136,000 results. Scroll down to find "30 Traits of a Jezebel Spirit," "4 Keys to Stop Tolerating . . . a Jezebel Spirit," and "How to Defeat the Insidious Spirit of Jezebel."[38] So what is this SOJ? Alas, there is no Wikipedia entry. Perhaps a key to understanding this mystery comes from a comment by Jessica on a post titled "Identify and Remove the Jezebel Spirit" (picturing Eve eyeing the apple as she lies on the ground as a scaly serpent). Jessica writes, "I'm just a little unsure about how to handle my mother-in-law. She definitely carries the spirit of Jezebel."[39]

Today, the most recognizable *Jezebel* is a hugely popular feminist

---

35. Felicity Dale, "Heroine of Faith: Jessie Penn-Lewis," *Charisma*, June 4, 2013, www.charisma mag.com/life/women/17939-heroine-of-the-faith-jessie-penn-lewis (accessed May 22, 2017).

36. Jennifer LeClaire, "How Jezebel Killed One of the Greatest Revivals Ever," *Charisma*, July 30, 2015, www.charismamag.com/blogs/the-plumb-line/23974-how-jezebel-killed-one-of-the-greatest-revivals-ever (accessed May 22, 2017).

37. Knox, *First Blast of the Trumpet*, 112.

38. Checked on August 13, 2015.

39. Marianne, "Identify and Remove the Jezebel Spirit," *Heaven Awaits*, https://heavenawaits.wordpress.com/identify-and-destroy-the-jezebel-spirit-sex-church-witchcraft (accessed May 22, 2017).

website that wears the name as a badge of honor. Indeed, if the real Baal-worshiping Jezebel of the Hebrew Bible were to become involved in American politics today, she would no doubt be more popular than old Elijah. He may be able to quote the Second Commandment in a televised debate, but she would appear in high fashion waving the Second Amendment.

Actually, some might argue that a high-fashion Jezebel has already entered the American political arena—a Jezebel who led a prayer on the first night of the Republican convention in Cleveland, July 18, 2016. Pastor Paula White had been one of Donald Trump's "spiritual advisors," and the headline said it all: "Pastor Paula White Fires Back at 'She's a Jezebel' Accusations." She admitted to being called names: "I hear I'm a Jezebel," but she denied the comparison.[40] One possible reason for such a moniker might relate to another headline about her: "Donald Trump's 'Spiritual Advisor' Sells Eternal Life for $1,144 by Stealing from Harry Potter."[41] The biblical Jezebel would have approved.

It is interesting that when seen through the lens of different eras and different cultures, biblical figures often appear in vastly different lights, not only Jezebel, but also other women who have been transformed through the generations, including the Woman of Samaria.

Shaming the Samaritan Woman

How better to defend the 2016 Republican nominee for president than to call forth the Woman at the Well. That was the approach taken by Jerry Falwell Jr., president of Liberty University:

---

40. "Pastor Paula White Fires Back at 'She's a Jezebel' Accusations," *AT2W Unveiling Truth*, October 14, 2012, www.atoast2wealth.com/2012/12/30/pastor-paula-white-fires-back-at-shes-a -jezebel-accusations-and-the-naysayers (accessed May 22, 2017).

41. Sarah K. Burris, "Donald Trump's 'Spiritual Advisor' Sells Eternal Life," *Alternet*, July 12, 2016, http://www.alternet.org/election-2016/donald-trumps-spiritual-advisor-sells-eternal-life -1144-stealing-harry-potter (accessed May 22, 2017).

"Jesus said we are all sinners. When they ask [whether Trump's personal life is relevant], I always talk about the story of the woman at the well, who had five husbands and was living with somebody she wasn't married to," Falwell told NPR. "They wanted to stone her and Jesus said, 'He who is without sin, casts the first stone.' I just see how Donald Trump treats other people and I was impressed by that."[42]

Yes, for sure. Unless we are without sin we ought not cast the first stone at the Woman at the Well. Isn't that exactly what Jesus said when his disciples returned from Sychar with their backpacks filled with rocks? Apart from Falwell's factual misstep, however, it is true that casting stones at this woman, has throughout history been a hermeneutical sport.

She was "a harlot, a Samaritan adulteress . . . enslaved to the flesh. Her spirit was dead . . . hopelessly carnal"[43]—all those stones thrown by John Piper. Abraham Kuyper decades earlier weighed in with a full backpack, describing her as "positively uncouth . . . calloused to appropriate feminine modesty . . . superficial, mundane and gullible."[44] "Even our own, John Calvin," says John McKinnon, "imagined her to have been a difficult and disobedient wife, who thereby 'constrained her husbands to divorce her.'"[45] Heinrich Bullinger elevated her to the highest plane, though not before hurling some of his own rocks: "A great consolation is found in the fact that a sinful woman who had been the cause of the ruin of many was now made an apostle and preacher."[46] This

---

42. Samuel Smith, "Jerry Falwell Jr. Wonders if Russell Moore Is a 'Closet Liberal Because He Doesn't Support Trump,'" *Christian Post*, July 21, 2016, www.christianpost.com/news/jerry-falwell -jr-russell-moore-closet-liberal-166825 (accessed May 22, 2017).

43. John Piper, "God Seeks People to Worship Him in Spirit and Truth," Bethlehem Baptist Church, *Piper's Notes: Sermon Library*, April 8, 1984, http://www.soundofgrace.com/piper84/ 040884m.htm.

44. Abraham Kuyper, *Women of the New Testament: 30 Devotional Messages for Women's Groups*, trans. Henry Zylstra (Grand Rapids: Zondervan, 1934), 45.

45. John C. McKinnon, "The Samaritan Woman," Beckley Presbyterian Church, September 22, 2013, http://fairlie2.tripod.com/sermons/id411.html (accessed May 22, 2017).

46. Cited in Tracy Kemp Hartman, *Letting the Other Speak: Proclaiming the Stories of Biblical Women* (New York: Lexington, 2012), 95.

sentence is appropriate for the apostle Paul who, by his own testimony, was himself the ruin of many prior to his conversion. But where do we find evidence for this woman "apostle" ruining even one person?

Is it a stretch to regard the Samaritan woman as one who had been widowed, divorced, or abandoned? Might she have fallen into a string of marriages that involved alcoholism and domestic violence? Is Jesus bringing up her past to prove her sinfulness, or is he concerned about her neediness? It is significant, as David Lose points out, that neither sin nor repentance is even mentioned. "There are any number of ways, in fact, that one might imagine this woman's story as tragic rather than scandalous," Lose continues, "yet most preachers assume the latter." Not Lose: "He [Jesus] has seen her plight—of dependence, not immorality. He has recognized her, spoken with her, offered her something of incomparable worth.[47]

Indeed, the text does not call on us to emphasize her sinfulness. I recently learned of a situation relating to a woman whose late father was a minister—a minister who had repeatedly been unfaithful to her mother and had sexually abused her. Now as an adult in her forties, she has been married and divorced four times, each husband being an alcoholic and abusive. Counselors commonly encounter such dysfunction among adults who have been abused as children. If this had been the situation with the Samaritan woman, does it naturally follow that she was also a harlot—a prostitute plying her trade in Sychar? She might have been, but there is simply no evidence at all to support such a conclusion. As to the other accusations, the story makes clear that she was not spiritually dead, hopelessly carnal, superficial, mundane, and gullible. That she was so disobedient that her husbands had no other choice but to divorce her sounds like a claim coming from an insecure man.

---

47. David Lose, "Misogyny, Moralism and the Woman at the Well," *Huffington Post*, September 19, 2011, www.huffingtonpost.com/david-lose/misogyny-moralism-and-the_b_836753.html (accessed May 22, 2017).

It is also significant that the alleged sin of the Samaritan woman was not always the focus of the story. In fact, Craig Farmer, in "Changing Images of the Samaritan Woman in Early Reformed Commentaries on John," points out that prior to the Reformation, she was regarded, at least in popular culture, as a serious seeker of truth, and the significance of the story was Jesus' self-revelation to her and her transformed life.[48] In fact, medieval hagiographers went so far as to present her as an evangelist who converted Nero's daughter and was soon thereafter martyred in Rome.

But certain theologians were less inclined to see her in positive terms. *How could a woman ask theological questions?* Thomas Aquinas wondered, since women are "unproductive lovers of ease." And why would Jesus throw pearls to swine? Didn't he tell her to fetch her husband, Aquinas asks, so that he could then transmit the deep spiritual truths to her at home?[49]

Augustine had found the woman ignorant because she thought Jesus, in speaking of "living water," was referring to the actual water in the well.[50] It is interesting that she is found ignorant for questioning what kind of water Jesus is talking about, while Nicodemus, a chapter earlier in John, gets a pass for asking whether being born again means going back through the birth canal into a mother's womb. No, Nicodemus. Dumb question. The words are figurative, not literal—not some sort of first-century version of *The Vagina Monologues*. And as for you, Augustine, throw your rocks at someone else.

Concluding Thoughts

Biblical interpreters have always had issues with strong women. Eve, Jezebel, and the Woman at the Well: they represent women who did

---

48. Craig S. Farmer, "Changing Images of the Samaritan Woman in Early Reformed Commentaries on John," *Church History* 65.3 (September 1996): 365–75.
49. See Farmer, *Changing Images*, 367.
50. Ibid., 368.

not conform to proper female decorum, and all of them—especially Jezebel—have served as warnings to women who would step out of line.

Stepping out of line started with Eve—her sin, her seeking after wisdom. But women through the ages who have stepped out of line have found ways to sidestep the "daughter of Eve" label. Anne Bradstreet is a case in point. "By successfully negotiating the difficulties of an orthodox path to feminine wisdom," writes Zachary Hutchins, "Bradstreet revises her legacy as a daughter of Eve. She exercised her creative abilities within the theological constraints of seventeenth-century New England." As such, she was able to build on "Eve's failure in the garden" and "to reinvent a woman's approach to wisdom."[51] In fact, Hutchins sees her as a pioneer. In an era when wisdom and public speaking easily earned a woman the label of heretic, Bradstreet showed the way for women's voices to be heard while maintaining orthodoxy.

All the same, she feared criticism from those who were smart enough to be suspicious. After all, Eve got into trouble seeking wisdom, but in the words of Hutchins, Bradstreet "did not keep faith with the Fall when she reframed Eve's pursuit of wisdom."[52] Bradstreet too sought wisdom and worried if "my prudence, judgment, I might now reveal" to the keepers of orthodoxy. Thus she concluded, "But wisdom 'tis my wisdom to conceal."[53] Not an easy task when there are a "thousand fancies buzzing in my brain," wishing for wings "to take my flight."[54]

In some respects, Bradstreet's words are reminiscent of Emily Dickinson's two centuries later. "Tell all the truth," she penned, "but tell it slant."[55] Indeed, for a woman in centuries past—and even today—the

---

51. Zachary McLeod Hutchins, *Inventing Eden: Primitivism, Millennialism, and the Making of New England* (New York: Oxford University Press, 2010), 131.

52. Hutchins, *Inventing Eden*, 131.

53. Charles Eliot Norton, ed., *The Poems of Mrs. Anne Bradstreet (1612–1672)* (New York: De Vinne Press, 1897), 54.

54. Anne Bradstreet, "Contemplations," stanza 26, *Poetry Foundation*, www.poetryfoundation. org/poems-and-poets/poems/detail/43699 (accessed June 15, 2017).

55. R. W. Franklin, ed., *The Poems of Emily Dickinson: Reading Edition* (Cambridge, MA: Harvard University Press, 1998), 1263.

better part of wisdom is in concealing wisdom and in giving a slant to the truth. But for others, however, wisdom and truth must be shouted from the housetops. Patricia Gundry minced no words in her volume *Woman Be Free!* And yes, the top title is capped with an exclamation point.

Eve, Jezebel, the Woman at the Well, Anne Bradstreet. Emily Dickinson, Patricia Gundry—and all of us who are spurred on by remnants of rebel blood surging through our veins. Call us names if you like. Daughters of Eve: a badge of honor. With wings we take flight. *Woman Be Free!*

Chapter 11

FAITHFULNESS IN A "COUNTERPOINT" WORLD

The Role of Theological Education

RICHARD J. MOUW

O ne of the many good things I associate with Stan Gundry is his creative work as the series editor of the "Counterpoints" series, featuring books in which evangelicals engage each other on different viewpoints regarding specific topics, such as, baptism, divorce, eternal security, church government, and many more. My own interests over the years have been guided by a commitment to "counterpoint" thinking, and I have been encouraged by Stan's leadership in this area. Not only has he promoted "counterpoint" discussion, but he has contributed to it directly in his own writings. And those of us who know about his personal journey are aware of the fact that he has paid a personal price on occasion for his insistence that specific evangelical subcultures be open to "counter" explorations.

In an interview published by *Christianity Today* in the 1990s, Mark Noll asked the well-known historian-theologian Jaroslav Pelikan to compare his time of teaching in the fairly conservative Lutheran environs where he had been trained with his later years on the faculty at Yale University. Pelikan, who eight years after this interview would move from Lutheranism to Eastern Orthodoxy, did not speak kindly about church-related institutions. The best way to serve the Christian community, Pelikan said, is to work at a secular institution: "You have to give the church what it needs," he said, "not what it wants. And in order to do that you have to leave its payroll. It hurts me to say this because I want to be part of a church where that doesn't have to be said. But show me one where it is not true."[1]

When Stan Gundry was forced to leave an evangelical payroll because of his support for an egalitarian perspective on gender relations, he did not abandon evangelical institutions, moving instead to the Zondervan company, where he expanded his leadership reach as a supporter of creative evangelical life and thought. And in doing so, he provided a fine example of staying on an evangelical payroll while working diligently at serving the genuine needs of the evangelical community.

Pelikan may have overstated the case about what it takes to provide intellectual leadership to a community about whom one cares deeply, but he is pointing to challenges that many of us in the evangelical scholarly world understand quite well. For more than three decades now, I have engaged in addressing those challenges as they are clearly on display in the world of theological education, both as a scholar and as an administrator, a vantage point from which I see myself as having walked alongside Stan as a fellow traveler.

Some Patterns of Evangelical Theological Education

Alasdair MacIntyre famously defined a tradition as a "historically extended, socially embodied argument."[2] Evangelicalism is certainly a

---

1. Mark A. Noll, "The Doctrine Doctor," *Christianity Today* 34.12 (September 10, 1990): 26, www.christianitytoday.com/ct/2004/decemberweb-only/12-27-42.0.html (accessed May 22, 2017).
2. Alasdair MacIntyre, *After Virtue*, 3rd ed. (Notre Dame, IN: University of Notre Dame Press, 2007), 222.

tradition in that sense, and those of us who think much about evangelical identity are acutely aware of belonging to a community that is regularly engaged in an ongoing historical conversation about the meaning of the gospel as a transforming presence in human life. And one of the topics we have regularly discussed—indeed, often argued about with much energy—is the role of the intellect in the Christian life and, more particularly, the importance of disciplined courses of study in preparing for kingdom leadership.

Evangelicalism is a loose coalition of groups and ministries that have their origins in various branches of historic pietism, and like our pietist forebears, we North American evangelicals stress the need for a religion of "the heart." To be a Christian, properly understood, is to experience the regeneration of the inner self, so that the claims of the gospel can be appropriated in a very personal way. To be sure, this experiential emphasis has not kept us from paying close attention to doctrine formulations. We care about how people speak theologically about the authority of Scripture, the atoning work of Christ, the Lord's return, and the like. But we also worry that doctrine as such can harden into a thoroughgoing "head knowledge."

This general concern about the relationship between personal experience and the life of the mind has, as I have already indicated, generated much discussion about the merits of higher education, particularly in preparing for ministry. In some cases in the not-too-recent past, the concern has taken the form of rejection of formal programs of ministry preparation. Here, for example, is the assessment of Peter Cartwright, a well-known nineteenth-century Methodist circuit-riding preacher, who describes an earlier time of itinerant preaching in America:

> Perhaps, among the thousands of traveling and local preachers employed and engaged in this glorious work of saving souls, and building up the Methodist Church, there were not fifty men that had anything more than a common English education, and

scores of them not that; and not one of them was ever trained in a theological school or Biblical institute, and yet hundreds of them preached the Gospel with more success and had more seals to their ministry than all the sapient, downy D.D.'s in modern times, who, instead of entering the great and wide-spread harvest-field of souls, sickle in hand, are seeking presidencies or professorships in colleges, editorships, or any agencies that have a fat salary, and are trying to create newfangled institutions where good livings can be monopolized, while millions of poor, dying sinners are thronging the way to hell without God, without Gospel.[3]

Cartwright's assessment here of formal theological training is harsh, but it is good to see it alongside a viewpoint on the other end of the spectrum, as exemplified in this report of the kind of training required during the nineteenth century by the newly established Christian Reformed denomination. In a volume published by Calvin College in 1926, Albertus Rooks, the college's dean at the time, offered this description of the preparatory program in the early days of theological education at the Grand Rapids school:

> In reflecting upon the course of study of that time in which stu-dents, fresh from the farm and shop, were required to take up, all at once, a half dozen languages—English, Dutch, German, Latin, Greek, Hebrew—and with the Philosophy and Logic and other branches, to carry on for four years and then to conclude with one oral examination in all these studies before the Faculty and Board of Trustees, I admire—and with me all those who know something of the difficulties of Higher Education admire— the ambition, the courage, and the perseverance of the men who

---

3. Quoted in Richard Hofstadter, *Anti-Intellectualism in American Life* (New York: Vintage, 1963), 102–3.

undertook and carried forth the study of all these languages and other branches of study at one and the same time.

True, some soon became discouraged and fell by the way, and no wonder; others plodded on but in the course of time succumbed to the heavy burden with a wrecked mind, and broken body and a discouraged heart. Those who surmounted the difficulties, especially of the earlier years of literary study, became men and servants of the Lord of no mean or ordinary power and ability.[4]

While most of the evangelical debates have typically occurred in a space somewhere between these two extremes, the arguments have still been quite passionate. One factor at work in these debates has been the question of the degree to which "practical training" should dominate preparation for ministry. F. W. Farr of the Nyack Missionary Training Institute set forth his framework for dealing with this issue in his 1887 declaration. "It is best to know and to do," he wrote, "but it is better to do without knowing than to know without doing."[5] And while the early Bible institutes and Bible colleges emphasized the necessity of formal educational programs, their curricula focused heavily on providing the requisite skills for engaging in the tasks of evangelism, foreign missions, congregational ministries, and other areas of "Christian work."

Another area of concern in the debates has been the degree to which persons teaching in theological training programs should be subject to doctrinal policing by sponsoring denominations and organizations. There are certainly some sad stories to tell in this regard, but the patterns that have been at work must be seen against the background of some historical realities. Evangelicalism has been shaped by the experiences

---

4. Albertus J. Rooks, "A History of Calvin College: 1894–1926," in *Semi-Centennial Volume: Theological School and Calvin College* (Grand Rapids: Semi-Centennial Committee, Theological School and Calvin College, 1926), 52.

5. Quoted in William C. Ringenberg, *The Christian College: A History of Protestant Higher Education in America* (Grand Rapids: Eerdmans, 1984), 165.

of many past theological protests and ecclesiastical battles. Very often, these struggles have taken place in specific denominational settings, where the control of seminaries (along with mission boards) has been a major factor in the struggles, with evangelicals ending up as the losers. Many present-day evangelical theological schools originated as alternatives to the status quo in theological education. Some were established by ethnic-confessional groups (Mennonite, Lutheran, Calvinist, "free church") denominations that opposed the existing patterns of North American theological education. Others were established by scholars who were "exiled" from schools where they had taught—J. Gresham Machen's founding of Westminster Seminary after departing from Princeton Seminary in the 1930s is an obvious case in point. Still others (e.g., Francis Asbury, Charles Fuller) saw their mission, in part at least, in providing an evangelical setting for preparing for leadership in mainline denominations.

While these historical experiences do not excuse what have often been rigid practices of the policing of theological faculty, they do need to be taken into account in understanding the patterns. Many evangelical groups still nurture painful memories of loss and exile, resulting in a fear of once again losing control of what goes on in their seminaries. This concern has in turn reinforced long-standing evangelical anxieties regarding the role of the intellect in the Christian life. At times these anxieties have undergirded the perception that the rest of the Christian world was being held captive to a dangerous modernistic rationalism. These days a similar antipathy is directed toward the widespread influence of postmodernism in the theological academy.

Yet another factor in the debates about theological education must be acknowledged. More than any other tradition—Catholic, Orthodox, the Protestant mainline—evangelicals have engaged in (quoting Alasdair MacIntyre again) "a historically extended, socially embodied conversation" regarding the proper locus of theological education. Where, at its best, should the requisite preparation for ministry take place?

The emergence of the Bible institute movement in North America posed that question in a concrete manner. While their "practical training" curricula were, in a sense, a rejection of the kind of "no need for formal education" perspective of the declaration quoted earlier from Peter Cartwright's celebration of the circuit riders, the rhetoric of the Bible schools was also directed toward the graduate-level theological schools. Seminaries have long insisted that a classical undergraduate education is a necessary prerequisite for immersion in the classical disciplines associated with the traditional "fourfold curriculum" of biblical studies, dogmatics, church history, and pastoral theology. The Bible schools dissented from this, arguing that not only was all of that unnecessary, but that it could actually be detrimental to what is necessary for training—to use an A. B. Simpson phrase—the "foot soldiers of God's army."[6]

Many of those early Bible schools eventually themselves moved into the world of graduate theological education. The Bible Institute of Los Angeles is now Biola University, with its Talbot School of Theology. And the Moody Bible Institute offers a full-fledged master of divinity degree, accredited by the Association of Theological Schools.

The locus debates are not over, however. Some megachurch pastors, along with many younger leaders of new-style "contemporary" congregations, insist that seminaries are irrelevant to their ministries. They "train their own" within the local church. Once I was invited to talk to a group of charismatic pastors, none of whom had a seminary degree, about how Fuller Seminary could serve their ministry needs, and one leader responded in a disdainful tone, "I'm not against academic training as such, but I have no use for theological schools. If I had a younger pastor who wanted more education, I would send him to Harvard Business School!" The "practical training is all we need" refrain plays on!

---

6. Quoted in Ringenberg, *Christian College*, 161.

Academy, Church, and Society

When Peter Cartwright boldly denounced formal theological education as quoted earlier, he cited the example of nineteenth-century circuit-riding preachers who regularly mounted their horses to bring the gospel to persons living beyond the reach of worshiping communities. Cartwright may have gone much too far in his views about what is needed for equipping leaders for ministry, but his commendation of the efforts of the circuit riders is certainly legitimate.

I once heard a lecture on evangelism by an Anglican theologian who was visiting North America from England. He was rather harsh in his criticisms of American evangelicals for, as he put it, our fondness for divorcing the task of evangelism from the ministry of the local church. The fault here, he insisted, was a serious weakness in our ecclesiology.

I was not able to contain my frustration with the way he made his point, so in the question-and-answer period, I pushed back. Yes, we need to develop a more robust ecclesiology, I said. But if the early years of our country we had required evangelism to be linked directly to inviting folks into the local church, we would have been in big trouble. Unlike the situation in the British Isles, we have in our recent past an active pioneering spirit reaching into large geographic spaces. People established isolated homes in unpopulated areas, far from any church buildings. If they were to be drawn to Christ, it was up to some individuals to make lonely journeys on horseback with Bibles in their knapsacks, eager to talk about the saving work of Christ.

The positive thing I want to emphasize in this example is what I see as a laudable sense of urgency in promoting the cause of the gospel: "O Zion, haste, thy mission high fulfilling." There is indeed some urgency about promoting the cause of the gospel. Eternal destinies are at stake. Given such a mandate, haste is a highly appropriate response.

Men and women with no formal theological training have regularly taken up the urgent cause of ministry with wonderful results. It is possible to serve the Lord effectively with minimal—or even no—educational preparation. Indeed, there are some gifted people in the Christian community whom *we* should study rather than insist that *they* engage in studies. To acknowledge that, though, points to the need for at least some of us to be engaging in research and teaching. The lessons we can learn from gifted leaders need to be written down and passed on to others. Not everyone can draw on the kind of natural talent and resources that were available to a Corrie ten Boom or a Mother Teresa. They are like musical prodigies who somehow know how to play the piano brilliantly with little formal training. That is not the normal way in which great pianists reach their peak. The rest of us need to read the guidebooks and manuals that can be produced by observing the "natural" geniuses at work. A commitment to "practical" ministries needs to be undergirded by sustained practices of teaching and learning.

A helpful analogy here is the hospital. The emergency room is an extremely important place for exercising practical skills. Hospital emergency rooms are arenas for much urgent activity. People who work there seldom have the leisure to look things up in books or consult learned journal articles as they struggle to save a life. But emergency rooms would not be effective if there were not also medical schools where people engage in research and teach and learn in a somewhat detached setting.

Church ministries do require emergency room type skills. A pastor will have to think of what to say to couples whose marriages are in trouble without stopping to read the marriage counseling manuals. A youth group leader will grope for the right response to a teen's blunt questions about God's love without being able to check out what Karl Barth or Dietrich Bonhoeffer says about the subject. But the skills we must develop for those ministries require a background knowledge of the church's "science." Like the teams in emergency rooms, people in ministry must rely on instincts that have been shaped by the discipline of study and reflection. But those who engage in the areas of research and teaching should never lose sight of the fact that what they are studying has life-and-death significance for the mission of the church of Jesus Christ.

A final factor in the debates worthy of mention here is the question regarding evangelicalism's mode of engagement with the larger cultures in which we are called to minister. One of the chief complaints of the leaders of the "neo-evangelicalism" that emerged in the immediate post-World-War-II period was the failure of evangelical Christians to speak to the key issues of the larger culture—except for their propensity to lay out detailed "Bible prophecy" scenarios that featured themes that encouraged separation from the mores of the larger culture.[7]

Much has changed since then. Evangelicals pay much attention these days to cultural issues. The debatable topics now have to do with the degree to which we can offer positive assessments of trends and patterns in the larger culture—an area of heated discussion when the focus is on the merits of seeker-sensitive worship. Missiology has been an important theological arena for exploring these matters, as evangelical scholars have been paying close attention to the implications of the gospel for diverse cultures.

Here, too, the world of theological education must stay closely connected to "the emergency room," focusing on how local churches can equip their members to engage the complexities of their daily immersion in complex cultural realities. This is why questions about the locus of theological education are significant ones. In the interactive dynamics of academy, church, and society, we enter an arena where urgent matters need to be informed by careful theological reflection.

I once spoke at a large congregation whose lead pastor was a graduate of Fuller Seminary. He expressed gratitude for his own educational training while at the same time explaining why he was not requiring any of his younger pastoral associates to attend seminary. "Take my youth pastor," he said. "He has a junior college degree, and he's married with two kids. There is no need for him to move his family to a theological

---

7. This complaint was featured, for example, in Carl Henry's magisterial *The Uneasy Conscience of Modern Fundamentalism* (Grand Rapids: Eerdmans, 1947).

school. He is great with our young people and can get his practical training on the job in our church setting."

I did not argue with him, but simply offered to be available if he ever wanted Fuller to serve his ministries. Several months later, he called me. His youth pastor was being pressed by teens in his youth group about how to engage in discussions about God with their Mormon friends in high school. "I think my young pastor needs help on the attributes of God," the senior pastor said. "I remember studying in seminary about God's communicable and incommunicable attributes. Can you recommend a theology book he can read on the subject?" I gave him a title. A few weeks later, he got back to me: "That was so helpful! Does Fuller have an online course in systematic theology that would help my young colleague take the next step?"

That incident captures what happened historically in my own Dutch Reformed tradition. In the immediate post-Reformation years in the Netherlands, many candidates for ministry received their training by working under the supervision of older pastors in local congregations, where they were schooled in biblical studies and dogmatics while cultivating practical skills "on the job." After a while, though, a mentoring pastor would recommend that they spend time with a neighboring minister, who was more accomplished in biblical languages and sermon preparation. Gradually a more formal curriculum developed, and full-time teachers were appointed—thus the birthing, in some settings, of theological schools. One can imagine a similar evolution taking place when a youth minister needs some theological help in answering the questions of some high school students.

Theological Education for a "Counterpoint" World

The reference to those high school students brings me back to the "counterpoint" topic with which I began. I am pleased that the teens in the youth pastor's group were engaging in discussions about God with their Mormon friends in high school. And I am grateful that the young minister, through his senior pastor, reached out to a seminary for help. The formation of a new generation of evangelicals for engagement with diverse viewpoints in our increasingly pluralistic culture should be a high priority on the agenda of present-day theological education.

I am writing this during a time when I have been giving visiting lectures at several evangelical liberal arts colleges. I am deeply impressed these days by the students I encounter on those campuses and also by the faculty and staff members who are serving their educational needs. I typically come away from those visits with a renewed interest in how seminaries are doing their part to strengthen the overall task of Christian higher education. I can cite examples of people and programs in the evangelical seminary world where this task is being carried out with great skill and sensitivity. But there is also much that I worry about.

A case in point. At a meeting of evangelical seminary leaders, one president complained about the lack of commitment in the present generation of theological students to the preaching ministry. "They're all over the place," he said. "Theology and film. Counseling. Cross-cultural outreach. Interfaith dialogue. But they don't show much interest in solid biblical preaching. We need men [this president did not believe women were called to ordained ministries] who are passionate about preaching God's Word!"

Another president responded that he was in fact quite impressed by students who were "all over the place" these days. Many of them have been well educated in evangelical colleges, he observed. They care about environmental concerns, about gender issues, about sexual trafficking, about social justice. Many of them have traveled internationally. "They come to seminary with a big vision of the kingdom," he said with much passion, "and they are not sure that standing in pulpits in local churches is the best way to address the huge global challenges. They have come to seminary to find out where they might serve most effectively in the kingdom."

I fully endorse his assessment about the "big vision of the kingdom." The best students I've encountered in seminary programs are those who are very conscious of being called to serve in a "counterpoint" world. They are sensitive to the realities of diversity: lifestyles, religious perspectives, and worldview commitments. They care about injustices and have a heart for the marginalized. Like the circuit-riding preachers of earlier centuries, they have a sense of the urgency of the work of the kingdom. For these contemporary seminary students, though, it is precisely this sense of urgency that compels them to study—drawing on the authoritative teachings of God's Word and the historical memories of the Christian community—in order to properly engage the "counterpoints" of today's global village.

The late Arthur Holmes, longtime philosophy professor at Wheaton College, put it well in one of his helpful discussions of the mission of the Christian college. To ask what we *can do with* a liberal arts education, he wrote, is to ask the wrong question. Instead, we should emphasize what a liberal arts education *can do to us*.[8] The same kind of question needs to be addressed regarding seminaries. More important than asking what we *can do with* programs of theological education is the question of what that kind of disciplined study *can do to us*.

Conclusion

I have alluded to the fact that we are living in a much more diverse "counterpoint" world than our spiritual ancestors experienced. When I was a child, for example, we prayed regularly at our daily family devotions for the missionaries our congregation supported in "Arabia." The little I knew then about Islam came mainly from the slides that accompanied the presentations those missionaries gave to the church

---

8. Arthur F. Holmes, *The Idea of a Christian College* (Grand Rapids: Eerdmans, 1975), 33.

when they were home on furlough. Today we have Muslim neighbors and my grandsons have Muslim friends in their public schools. How do we equip contemporary Christians to wrestle with diverse points of view without abandoning a firm commitment to the abiding truth of God's Word? Given the complex cultural forces that attempt to impose their influences on us, what formation is necessary to keep us faithful to the supreme lordship of Jesus Christ? These questions are crucial for the life and witness of present-day evangelicalism.

In my own "counterpoint" efforts, I have spent much time in interfaith and ecumenical dialogues. But I continue to see the internal evangelical dialogues as having much importance. We cannot properly engage the diversity of the world beyond our evangelical communities if we fail to learn how to talk with others about our disagreements within our own ranks. The Spirit has graced evangelicalism with many gifts expressive of unique spiritual and theological sensitivities and memories. The diversity of these gifts provides us with "counterpoints" that, if we wrestle effectively with them, can strengthen us for renewed patterns of service in Christ's kingdom.

Chapter 12

THE MISSIONAL NATURE AND ROLE OF THEOLOGICAL EDUCATION

CHRISTOPHER J. H. WRIGHT[1]

The vision of "a missional hermeneutic of Scripture" is being widely explored in a number of forums and writings during recent years. It is recognized that the phrase can refer to several interrelated approaches to the text. We may view the whole Bible from a missional point of view:

- as the *product* of God's mission through God's people in the world (these texts came into existence in the course of and as a result of that missional engagement in biblical history)
- as the *witness* to God's mission, rendering to us the grand narrative that spans the whole biblical arc from creation to new creation (these texts record the story of God's mission and bear witness to multiple facets of the great biblical drama in the six acts of creation,

---

1. It is a pleasure and privilege to contribute to this Festschrift in honor of Stan Gundry. Stan was among the first people at Zondervan to welcome me and invite me to write for them. He explored with me over a meal with Pieter Kwant the early reflections and questions that eventually came together in *The God I Don't Understand*. It is a relationship that, in common with many others, I have valued highly over the years.

rebellion, Old Testament promise, gospel, New Testament mission, and new creation)

- as the *tool* of God's mission (these texts came into existence partly in order to shape the people of God for their missional task in the world).

These themes have been thoroughly outlined and explored in other places.[2] It is the third theme that is our main focus in this essay. The church of today stands in spiritual continuity with the people of God throughout the Bible, as those whom God has called into existence in the great moments of election, redemption, and covenant to participate in God's mission in the world, for the sake of God's redemptive purpose for all nations and all creation. And in order to *be* such a missional community, God's people must *live* worthy of their calling (Ephesians 4:1). The missional calling demands an ethical response. There is a message to be proclaimed *and* a life to be lived, and they must go together. God's people need to be "fit for purpose"—God's purpose.

How are God's people to be thus shaped for mission? One clear answer from the Bible itself: through the teaching of those whom God has given to his people for that purpose. In both Testaments, God's people need godly teaching and godly teachers, and disaster strikes when both are lacking.

Now, the phenomenon we call "theological education" did not exist in Old Testament Israel or the New Testament church in the kind of formal structures and institutions we have developed in the history of Christianity. Nevertheless, inasmuch as theological education is one

---

2. See George R. Hunsberger, "Mapping the Missional Hermeneutics Conversation," in *Reading the Bible Missionally*, ed. Michael W. Goheen (Grand Rapids: Eerdmans, 2016), 45–67; Michael W. Goheen and Christopher J. H. Wright, "Mission and Theological Interpretation," in *A Manifesto for Theological Interpretation*, ed. Craig G. Bartholomew and Heath A. Thomas (Grand Rapids: Baker, 2016), 171–96. And in relation to the topic of his papers, see also Darrell L. Guder, "The Implications of a Missional Hermeneutic for Theological Education," in *Reading the Bible Missionally*, 285–98; Michael W. Goheen, "A Missional Reading of Scripture for Theological Education and Curriculum," in *Reading the Bible Missionally*, 299–329.

significant (and rather expensive!) dimension of the teaching ministry of the church, we are including it under that wider generic term. So then, when I use this phrase, "the ministry of teaching," I intend it to have a broad meaning. It includes the regular preaching of pastors in churches, other church-based courses of study and training, and also the formal world of theological education in Bible colleges and seminaries. These are all ways—formal and nonformal, short-term and long-term—in which the teaching ministry can take shape within the church.

A further point needs to be made at the outset. If teaching within God's people is for the purpose of shaping them for their mission in the world, then teaching needs to be *included* within the mission of the church and needs to be *seen to serve* the mission of the church. It is an intrinsic part of the task of bringing people to faith in Christ and mature discipleship and effective witness. It is included within the Great Commission itself, as we shall observe in a moment.

Theological Education and Mission

The New Testament shows the close partnership between the work of evangelism and church planting (e.g., the apostle Paul), and the work of nurturing churches (e.g., Timothy and Apollos). Both tasks are integrated in the Great Commission, where Jesus describes disciple-making in terms of evangelism (before "baptizing them") and "teaching them to obey all that I have commanded you." Theological education is part of mission beyond evangelism.[3]

The mission of the church on earth is to serve the mission of God, and the mission of theological education is to strengthen and accompany the mission of the church. Theological education serves *first* to train those who lead the church as pastor-teachers, equipping them to teach the truth of God's Word with faithfulness, relevance and clarity; and *second*, to equip all God's people for the missional task of understanding

---

3. Colossians 1:28–29; Acts 19:8–10; 20:20, 27; 1 Corinthians 3:5–9.

and relevantly communicating God's truth in every cultural context. Theological education engages in spiritual warfare, as "we demolish arguments and every pretension that sets itself up against the knowledge of God, and we take captive every thought to make it obedient to Christ."[4]

Those of us who lead churches and mission agencies need to acknowledge that theological education is intrinsically missional. Those of us who provide theological education need to ensure that it is intentionally missional, since its place within the academy is not an end in itself, but to serve the mission of the church in the world.[5]

In this essay, we shall attempt to answer three questions:

1. Why is the ministry of teaching so important in relation to the mission of the church?
2. What are the goals of the ministry of teaching in the Bible and how do they relate to our mission—particularly in relation to the goals of theological education?
3. How can we be more effective in our theological education, in equipping the church for mission?

Why Is the Teaching Ministry Important for the Mission of the Church?

THE BIBLE SAYS SO

The teaching of God's Word is integral to the growth and mission of God's people. The Bible provides robust support for this conviction.

---

4. 2 Corinthians 10:4–5.

5. Lausanne Movement, "The Cape Town Commitment." This is the statement from the Third Lausanne Congress on World Evangelization, Cape Town (October 2010), IIF.4 (biblical quotes are part of the original), www.lausanne.org/content/ctc/ctcommitment (accessed May 22, 2017). And we should add that such intrinsically and intentionally missional theological education will necessarily require a missional hermeneutic of Scripture, if the Bible is to be studied as the integrating center of all that is taught, learned, and practiced.

The Old Testament

The work of teachers and teaching is deeply rooted in Old Testament Israel. It was an essential part of the way God called, shaped, and educated his people. Professor Andrew Walls makes this remarkable affirmation: "The Old Testament is not only the first textbook of church history; it is the oldest programme of theological education on record."[6] Throughout the whole Old Testament, for a millennium or more, God was shaping his people, insisting that they should remember *and teach to every generation* the things God had *done* ("what your eyes have seen") and the things God had *said* ("what your ears have heard"). This is stressed again and again in Deuteronomy. God gave his people the Levitical priests as teachers of the Torah, and the prophets to call them back to the ways of God, and psalmists and wise men and women to teach them how to worship God and walk in godly ways in ordinary life. When reformations happened in Old Testament times (e.g., under Jehoshaphat, Hezekiah, Josiah, Nehemiah-Ezra), there was often a return to the teaching of God's Word by the Levites (e.g., Nehemiah 8). God's people were to be a community of teachers and learners, shaped by the Word of God, as we see so emphatically in the longings of the author of Psalm 119. Israel's mission was not to *go* to the nations (yet), but to *so live among the nations* that the name and character of Yahweh would become known among the nations. And teaching was necessary for that mission.

Jesus

It's not surprising then that when Jesus came, he spent years doing exactly the same—teaching, teaching, teaching his disciples as the nucleus of the new community of the kingdom of God. Even as a twelve-year-old boy, he showed that he was rooted in the Scriptures and able to engage with the rabbis in the temple.

---

6. Quoted in Andrew Walls, "Theological Education from Its Earliest Jewish and African Christian Beginnings," in *Handbook of Theological Education in Africa*, ed. Isabel Apawo Phiri and Dietrich Werner (Eugene, OR: Wipf & Stock, 2015), 3.

And in the Great Commission, he mandates his apostles to teach new disciples to observe all that he had taught them (Matthew 28:20)—which was a lot! Teaching was at the heart of Jesus' own mission and ministry, and he makes himself the model for his mandate. We are to make disciples the way Jesus made disciples—with patient teaching over time. It's no good just to bring people to conversion and leave it at that. The seed needs deep soil and good roots in order to bear fruit. Churches need not only to be planted through evangelism, but also to be watered through teaching. Both evangelism and teaching are Great Commission mandates. And both are clearly also God's will for his people. God is at work, not only bringing people to faith in Christ, but also bringing them to maturity in Christ through the work of the Holy Spirit within them, with his gifts, power, and fruit in their lives. The ministry of teaching within the church is a participating in the process by which God himself brings his people to the fullness of maturity and Christlikeness. It is one way in which our mission shares in the mission of God. Theological education, then, as the Cape Town Commitment says, is *intrinsically* missional, and should therefore be *intentionally* missional.

Paul

When we look at Paul, we notice that teaching was integral to his whole life as a missionary church planter. Often he had to leave a newly planted church quickly, under threat, but even then, he would write to them to encourage and teach them. And when Paul had the opportunity, as in Ephesus, he stayed for nearly three years, during which he transformed a group of twelve disciples into a city church with several households and functioning elders. He later tells them that he had taught them not only all that was helpful for them but "the whole will of God"—i.e., the whole scriptural revelation of God's great plan and purpose (Acts 20:20, 27).

And when Paul could not personally do the teaching, he ensured that it was done by others who were part of his missionary team, like

Timothy and Titus. Or Apollos (from Africa), who was learned in the Scriptures (i.e., the Old Testament) and a gifted teacher. Apollos gained further theological education at the home of Priscilla and Aquila (in Asia) and then went to Corinth (in Europe), where he systematically engaged in teaching that included Old Testament hermeneutics, Christology, and apologetics (Acts 18:24–28). Later, when the Christians in Corinth divided into factions boasting loyalty to Paul or Apollos, Paul wouldn't allow it. Yes, Paul and Apollos had had different parts to play. Paul was the evangelist church planter. Apollos was a theological church teacher. But they shared a *common mission*. Paul insisted that the evangelist (planter) and the teacher (waterer) have "one purpose"—or a single mission (in Greek, "they are one"; 1 Corinthians 3:5–9). The apostolic understanding and practice of mission clearly included systematic teaching of new believers, and the bulk of that teaching seems to have been a Christ-focused understanding of the mission of God as revealed in the Old Testament, leading to the inclusion of the Gentile nations, the vision and hope of Christ's return, and the restoration, reconciliation, and redemption of all creation.

So teaching within the church in all its forms, including what we would now call theological education, is an intrinsic part of mission. It is not an extra. It is not merely ancillary to "real mission." The ministry of teaching has to be included as part of our obedience to the Great Commission. The Bible itself commands it.

THE CHURCH NEEDS IT

The Cape Town Commitment identifies several ways in which we Christians have failed to live up to our calling. There is confession of *failure* (in repentance), as well as confession of *faith* (in affirmation). We have to confess that we Christians are not always particularly attractive in the way we live and behave, and that we simply do not look like the Jesus we proclaim.

The Cape Town Commitment puts it this way: "When there is no distinction in conduct between Christians and non-Christians—for example, in the practice of corruption and greed, or sexual promiscuity, or rate of divorce, or relapse to pre-Christian religious practice, or attitudes towards people of other races, or consumerist lifestyles, or social prejudice—then the world is right to wonder if our Christianity makes any difference at all. Our message carries no authenticity to a watching world."[7]

But what lies behind these areas of failure? Surely the moral confusion and laxity of the global church are products of a "famine of hearing the words of the LORD" (Amos 8:11), that is, a lack of biblical knowledge, teaching, and thinking—from the leadership downward. As in Hosea's day, there were many of God's people who are left with "lack of knowledge" of God—at least, no adequate and life-transforming knowledge. And this is so for the same reason as Hosea identified, namely, the failure of those appointed to teach God's word (the priests in his day) to do so (Hosea 4:1–9).

Without good biblical teaching rooted in a missional hermeneutic (that is, biblical teaching conscious of its own purpose, namely, to shape God's people for their mission in the world), people forget the story they are in, or never knew it in the first place. They may know their sins are forgiven and they are "on the way to heaven." But as for how they should be living now, engaging with God in God's mission in today's world—of that story and its demands and implications, they know nothing. Lack of missional teaching inevitably results in absence of missional interest or engagement.

Decades ago, John Stott believed it was this lack of biblical teaching, more than anything else, that was to blame for the ethical and missional weakness of the contemporary church. And he believed that the key remedy—"the more potent medicine," as he called it—was to raise the standards of biblical preaching and teaching, from the seminaries to the grassroots of the churches. Here is an extract from a document I recently

---

7. Lausanne Movement, "Cape Town Commitment," IIE.1

found among his papers, dated 1996, expressing his personal vision for the work of Langham Partnership (which he founded). He pulls no punches and spares no part of the global church in his illustrative samples. And he is crystal clear in his prescription and prophetically exalted in his vision of a different reality.

1. The Ambiguity of the Church

The statistics of church growth are enormously encouraging. But it is often growth without depth, and there is much superficiality *everywhere*. As in first-century Corinth, there is a tension between the divine ideal and the human reality, between what is and what ought to be, between the "already" and the "not yet." Thus the church is both united and divided, both holy and unholy, both the guardian of truth and prone to error.

Everywhere the church boasts great things, and everywhere it fails to live up to its boasts. Its witness is marred by conspicuous failures—for example, by litigation in India (Christians taking one another to court, in defiance of the plain teaching of the apostle Paul), by tribalism in Africa (so that appointments are made more according to tribal origin than to spiritual fitness), by leadership scandals in North America (revealing a lack of adequate accountability), by apathy and pessimism in Europe (the consequence of 250 years of Enlightenment rationalism), by hierarchy in the Chinese, Japanese, and Korean cultures (which owes more to Confucius than to Christ), by anti-intellectual emotionalism in Latin America, and everywhere by the worldly quest for power, which is incompatible with the "meekness and gentleness of Christ."

2. The Word of God

All sorts of remedies are proposed for the reformation and renewal of the church and for its growth into maturity. But they tend to be at the level of technique and methodology. If we probe more deeply into the church's sickness, however, we become aware of its need for more potent medicine, namely, the Word of God.

Jesus our Lord himself, quoting from Deuteronomy, affirmed that human beings live not by material sustenance only, but by the spiritual nourishment of God's Word (Deuteronomy 8:3; Matthew 4:4). It is the Word of God, confirmed and enforced by the Spirit of God, which effectively matures and sanctifies the people of God.

3. The Power of Preaching

If God reforms his people by his Word, precisely *how* does his Word reach and transform them? In a variety of ways, no doubt, including their daily personal meditation in the Scripture. But the principal way God has chosen is to bring his Word to his people through his appointed pastors and teachers. For he has not only given us his Word; he has also given us pastors to teach the people out of his Word (e.g., John 21:15–17; Acts 20:28; Ephesians 4:11–12; 1 Timothy 4:13). We can hardly exaggerate the importance of pastor-preachers for the health and maturity of the church.

My vision, as I look out over the world, is to see every pulpit in every church occupied by a conscientious, Bible-believing, Bible-studying, Bible-expounding pastor. I see with my mind's eye multitudes of people in every country worldwide converging on their church every Sunday, hungry for more of God's Word. I also see every pastor mounting his pulpit with the Word of God in his mind (for he has studied it), in his heart (for he has prayed over it), and on his lips (for he is intent on communicating it).

What a vision! The people assemble with hunger, and the pastor satisfies their hunger with God's Word! And as he ministers to them week after week, I see people changing under the influence of God's Word, and so becoming more like the kind of people God wants them to be, in understanding and obedience, in faith and love, in worship, holiness, unity, service, and mission.

That was John Stott's vision. But it is very close to how the apostle Paul also saw the primary task of those who were appointed as elders and pastors within the churches. And that brings us to the third reason that the teaching ministry is important for the mission of the church.

It Is the Priority for Pastors and Those Who Train Them

What should a pastor be *able to do*? What should a pastor-in-training in a seminary be trained and equipped to do? We can start to answer that question by consulting the list of qualifications that Paul gives for elders/overseers in the churches he had founded that were now being supervised by Timothy and Titus. We find extensive lists of qualities and criteria in 1 Timothy 3:1–10 and Titus 1:6–9.

What is striking is that almost all the items Paul mentions are matters of character and behavior—how they should live and conduct themselves and their families. Pastors should be *examples* of godliness and faithful discipleship. Only *one* thing could be described as a competence, ability, or skill: "able to teach" (1 Timothy 3:2). The pastor above all should be *a teacher of God's Word*, able to understand, interpret, and apply it effectively (as Paul further describes in 1 Timothy 4:11–13; 5:17; 2 Timothy 2:1–2, 15; 3:15–4:2). The pastor's personal godliness and exemplary life are what will give power and authenticity to this single fundamental task. The pastor must *live* what he or she *preaches* from the Scriptures. But preaching and teaching the Scriptures is the fundamental task and competence for those who are called into pastoral leadership in the church. That is very clear.

So then, if seminaries are to prioritize in their training what Paul prioritizes for pastors, they ought to concentrate on two primary things: (1) *personal godliness* and (2) *ability to teach the Bible*.

Now, of course, there are many other things that pastors have to do in the demanding tasks of church leadership. They will need basic competence in pastoral counseling, in leading God's people in worship and prayer, in management and administration of funds and people, in articulating vision and direction, in relating to their particular cultural context, etc. But above all else, Paul emphasizes what they must *be* (godly and upright in their personal lives), and what they must commit themselves to *do* (effectively preach and teach God's Word).

Yet equipping future pastors with that skill of careful, diligent, imaginative, and relevant preaching of the Bible seems sadly neglected in many seminaries. Or so it seems from the response I often get when, at a Langham Preaching seminar somewhere, I ask participants whom I know have already been to a seminary, "Did you not learn how to preach from Bible passages at seminary?" "Well," comes the answer many a time, "we did have a course called Homiletics, but it was just ten lectures on different kinds of preaching. We were never taught *how* to move from a Bible text to a biblical sermon, or given any practice and assessment in doing it." When I hear that, it points to a tragic abdication of what ought to be a primary responsibility—both for pastors themselves and for institutions that train them.

So, to be very frank at this point, whenever theological education neglects or marginalizes the teaching of the Bible or squeezes it to the edges of a curriculum that has become crammed with other things, then that form of theological education has itself become unbiblical and disobedient to the clear mandate that we find taught and modeled in both Testaments. Theological education that does not produce men and women who *know* their Bibles thoroughly, who know how to *teach and preach* the Scriptures, who are able *to think biblically* through any and every issue they confront, and who are *able to feed and strengthen* God's people with God's Word for God's mission in God's world—whatever else such theological education may do or claim or be accredited for, it is failing the church by failing to equip the church and its leaders to fulfill their calling and mission in the world. That kind of theological education is failing to fulfill the very biblical mandate for which it exists.

To conclude this first section, then, I am arguing that we must give greater priority to the ministry of teaching (and to the task of theological education within that broad ministry) (1) because of the biblical mandate and examples, (2) because of the dire need of the church, and (3) because of Paul's clear instruction that preaching and teaching the Scriptures should be a primary calling and competence of those who exercise pastoral leadership in churches.

What Are the Goals of the Ministry of Teaching?

As we have seen, the Bible affirms from very early on, and repeatedly in both Testaments, that God's people need teaching and teachers and that God's people are vulnerable and endangered when teachers are either absent, false, or unfaithful. But we need to take a step further and ask what the ultimate goals of such teaching are.

What, then, are the *intended outcomes* of faithful and effective teaching, according to the Bible? What goals are we aiming at? What results should we want to achieve through the ministry of teaching? And since theological education is an integral part of the wider concept of teaching within the church, what should be the outcomes of theological education if it is going to truly reflect the goals of teaching that the Bible itself envisages?[8]

I suggest three focal points. Each of the following sections is connected with a Bible character who was either commissioned to teach or who commissioned others to do so—Abraham, Moses, and Paul. And

---

8. These questions were very much brought to the fore at the Triennial Conference of the International Council for Evangelical Theological Education (ICETE) in Antalya, Turkey (November 2015), www.icete-edu.org/antalya/index.htm; the materials from the conference are available at: http://theologicaleducation.net/articles/index.htm?category_id=77 (accessed May 22, 2017).

in each case, there is a strong reason that such teaching matters in the context of our world.

Here, then, are three biblical outcomes of teaching:

1. **Mission**: in a world of many nations, the Abrahamic outcome
2. **Monotheism**: in a world of many gods, the Mosaic outcome
3. **Maturity**: in a world of many falsehoods, the Pauline outcome

Mission: In a World of Many Nations, the Abrahamic Outcome

In Genesis 18, we read, "Abraham will surely become a great and powerful nation, and all nations on earth will be blessed through him. For I have chosen him, so that he will direct his children and his household after him to keep the way of the LORD by doing what is right and just, so that the LORD will bring about for Abraham what he has promised him" (Genesis 18:18–19).

In a world going the way of Sodom and Gomorrah (Genesis 18:20–21; 19; Isaiah 1:9–23; Ezekiel 16:49–50), God wanted to create a community that would be different—not just religiously different, but *morally and socially distinctive* (committed to righteousness and justice). That is the reason God chose and called Abraham and commissioned him to teach his own household and descendants.

But then, *why* did God want such a community to exist in the world? Why did God plan to create a nation chosen in Abraham and taught by him? God reminds us of his own purpose in verse 18. It was in order to fulfill God's promise to Abraham that through him and his descendants, *all nations on earth would find blessing* (echoing, of course, Genesis 12:3). That is God's ultimate purpose.

There is, then, a *universal and missional context* here to the teaching mandate given to Abraham. And significantly, this instruction to Abraham comes in Genesis—long before the giving of the law in Exodus. Already, however, the *ethical* content of the law ("keep the way of the

LORD by doing what is right and just") is anticipated in the kind of teaching that Abraham was to give to his household after him. Abraham was to teach his people not only *about* God but also about the ethical character of God and how God wants people to *live*. In other words, this is missionally focused ethical teaching to shape a people through whom God can fulfill his mission among the nations—a long-term eschatological vision, no doubt, but clearly expressed in the syntax and logic of the verse. Notice the three statements in verse 19: "I have chosen him . . . he will direct . . . the LORD will bring about . . . what he has promised," joined together by two "so thats." God's election flows through human teaching within God's people toward God's ultimate mission of blessing all nations.

This in itself shows that teaching (whether in churches or in institutions of theological education) is never merely the imparting of cognitive knowledge, but includes the *shaping of character and behavior.* The language of "walking in the way of the LORD" is common across the Torah, the Prophets, the Psalms and wisdom literature.

So the *ethical purpose* of teaching in Old Testament Israel is governed by *the missional purpose* behind Israel's existence in the first place. In the midst of the nations, *this* nation is to be *taught* how to live as the redeemed people of God, ultimately for the sake of the nations and as part of the mission of God for the nations.

The ministry of teaching within God's people, including theological education, is, as the Cape Town Commitment puts it, *intrinsically* missional. Its whole purpose is to serve the mission of the church. So therefore it ought also to be *intentionally* missional, since it seeks to train the people of God for their mission of life and work in the midst of the nations.

MONOTHEISM: IN A WORLD OF MANY GODS, THE MOSAIC OUTCOME

There is a strong emphasis on teaching in Deuteronomy. God's word in its broadest sense (the knowledge of God's mighty acts, along with an understanding of God's law) must be *constantly taught to the people*, the whole people, and every generation of the people.

Moses himself is repeatedly presented in the book as the one who teaches Israel the requirements of their covenant God (to be followed by the Levitical priests; 33:10). And the primary content of Moses' teaching was that YHWH the God of Israel was *the one and only, unique and universal God, beside whom there is no other* (4:35, 39). For that reason, the first and greatest commandment, as Jesus said, is to love that one whole single God with your one whole single self—with heart and soul and strength (6:4–5).

And that primary love command is immediately followed by *the necessity of teaching*—teaching that is to apply to the personal realm (hands and foreheads), the family realm (the doorposts of the home), and the public arena (the gate).

> Hear, O Israel: The LORD our God, the LORD is one. Love the LORD your God with all your heart and with all your soul and with all your strength. These commandments that I give you today are to be on your hearts. Impress them on your children. Talk about them when you sit at home and when you walk along the road, when you lie down and when you get up. Tie them as symbols on your hands and bind them on your foreheads. Write them on the doorframes of your houses and on your gates.
>
> *Deuteronomy 6:4–9*

Such teaching was necessary because of the polytheistic culture that surrounded the Israelites. Monotheism, in its proper biblical sense (i.e., not just the arithmetical conviction that there is only one God, but the specific affirmation of the identity and universality of YHWH the God of Israel), is *not* an easy faith to inculcate or sustain (as the rest of the Old Testament shows). But since this crucial affirmation is both the primary *truth about God* and the primary *obligation and blessing for*

God's people (the privilege of knowing, loving, and worshiping the one true creator and redeemer God), then whatever threatens that biblical monotheistic faith must be vigorously resisted at any cost. Idolatry is the greatest threat to biblical mission, for God's people cannot bear witness to the true and living God if they are obsessed with the worship of the gods of the cultures around them (whether in Old Testament Israel or in today's church).

So, the whole of Deuteronomy 4 is a sustained challenge to *avoid idolatry*, and the emphasis on *teaching* within the chapter is strong and repeated. It is worth reading the chapter carefully and noting how the two themes (idolatry and teaching) are interwoven, since each is integral to the other. The way to avoid idolatry is to pay attention to the teaching, and the purpose of the teaching is to keep future generations from idolatry. The intention, goal, and outcome of the teaching that God wanted to happen in Israel were to keep people from idolatry and preserve their monotheistic faith and covenant obedience.

If Israel was to be true to their mission among the nations, in such a way that the nations would ultimately come to worship the one true living God, then they—Israel—must preserve the knowledge and worship of YHWH alone. For that reason, there must be *teaching* from generation to generation of all that the God of Israel had *done* and all that the God of Israel had *said*. Teaching was essential to preserving their monotheistic stewardship, the knowledge of God that God had entrusted to Israel. The "theological education" of Israel had the missional intention of preserving their monotheistic faith for the sake of the nations who had yet to come to know this truth about the living God.

MATURITY: IN A WORLD OF MANY FALSEHOODS, THE PAULINE OUTCOME

When we talk about church growth, we usually mean numerical growth through successful evangelism and church planting. But if you had asked the apostle Paul, "Are your churches growing?" I think he would not have understood the question in that way. For Paul, evangelistic growth was simply "gospel growth." So he could write, "The gospel is *bearing fruit and growing* throughout the whole world—just as it has been doing among you since the day you heard it and truly understood God's grace" (Colossians 1:6, emphasis added).

The kind of church growth Paul prayed for was *growth in maturity*. Here's how Paul described the kind of qualitative church growth he prayed for in his churches:

> We continually ask God to fill you with the knowledge of his will through all the wisdom and understanding that the Spirit gives, so that you may live a life worthy of the Lord and please him in every way: bearing fruit in every good work, growing in the knowledge of God, being strengthened with all power according to his glorious might so that you may have great endurance and patience.
>
> *Colossians 1:9–11*

In those few verses, Paul prays for three kinds of maturity:

- Paul wants the believers in Colossae *to know God's story* (verse 9; the will and purpose of God); this involves head knowledge of the whole great narrative of God's plan revealed in the Scriptures.
- Paul wants them *to live by God's standards* (verse 10); this involves their practical lives and moral choices and behavior.
- Paul wants them *to prove God's strength* (verse 11); this involves their spiritual commitment to Christ and perseverance in spite of suffering.

So for Paul, growth in maturity could be measured (1) by increasing knowledge and understanding of the faith, (2) by a quality of living that was ethically consistent with the gospel and pleasing to God, and (3) by perseverance under suffering and persecution. And all of those would be necessary if the believers in Colossae were to participate in God's mission in the surrounding pagan culture of their region.

But how will such Christian maturity be attained? Not surprisingly, through sound teaching by those whom Christ has gifted to the church. We could go to the Pastoral Epistles and prove this point repeatedly through the many places where Paul instructs Timothy and Titus to be teachers themselves and also trainers of teachers—all with a view to *opposing false teachings and practices* of all kinds. Back then, as today, Christian believers were surrounded by competing worldviews and seductive alternatives to the true confession of faith. All kinds of false teaching were around. Back then, as today, the apostolic remedy for, and protection against false teaching, was sound teaching rooted in the Scriptures.

Paul is even more clear about this in Ephesians. There he affirms that the teaching ministry in the church (within which we could now include the work of theological education) is *a Christ-ordained gifting.* Theological education is not an end in itself—this is the temptation of academia, which can easily become an idolatrous seduction—but rather *a means to an end,* namely, the goal of equipping God's own people for *spiritual maturity* and effective mission in the world.

> So Christ himself gave the apostles, the prophets, the evangelists, the pastors and teachers, to equip his people for works of service, so that the body of Christ may be built up until we all reach unity in the faith and in the knowledge of the Son of God and become mature, attaining to the whole measure of the fullness of Christ.
>
> Then we will no longer be infants, tossed back and forth by the waves, and blown here and there by every wind of teaching and by the cunning and craftiness of people in their deceitful scheming. Instead, speaking the truth in love, we will grow to become in every respect the mature body of him who is the head, that is, Christ. From him the whole body, joined and held together

by every supporting ligament, grows and builds itself up in love,
as each part does its work.

Ephesians 4:11–16

Let's apply that text for a moment to the world of theological education, where future pastors are trained.

Doubtless some young graduates come out of seminary thinking they are God's gift to the church. Well, they are right—but not in the sense they may imagine! They are not so much the gifted ones as *the given ones*. God has not given *to* them all the gifts to do all *the* ministry themselves; rather God has given *them* as people (with their particular gifts) *to equip others for their ministry.*

So, the job of pastor-teachers, according to Paul (their unique ministry gifting, in other words), is precisely to equip the rest of the people of God (the saints) for *their* ministries—their many ways of serving God in the church and in the world. So, in theological education, we do not train people for a clerical ministry that is an end in itself, but for a *servant* ministry that has learned how to train disciples to *be* disciples in every context in which they live and move.

I sometimes say to congregations, "I hope you do not think you come to church every Sunday to support the pastor in his or her ministry. It is precisely the other way around. The pastor comes to church every Sunday to support *you in your ministry*, which is out there in the world, in the front lines of your everyday life and work. *You* have the ministry, *you* have the mission, where it really counts. You need to be fed and taught and equipped for whole-life discipleship out there in the world, and it is the pastor's job to do that. Make sure he or she does it, and pray for them until they do!"

Are we teaching future pastors to think like that? Do we give them the missional task of training others for ministry and mission? Do we encourage and equip them to shape their preaching and teaching and pastoral ministry for that goal—to be equippers of the saints for their

244

ministry? Do we inculcate in them the understanding that their own mission is not to *do* all the mission or ministry, but to train and equip the rest of God's people for mission and ministry in the world?

This is a perspective that John Stott repeatedly pointed out through fifty years of writing (sadly on largely deaf ears). He insisted that, in biblical terms, pastoral ministry is not *the* ministry (certainly not the only one), nor are pastors the only people who "do ministry."

> We do a great disservice to the Christian cause whenever we refer to the pastorate as "the ministry." For by our use of the definite article we give the impression that the pastorate is the only ministry there is . . .
>
> There is a wide variety of Christian ministries. This is because "ministry" means "service," and there are many different ways in which we can serve God and people. Acts 6:1–4 provides a firm biblical basis for this conviction . . . It is essential to note that both distributing food and teaching the word were referred to as ministry (*diakonia*). Indeed, both were Christian ministry, could be full-time ministry, and required Spirit-filled people to perform them. The only difference between them was that one was pastoral ministry, and the other social. It was not that one was "ministry" and the other not; nor that one was spiritual and the other secular; nor that one was superior and the other inferior. It was simply that Christ had called the Twelve to the ministry of the word and the Seven to the ministry of tables . . .
>
> It is a wonderful privilege to be a missionary or a pastor, *if God calls us to it*. But it is equally wonderful to be a Christian lawyer, industrialist, politician, manager, social worker, television scriptwriter, journalist, or home-maker, *if God calls us to it*. According to Romans 13:4, an official of the state (whether legislator, magistrate, policeman, or policewoman) is just as much a "minister of God" (*diakonos theou)* as a pastor . . .

At the same time, there is a crying need for Christian men and women who see their daily work as their primary Christian ministry and who determine to penetrate their secular environment for Christ.[9]

And consequently, there is also a crying need for institutions of theological education to train future pastors to be *equippers*, pastors who have a high view of the calling and ministries of all God's people, including the vast majority (98 percent) who are *not* pastors, etc., but who are out there as salt and light in the world.

To summarize then, God has ordained that there should be teachers and teaching among the people of God:

- so that God's people as a whole should be a community fit for participation in *God's own mission* to bring blessing to the nations (the Abrahamic goal)
- so that God's people as a whole should remain committed to *the one true God* revealed in the Bible (as YHWH in Old Testament Israel, and incarnate in Jesus of Nazareth in the New Testament), and resist all the surrounding idolatries of their cultures (the Mosaic goal)
- so that God's people as a whole should *grow to maturity* in the understanding, in the obedience and the endurance of faith, and in effective mission in the world (the Pauline goal)

Now, then, if we think particularly of the world of theological education and the work of Bible colleges and seminaries, the question we must ask at this point is this: What kind of graduates would we need—to be producing from our programs—if we wished to show that our theological education is being effective and fulfilling its biblical

---

9. John Stott, *The Contemporary Christian* (Downers Grove, IL: InterVarsity, 1992), 140–42, italics original.

purpose? What should be our goal in our theological training if we want to be faithful to the purposes for which God has ordained and provided for the teaching ministry among his people? What outcomes should we want to emerge from our theological education investments?

Surely it means we ought to be seeing men and women who graduate and go out into their own preaching and teaching ministry in the churches and who are:

- committed to mission (in all its multiple biblical dimensions)—eager to participate with God in his mission and to lead the communities they serve in the mission entrusted to the church
- faithful to biblical monotheism—totally committed to the God of the Bible alone and able to discern and resist the false gods that surround us; this includes not only the ability to understand and defend the uniqueness of Christ in contexts of religious plurality (and where necessary to bear costly witness to that faith), but also the spiritual insight to discern many idolatries that are more subtle in all cultures (e.g., consumerism, ethnocentrism, etc.)
- marked by maturity in understanding, ethics, and perseverance— able to do the things Paul urges Timothy and Titus to do; men and women who are taking care of their lives and their doctrine and building up others in maturity through godly example and steady biblical teaching

So I ask, Is that actually the kind of goal we have in mind as we shape our curricula, construct our syllabi, develop our lecture courses, and hold our seminars and workshops—across the whole range of our theological disciplines and departments? Is that what we are trying to achieve?

Are we aiming to produce people who are *biblically mission-minded, biblically monotheistic, and biblically mature*?

If that is our aim, then one necessary component of achieving it will be to bring the Bible back to its central place both in the regular teaching and preaching ministry of local churches and in the world of theological education in seminaries. And that leads us to our final question and answer.

How Can We Make Our Ministry of Teaching Effective for Mission?

I believe the only legitimate answer to that question is to call for a recentering of the Bible itself in all our ministry of teaching, and to do so with a more missionally integrated way of teaching it.

The Cape Town Commitment calls for this, quite emphatically, twice:

> We long to see a fresh conviction, gripping all God's Church, of the central necessity of Bible teaching for the Church's growth in ministry, unity and maturity. We rejoice in the gifting of all those whom Christ has given to the Church as pastor-teachers. We will make every effort to identify, encourage, train and support them in the preaching and teaching of God's Word.[10]

> We long that all church planters and theological educators should place the Bible at the center of their partnership, not just in doctrinal statements but in practice. Evangelists must use the Bible as the supreme source of the content and authority of their message. Theological educators must re-center the study of the Bible as the core discipline in Christian theology, integrating and permeating all other fields of study and application. Above all, theological education must serve to equip pastor-teachers for their prime responsibility of preaching and teaching the Bible.[11]

---

10. Lausanne Movement, "Cape Town Commitment," IID.1.d.1.
11. Ibid., IIF.4.d.

So the Cape Town Commitment, like the Great Commission itself, brings theological education into the sphere of Christian mission and then urges that it should be biblically rooted and centered.

In calling for a recentering and reintegrating of the Bible, I mean two things: (1) an integrated way of reading, studying, preaching, and teaching the Bible itself; and (2) integrating a biblical perspective into all other areas of study.

Missional Integration of Biblical Studies

The discipline of biblical studies has become very fragmented in many seminaries—first of all, into Old Testament and New Testament, but then also into further canonical sections of those, and then further into a whole range of critical disciplines, languages, etc.

As a result, sadly, it is possible for students to gain great expertise in various parts of the Bible without having a thorough and integrated understanding of *what the Bible is as a whole.*

We need to help theological students—and ordinary Christians in our churches—to know that the Bible is:

- not just a book full of *doctrines* for systematic theologians to rearrange and order properly
- not just a book full of *promises* for Christians to gain some comfort and "blessed thoughts" from each day
- not just a book full of *rules* for some kind of ethical applications to the problems of life around us, by whatever system of hermeneutics we employ to get our ethics from in the Bible

Rather, God has given us his Word as a whole canon of Scripture that is, fundamentally, a story—the grand narrative of God, creation, and the history of the world. The Bible has a coherent plot: a beginning, a problem, a promise of a solution, a climax and resolution, and a final ending (which is a new beginning). The Bible is like a great "drama" in six acts or stages: Creation, Rebellion, OT Promise, Gospel, NT Mission, New Creation, or as Craig Bartholomew and Michael Goheen shape it: Creation, Fall, Redemption Initiated, Redemption Accomplished, Mission of the Church, Redemption Completed.[12]

Reading and studying the Bible with this overarching framework in view at all times keeps us working with the direction of the text itself and *aligned with the mission of God*, which is why the narrative approach has been broadly adopted by those seeking a missional hermeneutic.

While, of course, it is necessary to get down deep into the exegesis of biblical texts from every part of the canon (with all the specific and detailed work it requires and all the disciplines we can bring to bear on the task), we must bring students back to the surface often—to survey their particular text within the wider flow of the whole narrative. What has already come before this text, where it is leading, where it fits in the canonical framework, how it is integrated into the whole Bible story. I would love to see all seminaries teach a required preliminary course on what it means to take the Bible as a whole, for what it is—the grand narrative of God's mission—before getting down to the more narrowly focused work of exegetical and critical studies.

What does this integrated reading of the Bible as a whole story do?

It tells us the story we are in. We are *in* the story of the Bible—participating in act 5. We must live in the light of all the Bible tells us in its first four stages (acts 1–4) and in anticipation of what God will do at act 6. We live "within the story," which means participating in the mission of God that the story is telling.

So living as a Christian is not just a matter of "applying this verse to my life" (as if my life is the central reality, and the Bible must be applied in an adjectival way), but rather asking, "Where does my life fit into this

---

12. See Craig G. Bartholomew and Michael W. Goheen, *The Drama of Scripture: Finding Our Place in the Biblical Story* (Grand Rapids: Baker Academic, 2014).

great drama in a way that is consistent with the story of what God has done and plans to do? How am I implicated in this text, as a participant in the story of which I am a part and to which I belong?" Those are fundamentally missional questions to ask.

It shapes our worldview. Worldviews are basically shaped by narrative. That is true of all religions and philosophies. They have a "narrative" by which they seek to answer questions about ourselves and the world in the past and present and what they expect in the future. The Christian faith, as a coherent worldview, answers all the fundamental worldview questions *from within the Bible story as a whole* (from creation to new creation, with Christ at the heart of it). Once again, the Cape Town Commitment emphasizes this narrative nature of biblical revelation and theology:

> *The story the Bible tells.* The Bible tells the universal story of creation, fall, redemption in history, and new creation. This overarching narrative provides our coherent biblical worldview and shapes our theology. At the center of this story are the climactic saving events of the cross and resurrection of Christ which constitute the heart of the gospel. It is this story (in the Old and New Testaments) that tells us who we are, what we are here for, and where we are going. This story of God's mission defines our identity, drives *our* mission, and assures us the ending is in God's hands. This story must shape the memory and hope of God's people and govern the content of their evangelistic witness, as it is passed on from generation to generation.[13]

So, then, the task of recentering the Bible in the ministry of teaching, including theological education, means that we help our congregations and our students:

---

13. Lausanne Movement, "Cape Town Commitment," I.6B.

- to inhabit the Bible story and see it as *The Story* within which we live; we have to live in the world, but we do not live by the world's story
- to adopt the Bible's worldview—in marked contrast to the worldview of whatever cultures surround us

Biblical Centering of the Whole Curriculum

This may seem the more challenging task, since it is inviting those who are not biblical specialists but teachers of systematic theology, ethics, church history, pastoral studies, etc., *to see the overall biblical narrative as the governing paradigm* for their disciplines.[14]

This does not mean the Biblical Studies department simply takes over the whole curriculum—any more than a missional integration means the Mission department takes over the whole faculty! Rather, it takes seriously our evangelical affirmation that the Bible is our sole authority for all our life and doctrine—i.e., including all that we teach.

I think this means, for example, that the teaching of "Christian Doctrine" should show how the grand house of Christian theology in fact reflects the implications of every part of the revelation contained within the great Bible story. Systematic theology simply draws out the systems and themes and their implications that are built on the whole story of what God has done and will do, according to the whole Bible. Doctrines express the truth revealed and the life required by that story, but the story has preeminence. That's why it is the "canon" of Scripture.

It means, for example, that "Church History" should be seen as the outworking of God's mission in act 5 of the Bible story. The church has been living in act 5 since the day of Pentecost. So we can study and evaluate the subsequent history of the church in terms of its faithfulness or otherwise to the patterns already set in acts 1–4 and the expectation

---

14. See for much more thorough analysis Michael W. Goheen, "A Missional Reading of Scripture for Theological Education and Curriculum," in *Reading the Bible Missionally*, 299–329.

of act 6. We need to constantly assess the story of the church in the light of the story of the Bible—which is uncomfortable, but necessary.

It means, for example, that in "Ethics," we help our congregations and students to bring every ethical issue into the light of every part of the Bible story—asking what light is shed on the issue by the implications of the great facts and truths of each section—all six acts. That is, we help them to *think biblically* about any issue rather than be given answers to every issue.

The problem is that in theological education, we are tempted to multiply the number of bolt-on courses on this or that new social or ethical issue that has just arisen in the world. Something else becomes "a big issue" in our context, and we feel we must add a lecture course on it to our already overburdened curriculum, often squeezing out the biblical courses to make room. But of course, as soon as the students graduate and leave college, some other "big issue" will hit them. Now they are stumped because they "didn't take a course on that subject at seminary."

Rather, we need to teach people how to *think biblically* about any and every issue that will arise. They need to have learned how to bring every issue into the light of all the key points along the Bible narrative and how to hear the major "voices" of the biblical canon. The Bible may not have a direct answer (chapter and verse) to the new problem, but by systematically shining the light of biblical revelation along the whole sweep of the canon onto the issue, they can generate an informed ethical response that can have some claim to being "biblical."

I would love to see such a "whole Bible approach" become characteristic of all theological education—across all disciplines—and indeed of all biblical preaching and teaching that is planned over time in our churches. We should be learning together to read the Bible as a whole and to root our theology and our practice deeply in the "whole will of God." We need to help our students and congregations see that the Bible is not just an *object* of their study, limited to when they are doing "biblical studies," but rather that the Bible becomes the *subject* of their thinking about everything. That is to say, the Bible is not just some-thing we "*think about*," but rather something we "*think with*." The Bible informs and guides the way we think about everything else—whether in the classroom or in all the rest of life in the world.

I want to conclude by saying, "I have a dream . . ." At least, I once *had* a dream, which I used to muse on when I was the principal of All Nations Christian College in the UK. I dreamt of a "Bible college" that would be exactly and only that—a place where we would teach and study *only the Bible* together in depth, sequentially from the very beginning, and let everything else flow out of the exegesis, interpreta-tion, and application of the biblical text—inviting the experts in other disciplines to contribute as appropriate. And immediately you would be forced, not only to be rooted in what the Bible says, but also to engage with all the issues that the Bible itself engages. You would have to deal with monotheism and cosmology, issues of science and faith, the nature of humanity, the meaning and purpose of sex and marriage, the problem of evil, gender relations and disorder, creation care and ecological chal-lenges, violence and corruption, ethnic diversity and conflict, urban development and cultural progress . . .

And that's before you even get past Genesis 1–11!

Chapter 13

THE BLESSED ALLIANCE

Already But Not Yet

CAROLYN CUSTIS JAMES
AND FRANK A. JAMES III

Nearly twenty years ago, while we were minding our own business, Stan Gundry quietly and graciously disrupted our lives. As Zondervan's editor-in-chief, Stan was prospecting for new talent and made a swing through the city beautiful—Orlando, Florida. As was his practice, he visited the seminary where Frank taught in search of scholars who could write something more than arid technical dissertations. That was when Frank met Stan for the first time.

The name Gundry wasn't new to either of us at the time. But it was the other Gundry, Stan's brother Bob, whom we both knew. Frank had been a colleague of Bob Gundry at Westmont College for two years. Carolyn had a much longer history with the Gundry family that began when she was an undergrad at Westmont. For years, Frank heard stories from her about how Bob's life-changing classes opened up a whole new world of biblical studies and ignited a passion in Carolyn to dig deeper into Scripture that has only grown stronger.

Little did we know that this second Gundry brother was going to change both our lives. The conversation between Frank and Stan took a propitious turn when Frank remarked, "I think you might be interested in what my wife is doing."

That comment resulted in an invitation for Carolyn to submit a book proposal to Stan. Not only was that proposal the beginning of her writing career, it was also the start of a friendship with Stan, who shared Carolyn's desire to cast a bolder vision for women and girls that is grounded in Scripture. He became Carolyn's strongest ally and mentor within the publishing community. To this day, she credits Stan with launching her publishing career by his readiness to go to bat for an untested female writer who wanted to break from the pack of typical books being written for Christian women. Stan's and Carolyn's shared commitment to greater depth in publishing for women is one of many examples we've observed of the Blessed Alliance between men and women. With this historical context, it seemed good to us that the best way to honor Stan Gundry would be to explore the Blessed Alliance more fully.[1]

We propose to engage this topic under three general rubrics: What is the Blessed Alliance? What is it supposed to do? What does it look like in real life?

What Is the Blessed Alliance?

The Blessed Alliance (a term Carolyn first coined in *Lost Women of the Bible*[2]) is derived from the story of creation, where God is vision-casting for his world and unveiling a bold kingdom vision for humankind:

> Then God said, "Let us make mankind in our image, in our likeness, so that they may rule over the fish in the sea and the birds

---

1. Although the Blessed Alliance is a major theme that Carolyn has developed in her books, more work remains to be done on this important biblical theme.

2. Carolyn Custis James, *Lost Women of the Bible: The Women We Thought We Knew* (Grand Rapids: Zondervan, 2005).

in the sky, over the livestock and all the wild animals, and over all the creatures that move along the ground."

> So God created mankind in his own image,
>> in the image of God he created them;
>> male and female he created them.
>
> *Genesis 1:26–27*

God was so delighted with his creation that after creating the first male and female image bearers, "God *blessed* them" (Genesis 1:28, emphasis added) and then with a ringing endorsement declared his whole creation to be *emphatically* and *exceedingly* "good" (1:31). The partnership God created between his male and female image bearers is the Blessed Alliance.

Although there are more dimensions to the Blessed Alliance than a single chapter can address, we want to focus on the rich relational nature of the Blessed Alliance.

A Relational God Begat Relational Humans

Any discussion of the Blessed Alliance must begin with the *imago Dei*. But as it turns out, understanding (and reflecting) God's image is harder than it sounds. The image of God is one of those teachings that most evangelicals affirm but if pressed are not exactly sure what it means. All are happy to be included, but they don't know what to do with this designation. As theologians are wont to do, they have endlessly debated the meaning of the *imago Dei* for centuries. Some argue that the image of God is primarily about the rational abilities of humans. Others see the exercising of dominion as the essence of the image of God.[3] It may very well be that all the views contain a measure of truth,

---

3. Generally, there are three main approaches: (1) The substantive view locates the image of God within the very nature of human beings, usually referencing rational abilities. Thomas Aquinas is often seen as a prominent exponent. (2) The functional view locates the image of God in what humans do, especially the exercise of dominion. A modern advocate is Leonard Verduin, *Somewhat*

but they do not begin to capture all the good that God is bestowing on humanity. The traditional discussion arrives at a description rather than a bold, compelling sense of mission.

Trying to understand the meaning of the *imago Dei* is further complicated because we are not dealing with propositions in a syllogism. Rather, the foundational texts in Genesis are more akin to poetry than propositions. And so theologians are faced with the daunting task of trying to deduce theological conclusions from a bit of inspired poetry in the first few chapters of Genesis.[4] While this is a formidable challenge, it is still possible to reach relevant conclusions.

One can't really begin to understand the image of God without understanding something about who God is. While all theological constructs about the nature of God fall short, scholars can agree that the God of the Bible is nothing like Aristotle's "Unmoved Mover"—although some theological statements might give a different impression.[5] Rather, the God of the Bible is deeply personal, as is hinted at in Genesis 1:26, when God declares, "Let *us* make mankind in our image" (emphasis added).[6] In modern theological parlance, one may speak of a "social Trinity," which is to say that God is inherently relational and that there are intrapersonal relationships within the Godhead itself. So it follows that an inherently relational Creator would create relational beings, who together not only relate to the Creator but, by necessary implication,

---

Less Than God: The Biblical View of Man (Grand Rapids: Eerdmans, 1970). (3) The relational view sees the image of God in the relationship with God and with other humans. Karl Barth is especially identified with this view. See Millard J. Erickson, *Christian Theology* (Grand Rapids: Baker, 1985), 498–517.

4. Walter Brueggemann (*Genesis: A Bible Commentary for Teaching and Preaching* [Louisville: Westminster John Knox, 2010], 22) calls Genesis a "poetic narrative." Henri Blocher (*In the Beginning: The Opening Chapter of Genesis* [Downers Grove, IL: InterVarsity, 1984], 50–59) characterizes the creation account as an artistic, literary representation of creation.

5. The Westminster Confession of Faith (2.1) employs language that harkens back to Greek philosophical terminology, when God is described as "infinite in being and perfection, a most pure spirit, invisible, without body, parts or passions, immutable, immense, eternal, incomprehensible, almighty …"

6. This is not to suggest that 1:27 is a definitive proto-trinitarian reference. However, the plural pronouns do suggest some mysterious plurality in the creation of humanity; see Stanley J. Grenz, *Theology for the Community of God* (Nashville: Broadman and Holman, 1994), 227.

relate to other image bearers. Thus to bear the image of God involves not only the vertical relationship between humans and God, but also the horizontal relationships among human beings.

Another obvious conclusion is that the image of God is exclusive to humans. The biblical text is quite clearly asserting that "to be human is to bear the image of God."[7] Clearly, human beings are the highest expression of God's creativity. They alone are the image of God. This *'adam* (humanity) is ontologically different from all other creatures in a number of obvious ways. The image of God uniquely binds humanity to our Creator. Unlike the rest of creation, our identity, character, meaning, and purpose in the world are directly linked to who God is. This is not a static definition, but a dynamic engagement between the Creator and his glorious creation. It is of special significance that this is a creature with whom God can have an intimate relationship, with whom he can have a personal conversation—speaking, listening, and engaging. Gordon Wenham captures this idea when he states, "The image is a capacity to relate to God. Man's divine image means that God can enter into personal relationships with him, speak to him, and make covenants with him."[8]

Whatever else might be said of the *imago Dei*, it is clear that the Genesis account of human creation is saturated with the language of relationship. This distinctive ability to have an intimate relationship with God and with other human beings is "blessed" by God. One might even say that God's blessing is, at least in part, tantamount to an expression of his delight at the prospect of relationship with his image bearers.

GENDER AND THE *IMAGO DEI*

Given the patriarchal context within which the Bible was written, it is quite remarkable that the *imago Dei* is expressly connected to gender—male and female. Having said that, it is important to give

---

7. Victor Hamilton, *The Book of Genesis: Chapters 1–17* (Grand Rapids: Eerdmans, 1990), 137.

8. Gordon Wenham, *Word Biblical Commentary: Genesis 1–15* (Waco, TX: Word, 1987), 31.

careful attention to what this creation narrative says and does not say. For instance, the biblical creation account does not refer only to the creation of males, as some translations imply, but rather speaks more broadly of the creation of *human beings* in general.[9]

The countercultural significance of this cannot be overstated, given the fact that within patriarchy, males are given primacy over females, whose significance is derived laterally from their relationships with males (fathers, husbands, sons). According to the biblical creation narrative, however, male and female are fully equal. Their individual significance (unrivaled in all creation) is vertically derived solely from their Creator. Their flourishing as human beings and the success of the *missio Dei* revolves around the strength and beauty of their relationships with their Creator and with each other.

It is also important to note that this text is *not* primarily about marriage, as is sometimes suggested, especially with regard to Genesis 2.[10] We need to be careful not to read contemporary presuppositions back into the text. The Genesis account is actually far more foundational than the institution of marriage. This is the story of the origin of male and female as gendered beings and of the divine purpose for which they were created. The first explicit reference to marriage comes only at the end of chapter 2 (verses 24–25), where the narrator explains the implications for marriage in a surprisingly strong anti-patriarchal statement.[11] This is theologically important because it recognizes that the *imago Dei* extends to every human being, married or not, from birth to death.

The specific reference to male and female has further astonishing implications for understanding the *imago Dei* and thus the Blessed

---

9. Robert Alter, *Genesis: A Translation and Commentary* (New York: Norton, 1996), 5.

10. See Bruce K. Waltke, *An Old Testament Theology: An Exegetical, Canonical, and Thematic Approach* (Grand Rapids: Zondervan, 2007), 232–47.

11. "That is why a man *leaves his father and mother and is united to his wife*, and they become one flesh" (Genesis 2:24, emphasis added). This is a reversal of fundamental patriarchal practices still in effect in many cultures today, where a wife goes to live with her in-laws, becomes the property of her husband's family, and comes under their authority. This one biblical statement runs counter to the patriarchal tradition and thus undermines this social system.

Alliance. It would appear that the second clause (Genesis 1:27b; "male and female he created them") further explains the first clause (1:27a; "God created mankind in his own image"). Thus, Karl Barth concludes that "man together with woman is the man [humanity] who is the image of God."[12] This is an extraordinary assertion that locates the discussion of the image of God (and the Blessed Alliance) on a whole new plane.

One should not take this insight to mean that men and women do not bear the image of God individually, but it does rightfully suggest that the essence of the image of God lies in the male/female dynamic of humanity.[13] This underscores the fact that God designed the relationship between males and females at a core level to be the reflection of God. Thus the relationship of male and female humanity is "the great paradigm of everything that is to take place between [a human being] and God, and also everything that is to take place between [human beings] and [their] fellows."[14]

The *Ezer*-Warrior

It is also somewhat startling that the biblical account of creation stands in stark contrast to the Mesopotamian creation stories.[15] One of the most distinctive aspects of the biblical creation story is that it contains a separate account of the creation of the female. Ancient Near Eastern creation stories *subsume* the female under the creation of the

---

12. Karl Barth, *Church Dogmatics*, III.1. (Peabody, MA: Hendrickson, 2010), 203; cf. Genesis 5:1.

13. See Grenz, *Theology for the Community of God*, 231.

14. Barth, *Church Dogmatics*, III.1., 186. "Everything else that is said about man[kind], namely, that he is to have dominion over the animal kingdom and the earth, that he is blessed in the exercise of the powers of his species and the exercise of his lordship, and that is to draw nourishment from the plants and trees, has reference to this plural: he is male and female."

15. Brueggemann (*Genesis*, 24) notes, "There is no doubt that the text utilizes older materials. It reflects creation stories and cosmologies of Egypt and Mesopotamia. However, the text before us transforms these materials to serve a quite new purpose." See also A. Heidel, *The Gilgamesh Epic and Old Testament Parallels* (Chicago: University of Chicago Press, 1949), 212. Wenham (*Genesis*, xlviii) affirms that the Genesis account has a "probable dependency on the Mesopotamian version of origins." It is well-known that the ancient peoples had their own creation stories and that there are some notable parallels with the biblical creation narrative.

male.[16] So the biblical account is theologically distinct because it runs counter to the prevailing patriarchal culture. In effect, this implies that the female is not subservient or merely ancillary to the male as in patriarchal cultures, but rather underscores the significance of the woman as an ally to the man.

In Genesis 2:18, we read, "The LORD God said, 'It is not good for the man to be alone. I will make a helper [*'ezer*] suitable [*kenegdo*] for him.'" God describes the woman as *'ezer*, which allows for some further theological deductions. For centuries, this term has been *under*translated as "helper," implying that the woman functions as the subordinate to the male. The King James Version (1611) contributed to the downsizing of the female by translating *'ezer kenegdo* (Genesis 2:18, 20) into Old English as a "help meet [fit or suitable] for him." The poet John Dryden (1674) took it from there by adding a hyphen that moved the description of the *'ezer kenegdo* one step closer to becoming a single word. The hyphen disappeared in the nineteenth century, leaving us with "helpmeet." The unfortunate impact was to turn the focus for women exclusively on marriage and motherhood and away from the Creator's vision for her to bear his image and join the man in full partnership to fulfill the global mission God entrusted to them together. Not only that, but the narrowing of a woman's calling to marriage and motherhood excludes significant stretches of every woman's life and leaves out countless women entirely if they never marry or give birth.

Not often appreciated is the fact that every time the word *'ezer* appears in the biblical text, military language defines the context. When God's people are being oppressed or are under threat from an enemy, it is God who comes to the rescue as the ultimate *'Ezer* for his people. Etymologically, the verb behind *'ezer* is *'azar*, which means "save from danger" or "deliver from death."[17]

The military nature of the word *'ezer* has led to the conclusion that

---

16. See Hamilton, *Genesis*, 177.
17. See Hamilton, *Genesis*, 176.

the *'ezer* is a warrior.[18] The renowned Hebrew scholar Robert Alter writes that *'ezer kenegdo* "connotes active intervention on behalf of someone, *especially in military contexts*" (emphasis added).[19] If the woman is an *'ezer*-warrior, then certain relational questions arise: Why is a military partner needed, and what is the relational dynamic between the male and his combat partner.

Contrary to common interpretations, even the Garden of Eden was not a safe place. It contained dangerous trees and a treacherous enemy preparing to attack. Claus Westermann notes that "creation stories did not arise out of a curiosity about origins but from a sense of the menace to human existence in an endangered world."[20]

As the reader discovers in Genesis 3, there is a clear and present danger in the garden. Thus having a warrior by the man's side is a valuable and (according to the Creator) a necessary blessing. The image of God is reflected in the relationship of mutual protection and engagement in the challenges that lie ahead. It should not escape our notice that, given the very real and powerful enemy about to confront God's image bearers, the "help" the Creator provides is not another male. He creates the female. Truly there is mystery to this, but it is hard to avoid the conclusion that the "help" the *'ezer* brings is, in the opinion of the Creator, strategically the very best possible solution to the man's aloneness in every sphere.

The *'ezer* is not inferior or helpless, nor a dependent needing him to protect, provide, and think for her. *Kenegdo* establishes the *'ezer* as the man's match in every respect,[21] while at the same time, uniquely

---

18. See chapter 9 in Carolyn Custis James, *When Life and Beliefs Collide: How Knowing God Makes a Difference* [Grand Rapids: Zondervan, 2000], as well as chapter 5 in *Half the Church: Recapturing God's Global Vision for Women* [Grand Rapids: Zondervan, 2010].

19. Alter, *Genesis*, 9.

20. Claus Westermann, "Genesis," in *The Oxford Companion to the Bible*, ed. Bruce M. Metzger and Michael D. Coogan (Oxford: Oxford University Press, 1993), 246.

21. *Kenegdo* "suggests that what God creates for Adam will correspond to him. Thus the new creation will be neither a superior nor an inferior, but an equal. The creation of this helper will form one-half of a polarity and will be to man as the South Pole is to the North Pole" (Hamilton, *Genesis*, 175).

other. She was created to be a warrior who joins the man in ruling and subduing all creation and in bringing her full strength and wisdom to bear on the mission God entrusts to his image bearers.

Such military imagery is intensely relational. One only needs to consider the iron-clad bond returning military veterans have with their fellow soldiers. Their loyalty to each other exceeds their patriotism. It means they willingly venture into harm's way and make heroic sacrifices—even die—for each other. Even the wounded who are air-lifted from battle fronts to the safety of the hospital are determined to return to their troops. They stand strong in battle because they stand together. It is safe to say that if anything, the military connotation of 'ezer intensifies the relational bond God designed to exist between his sons and daughters.

What Is the Blessed Alliance
Supposed to Do?

Because the human—as male and female—uniquely reflects the relational God, they are "blessed" and given the unique responsibility of ruling and cultivating all of God's creation as God's representatives. The creation of the female was not merely a means to an end. The woman was *not* created so that the male could fulfill the creation mandate. The divine mandate was directed to both, because they together in relationship were the image of God and as such are tasked jointly with having dominion over God's creation. They were fully equal in this responsibility,[22] and both were essential to fulfilling this mandate from the Creator.

As God's unique image bearers, both males and females need each other to carry out God's mandate to rule and subdue in a way that

---

22. Katherine Doob Sakenfeld ("Eve," in *Oxford Companion to the Bible*, 207) states, "The woman is created to be a companion corresponding to (not originally subordinate to) the man."

reflects the Creator. Their mode of operation must be collaborative, creative, resourceful, problem solving, visionary, loving, gracious, productive, ethical, and intent on the whole earth's flourishing. Thus the responsibility to reflect God is a defining characteristic of both males and females. Above all, the Creator is the reference point for who they are and all they do.

Scientists describe an astrological phenomenon known as a *syzygy*. A syzygy forms when gravity pulls three celestial bodies into alignment. The syzygy illustrates beautifully that God is the nonnegotiable center, and male and female align with each other by *first* aligning with him. God is thus at the heart of the Blessed Alliance. Our alliance dissolves and we are carried wildly off course when we make anyone else—father, husband, pastor, professor, political leader, Christian celebrity—the center.

It is a two-tiered relationship between male and female and their relationship with Creator. The image of God has both a horizontal and vertical dimension. It is at once a blessing from God, and by its relational nature it in turn blesses God's creation. The divine blessing God bestows on this male and female Blessed Alliance is designed to ripple out and bless the whole world. But this kind of human rule is a vassal under a supreme ruler. With this feudal-like understanding, it also meant the rule of the supreme king entailed "responsibility for the well-being of his subjects."[23] The implication of the creation narrative is that the creation mandate requires both male and female. According to God's vision for humanity, we become our best selves when as men and women we work together for God's purposes. Human singularity is clearly not the divine design for accomplishing the creation mandate. It was not given to the male, and then, as an afterthought, God graciously included the female. The mandate is inherently designed and intended to be carried out by male and female in relationship to the other. In

---

23. Westermann, "Genesis," 246.

this way, there is a "reflection" of the relational triune God. "It is not good for the male to be alone," because accomplishing the purposes of the relational creator God requires relational human beings, male and female, to accomplish the mandate together.

What Does the Blessed Alliance Look like in Real Life?

The poetic structure of Genesis does not provide us with an indication of how much time transpired between the declaration that they "were both naked, and they felt no shame" (Genesis 2:25) and those ominous words, "Now the serpent was more crafty than any of the wild animals the LORD God had made" (3:1). And with the Enemy's first assault on God's image bearers, all hell breaks loose. The reader does not get to see a Blessed Alliance in action. Instead, the syzygy breaks apart as they become alienated from their Creator and at odds with one another as they pursue their own God-likeness without God.

This is the point in the story where you may want to put your head down and weep. It's okay if you do.

When Good Goes Bad

Even before the fall, the alliance God envisioned wasn't automatic or even instinctive. When the serpentine threat appears, the man and the woman fail to join forces to ward off the enemy or protect one another. They don't speak truth to each other or center their focus on their Creator. In the aftermath, instead of ruling creation for the flourishing of all, God's image bearers turn their ruling and subduing on each other, and a power struggle ensues. This is the birth of the patriarchal system that quickly takes root and persists (in one form or another) to this day.

The blessing turns into a curse. The Bible itself provides an endless supply of stories depicting stomach-turning failure after stomach-turning failure. These stories are tragic reminders of how far humanity has strayed from God's purposes.

After years of childlessness, the great patriarch Abraham and his barren wife Sarah commandeer the womb of an Egyptian slave girl in their desperation for a son. In today's world, this is called sex trafficking. Abraham's nephew Lot was willing to subject his two virgin daughters to an angry mob of sexual predators. Abraham and Sarah's grandson Jacob proves to be a chip off the old block. He marries sisters, Leah and Rachel, who engage in a fierce sibling rivalry to produce sons for their shared husband. To increase their count of sons, they force their slave girls into the competition. Jacob goes along and sires four more sons through them.

Then there is King David, the "sweet" psalmist who was a man after God's own heart, yet with appalling feet of clay. He rapes the young Bathsheba, and when she reveals she is pregnant, he arranges the death of her husband, Uriah.

The abuses foisted on women and children in ancient Israel are so great that God sends his prophets to cry out against them. Woe to those who "deprive the poor of their rights and withhold justice from the oppressed of my people, making widows their prey and robbing the fatherless" (Isaiah 10:2).

The collapse of the Blessed Alliance resulted in the devaluing of women and girls then and now. Every day we are bombarded with accounts of just how far we've strayed: sex trafficking, honor killings, child marriages, rape as a weapon of war, date rape on college campuses, domestic abuse, pornography, and sex-selective abortions of girls are but a few of the nightmares that have come to life. So many little girls (some estimate more than 160 million) have gone missing in China and India that gender ratios in both countries are dangerously out of balance and pose a grave global crisis as those cultures become increasingly masculinized.

Would that it were otherwise, but Christians have not always been innocent bystanders in this ongoing tragedy. We've dragged a lot of historical baggage into the new millennium. The same theological shapers of our evangelical heritage, while contributing much to the Christian faith, have also reinforced the gulf that exists between men and women today—both in society and in the church in ways that even open the door for violence and abuse against women. Augustine declared that women do "not possess the image of God" except insofar as she is joined to a male.[24] For Tertullian, the woman "is the devil's gateway."[25] Following Aristotle, Thomas Aquinas saw females as "defective and misbegotten."[26] The esteemed Reformer John Calvin asserted that women were made in God's image only in the "second degree."[27] Epitomizing the historical consensus of the church, the reforming abbot Odo of Cluny defined women as *saccus stercoris*, which translates to "a sack of shit."[28]

Those who cling to a fallen patriarchal paradigm, even in its most polite forms, are captive to cultural norms of the pagan past and fall vastly short of what God envisioned for us. Not only that, but the church is deprived of desperately needed gifts, wisdom, and strengths when her daughters are sidelined. God meant it when he declared that it is "not good for the man to be alone." Men need their *'ezer* sisters.

---

24. Augustine (*On the Trinity*, XII.7.10) states, "Woman does not possess the image of God in herself but only when taken together with the male who is her head, so that the whole substance is one image. But when she is assigned the role as helpmate, a function that pertains to her alone, then she is not the image of God. But as far as the man is concerned, he is by himself alone the image of God."

25. Tertullian (*On Female Fashion*, I.1) states, "You are the devil's gateway" (*tu es ianua diaboli*).

26. Aquinas (*Summa Theologica*, I q. 92 a. 1 ad 1) states that with respect to her individual nature, the "woman is defective and misbegotten" (*femina est aliquid deficiens et occasionatum*).

27. John Calvin, commenting on Genesis 2:18, affirms that the woman was created in the image of God, "though in the second degree."

28. Cited in Alexander Waugh, *God* (New York: St. Martin's Press, 2002), 127; see also Fiona J. Griffiths, "Women and Reform in the Central Middle Ages," in *The Oxford Handbook of Women and Gender in Medieval Europe*, ed. Judith M. Bennett and Ruth Mazo Karras (Oxford: Oxford University Press, 2013), 452; Karen Armstrong, *The Gospel According to Woman: Christianity's Creation of the Sex War in the West* (New York: Anchor, 1991), 23; Joan Smith, *Misogynies* (New York: Fawcett Columbine, 1989), 6.

Glimpses of the Blessed Alliance

Thankfully, there is more to the story. Although it is deeply troubling that the Blessed Alliance is not yet fully manifest in the church, the good news is that there is an eschatological "already but not yet" dimension in the Blessed Alliance. You have to look closely, but there are beautiful glimpses of the Blessed Alliance all throughout Scripture and in the lives of God's image bearers around us. When we take a deep dive into the stories of women and men in the Bible, there are marvelous hints of the Blessed Alliance at work.

Even within the full-blown patriarchal culture of the Old Testament, where widows without sons were powerless, perpetually at risk, and at the bottom of the human food chain, the Blessed Alliance could be seen. Naomi and Ruth were childless widows reduced to scavenging for food when their story intersected with Boaz, a man of enormous power and stature who turned out to be a different, countercultural kind of man. Against all odds, Boaz and two culturally powerless women become unlikely allies who advance God's purposes for the world.

The same strong Blessed Alliances surface in stories of Deborah, Barak, and Jael; of Esther and Mordecai; of Mary and Joseph; of Jesus and Mary of Bethany, Jesus and Mary Magdalene; of Paul and the women of Philippi. In each story, the same indispensable elements are present—an unbending centering on God and his purposes, sacrificial choices to strengthen and benefit others, and the mutual flourishing of all parties as they live out their true calling as image bearers of their Creator.

Growing up in Portland, Oregon, Carolyn witnessed a quiet example of an "already" Blessed Alliance between her pastor-father and an elderly Swiss missionary. Carolyn did not have a word for it at the time, but she witnessed how Edith Nanz Willies, widowed after many years on the mission field, ministered to her father in a particularly stressful time in his ministry. Mrs. Willies sensed his burdens, came alongside him, and became a voice of wisdom, strength, and encouragement. Conservative when it came to his views of female leadership in the church, her father could not deny that Mrs. Willies had "pastored the pastor."

Conclusion

Jesus came to inaugurate the kingdom of God on earth. And a key component of his mission is the restoration of the Blessed Alliance among his image bearers. That alliance is central to how they convey to the world the beauty of the Trinitarian oneness enjoyed by the Father, Son, and Holy Spirit. It was on Jesus' heart when he prayed "that they may be one *as we are one*" (John 17:11, emphasis added).

The apostle Paul reinforced this creation vision of a Blessed Alliance with a metaphor. In Galatians, he describes the Blessed Alliance—God's people united for God's purposes—as one all-inclusive *family* where cultural distinctions are erased. To a gathering of believers that included both men and women, he declared the most earthshaking, countercultural statement, that *"you are all sons of God* through faith . . . There is neither Jew nor Greek, there is neither slave nor free man, there is neither male nor female; *for you are all one in Christ Jesus . . .* heirs according to the promise" (Galatians 3:26, 28–29 NASB, emphasis added). Addressing a mixed audience in a patriarchal culture with a statement like that was nothing short of revolutionary. In a culture where sons are everything, telling women they too are sons in God's eyes was giving them full stature, equality, and rights in his kingdom—everything their brothers enjoy.

The picture of the Blessed Alliance is one of men and women joining forces, making extraordinary sacrifices, taking life-threatening risks, standing back-to-back in solidarity, and thus flourishing as God's image bearers. Much is riding on the oneness of the family of God, the unity of the body of Christ, and the ability of men and women to join forces to serve God together. If anything, the Blessed Alliance underscores the foundational fact that men and women *need* each other. The issue isn't the sharing of power or about who leads and who follows, but rather how *together* we can apply ourselves, heart and soul, to the monumental task that God has placed before us. God has entrusted men and women to rule and subdue creation as God's vassals. Let's not fail in our sacred responsibilities.

Thanks, Stan, for being a blessed ally—already.